QUEERING URBAN JUSTICE

Queer of Colour Formations in Toronto

T0341538

Queering Urban Justice foregrounds visions of urban justice that are critical of racial and colonial capitalism and asks: What would it mean to map space in ways that address very real histories of displacement and erasure? What would it mean to regard Queer, Trans, Black, Indigenous, and People of Colour (QTBIPOC) as geographic subjects who model different ways of inhabiting and sharing space?

The volume describes city spaces as sites where bodies are exhaustively documented while others barely register as subjects. The editors and contributors interrogate the forces that have allowed QTBIPOC to be imagined as absent from the very spaces they have long invested in. From the violent displacement of poor, disabled, racialized, and sexualized bodies from Toronto's gay village, to the erasure of queer racialized bodies in the academy, *Queering Urban Justice* offers new directions to all who are interested in acting on the intersections of social, racial, economic, urban, migrant, and disability justice.

JIN HARITAWORN is an associate professor in the Faculty of Environmental Studies at York University.

GHAIDA MOUSSA is a PhD candidate in the Social and Political Thought Program at York University.

SYRUS MARCUS WARE is a PhD candidate in the Faculty of Environmental Studies at York University.

RÍO RODRÍGUEZ is a Toronto-based latinx queer educator working in queer, trans, and POC communities.

Queering Urban Justice

Queer of Colour Formations in Toronto

EDITED BY JIN HARITAWORN, GHAIDA
MOUSSA, AND SYRUS MARCUS WARE,
WITH RÍO RODRÍGUEZ

UNIVERSITY OF TORONTO PRESS
Toronto Buffalo London

ISBN 978-1-4875-0374-1 (cloth)   ISBN 978-1-4875-2285-8 (paper)

Library and Archives Canada Cataloguing in Publication

Queering urban justice : queer of colour formations in Toronto / edited by
Jin Haritaworn, Ghaida Moussa, and Syrus Marcus Ware, with Río
Rodríguez.

Includes bibliographical references.
ISBN 978-1-4875-0374-1 (cloth). – ISBN 978-1-4875-2285-8 (paper)

1. Minority gays – Ontario – Toronto – Social conditions.   I. Haritaworn,
Jinthana, editor   II. Moussa, Ghaida, editor   III. Ware, Syrus, editor
IV. Rodríguez, Río, 1987–, editor

HQ73.3.C32T67 2018   306.76'608   C2018-902600-6

This book has been published with the help of a grant from the Federation
for the Humanities and Social Sciences, through the Awards to Scholarly
Publications Program, using funds provided by the Social Sciences and
Humanities Research Council of Canada.

University of Toronto Press acknowledges the financial assistance to its
publishing program of the Canada Council for the Arts and the Ontario
Arts Council, an agency of the Government of Ontario.

Canada Council   Conseil des Arts
for the Arts   du Canada

ONTARIO ARTS COUNCIL
CONSEIL DES ARTS DE L'ONTARIO
an Ontario government agency
un organisme du gouvernement de l'Ontario

Funded by the   Financé par le
Government   gouvernement
of Canada   du Canada

Contents

Acknowledgments

It takes a village, or maybe a city, to edit a collection of this nature. We would like to thank our ancestors, and the many QTBIPOC who have come before us, teaching us when to walk confidently, when to tread softly, and how to take up space differently in a white-supremacist, cis-heteronormative, anti-Black settler society. Some of you have transitioned out of recognition, while others have left your unforgettable marks.

The Marvellous Grounds project that this book is part of was conceived in the spirit of activist scholarship, which in antiracist and anti-colonial feminist and queer communities has been defined as "the production of knowledge and pedagogical practices through active engagements with, and in the service of, progressive social movements."[1] We thank the social movements, both organic and professional, that have given rise to the intellectuals whom we draw on and publish in this book. And we thank the community members who have contributed chapters here and elsewhere for trusting us with their writing.

In writing this book, we have experimented with various ways of sharing not only knowledge but also the risks, labour, and benefits of being knowledge producers, both with each other and with community members outside the academy. The book, as well as its sister volumes (a second forthcoming book collection on QTBIPOC archives and the *Marvellous Grounds* online journal), have indeed provided many opportunities to use and redistribute the resources of the academic industrial complex – from funding to writing and editing skills to the communal

---

1 Julia Chinyere Oparah and Margo Okazawa-Rey, *Activist Scholarship: Antiracism, Feminism, and Social Change* (London: Routledge, 2016), 3.

space within which to launch and celebrate these works. It has been important for us to resist the competitive values assigned to us – from individual brilliance to exceptionalism – and work collectively. Dominant ways of collecting stories often reinforce power – from who is credited as author or researcher, as opposed to research subject or research assistant, to whose histories are passed on and whose are not, to what is published and what is not. In contrast, it takes a collective to collect work that is collective, and to undo the dominant knowledge and methods of knowledge production, that are not only hierarchical and exploitative but also deeply alienating (of authors from their labour and of us from our communities).

We would like to express profound gratitude to the contributors to this collection, who have worked with us for multiple years in shaping the stories we are telling about QTBIPOC spaces in Toronto. You have all taught us so much about the struggles and triumphs, the solidarities and complexities, and, most of all, the radiance of QTBIPOC in the city. We extend a heartfelt thank you to the community groups, arts and advocacy groups, and individuals that have featured our work and collaborated with us in the past few years.

As a team of editors, we would like to thank each other as well as our many collaborators. Amandeep Kaur Panag and Nadia Kanani provided valuable research assistance on other rounds of this project. Alvis Choi was a shining light and constant source of brilliance without whose consistent support this book would not have been possible. Many activist QTBIPOC students at the Faculty of Environmental Studies and at other programs at York University transcribed interviews and shared classrooms with us where this work was being taught. Our colleagues Honor Ford Smith, Gloria Swain, Lisa Myers, Deborah Cowen, and Ren-yo Hwang cheered us on and shared important spaces with us.

Ghaida thanks her co-editors of this collection, who, through the gracious mentorship of Jin Haritaworn, created a space where each member's successes were celebrated – a refreshing representation of what collective work can look like. Ghaida is endlessly grateful to the people who welcomed and helped raise this little-town kid in the big city. Among them, special thanks go out to Nadijah Robinson, Kavita Bissoondial, Nakita Sunar, kumari giles, Nora Al-Aleiwi, Nadia Habib, Nishant Upadhyay, Nayrouz Abu Hatoum, Shushan Araya, and Karen Cocq. Ghaida also wishes to give thanks to Sam Whittle for her unwavering and generous love and her reminders of the power of vulnerability and an open heart. She also cannot thank her parents enough for teaching her to move through life with integrity and for their eternal support and wisdom. Finally, a big, heartfelt "Thank you for all you are" goes out to all the femmes in my life.

Syrus wishes to thank his twin, Jessica Lee Ware, for her ongoing support and encouragement; his grandparents, Gwen and Harold Irons, for their love; and his daughter Amelie Ware-Redman for her reminders that life should be a lot more fun than work. He would also like to thank Melisse Watson, Lamia Gibson, Sean Lee Popham, Alanna Kibbe, and Giselle Dias for holding him well while he struggled through disability and work responsibilities. Syrus would also like to thank the brilliance of the Marvellous Grounds collective, his co-editors, and collaborators. Syrus would especially like to thank his supervisor and mentor, Jin Haritaworn, for the ways that they have created innovative ways to re-remember critically the histories of QTBIPOC communities in Toronto. They have modelled activist scholarship at its finest, and we have all learned so much from this process.

Jin would like to thank all the community members who submitted contributions, from academic chapters to interviews, personal essays, dance choreography, song, film, letters, oral histories, roundtables, teach-ins, poems, and photography. It has been a humbling experience to start my first five years in Toronto learning from the many activist and artistic movements that have informed QTBIPOC spaces in the city. I am grateful to Ghaida, Syrus, and Río for working on this project with me and for sharing the wealth of your experience as leaders in the city with me and with our readers. You continue to impress me with your brilliance, your resilience, and your desire to make this work a good experience for everyone involved.

A thank you to University of Toronto Press and the editorial team, especially Douglas Hildebrand, for welcoming us, honing this collection, and enabling QTBIPOC voices that are often excluded from print.

This project received funding and support from the Social Sciences and Humanities Research Council of Canada; the Ontario Ministry of Research, Innovation and Science; and the Faculty of Environmental Studies at York University.

This book has been published with the help of a grant from the Federation for the Humanities and Social Sciences, through the Awards to Scholarly Publications Program, using funds provided by the Social Sciences and Humanities Research Council of Canada.

Toronto, August 2017

QUEERING URBAN JUSTICE

Queer of Colour Formations in Toronto

Introduction: Queering Urban Justice

JIN HARITAWORN, GHAIDA MOUSSA, RÍO
RODRÍGUEZ, AND SYRUS MARCUS WARE

Toronto is arguably one of the world's queer of colour capitals – a place that people move to in order to *be* queer of colour and *in* queer of colour community. Vice versa, it is one of the rare cities where organizing by queer and trans Black, Indigenous, and people of colour (QTBIPOC) has reached a critical enough mass to shape and, often, lead local landscapes of art and activism. Well-known, large-scale community-building projects include Blockorama/Blackness Yes!, a day-long, annual arts festival founded in 1999, which has for almost two decades been a site of Black queer intervention into the city's increasingly whitewashed Pride celebrations, and Asian Arts Freedom School, a hub of political art-making founded in 2006.

But anti-racist and anti-colonial impulses in queer and trans leadership in Toronto go back to at least the 1960s. In the 1970s and 1980s, the city was a hotbed of intersectional organizing, with Black, Indigenous, and racialized people centrally involved in mobilizing around class, HIV/AIDS, education, anti-apartheid, and disability justice, and addressing systemic marginalization and oppression in and beyond queer and trans communities. Organizing has taken many forms, from letter-writing in support of anti-apartheid activists like Simon Nkoli to the creation of multidisciplinary arts events like Mayworks, an annual arts festival celebrating working-class culture; Desh Pardesh, an arts and culture festival focused on the South Asian diaspora; and, more recently, the Counting Past Two Transsexual, Intersex and Transgender Film/Video/Arts Festival. By the late 1990s, Black queer and trans-focused spaces like Blockorama, Manhattan, and AYA were well established in the city.

Despite the fact that Black queers, in particular, have left their "indelible mark" on Toronto, they always remain newcomers in its official maps and archives (Walcott 2006, 129; see also Douglas et al. 1997;

Tinsley 2008). Just like urban justice campaigns, discussions of queer spaces and histories generally fail to take seriously non-white queers as historical or geographical subjects. Revisiting the question of urban justice through a range of gendered and racialized lenses, *Queering Urban Justice* joins some of these missing dots. The book explores the unique contributions that subjects who often fall through the identitarian cracks of neo-liberal multiculturalism have made to artistic, social, and political life in the city and the lessons that they offer to social movements across borders. It puts into conversation mental and affective maps that acknowledge "that places and those who inhabit them are … fictions" (Brand 2001, 17) and that, therefore, new ways of animating and distributing space are both necessary and possible.

Queering Urban Justice illuminates the void marked by spatial and temporal interventions and formulations that rarely reach the status of the observable and conservable. It gathers these formulations intentionally, to foster political power among those who have been marginalized within archival hierarchies (Derrida and Prenowitz 1995). The chapters ahead variously contest the archive, actively claim control over it, or intentionally remain in the realm of the "repertoire" – how Diana Taylor (2003) describes the oral traditions, cultural productions, community organizing, and everyday uses of space that characterize embodied memory transmission in subaltern communities. The chapters convey "palimpsestic glimpses" – the term that Jacqui Alexander (2005) adapts to describe times and places that are continually erased and overwritten – of what QTBIPOC formations have looked like in the city and what the city in turn looks like through the palimpsestic prisms of those who exceed its design.

As curators, we seek to lend weight to histories and presents that already possess a critical mass. The authors gathered here have various relationships to the ongoing realities of settler colonialism, anti-blackness, and border imperialism that shape space on Turtle Island. These complex and often contradictory relationships are reflected in shifting and changing names and coalitions, which are chosen, entered, claimed, and discarded in acts of linguistic self-determination according to what the current context demands. The acronym QTBIPOC in this Introduction highlights these complexities.[1]

---

1 We honour the importance of linguistic self-determination for those who generally remain the object rather than the subject of discourse in academic, artistic, activist, and other realms where racial, gender, sexual, class, and other hierarchical meanings are made and contested. For example, this Introduction oscillates between *black* and *Black*, depending on the authors' preferred spelling of the word.

What these artistic, political, and intellectual projects have in common is that they channel a "permanent readiness for the marvellous," in the words of Afro-Surrealist Aimé Césaire (2000, 15). A Martiniquan living in France, Césaire recognized the powerful potential of art in prefiguring futures beyond racism and colonialism. It is in this insurgent spirit that, in 2015, we founded Marvellous Grounds, the QTBIPOC archiving collective that has jointly curated this book.[2] The authors and artists who have entrusted their work to us echo this permanent readiness to imagine futures that do not merely diversify the status quo. Not only do they "unmap" the capitalist logics according to which space is carved out and distributed (Razack 2002), they also reclaim and repossess architectures that were not made with Black and brown sexually and gender non-conforming people in mind. They imagine futures beyond displacement and dispossession – futures beyond racial and colonial capitalism.

Queering Urban Justice intervenes in power-evasive discussions of the urban and in single-issue approaches to space, politics, and identity. It does so by engaging a range of concepts and conversations, including affect, Black liberation, coming out, community accountability, criminalization, diasporic intimacy, disability justice, domesticity, gay imperialism, homonationalism, multiculturalism, pinkwashing, protest, respectability, social movements, solidarity, and sovereignty. Read together, the following pages revisit conversations about queer space and queer archives, anti-blackness, settler colonialism, and border imperialism (see Walia 2013). They make space for an up-and-coming generation of writers and critics who are ready to leave their mark in and beyond disciplinary confines such as gender, queer, and sexuality studies; critical race and ethnic studies; Black studies; disability studies; urban and environmental studies; geography; and critical prison studies. All our contributors are activist scholars who mobilize theory to

---

2 Marvellous Grounds is a QTBIPOC mapping and archiving project coordinated by Jin Haritaworn. Contributors have included Alvis Choi, Ghaida Moussa, Amandeep Kaur Panag (member 2016–17), Río Rodríguez (co-coordinator 2014–16), and Syrus Marcus Ware. As a collective that shares responsibility for disseminating this work, we have co-edited both this book and a series of sister volumes specifically geared to a non-academic readership (see, e.g., Rodríguez and Kaur Panag 2016). We have received support in the form of an Insight Development Grant from the Social Sciences and Humanities Research Council of Canada, an Early Researcher Award from the province of Ontario, and small grants from the Faculty of Environmental Studies at York University.

dream up better futures. As such, the book models new ways of thinking and enacting the city that disrupt false dichotomies between the
grassroots and the academy and that are in the service of community-
building, healing, and survival.

The authors gathered here contribute to a vibrant body of queer of
colour studies, while also pushing this scholarship to address questions
of urban justice and to move beyond its US centricity (El-Tayeb 2012;
Ferguson 2004; Manalansan 2005). It is important to note that this scholarship is, in turn, indebted to an older body of women of colour writing,
whose rich genealogy it shares (e.g., Alexander 2005; Bacchetta 2009; Silvera 1991). Thus, the embattled subjectivities that we are writing about
here have ancestors whose kindred locations are invoked in titles such as
This Bridge Called My Back: Writings by Radical Women of Colour (Moraga
and Anzaldúa 1981) and *But Some of Us Are Brave: All the Women Are
White, All the Blacks Are Men – Black Women's Studies* (Hull, Scott, and
Smith 1982). In Toronto, this shared genealogy is demonstrated by the
spatial overlap and, at times, identity between women of colour and
queer of colour organizations in the 1980s, such as Sister Vision: Black
Women and Women of Colour Press and Zami, which indeed met, plot-
ted, and schemed at the same kitchen table (see chapter 3 by Dryden).
Indeed, few of the spaces discussed in this book would be thinkable
without the tools given to us by intersectionality feminism, which in
Toronto has always been a serious political practice as well as an important theory (see, e.g., chapter 5 by Chin, chapter 6 by Ejiogu and Ware,
and Ware's interview with Tabobondung in chapter 11).

Writers on the intersection of race and sexuality have encouraged
us to trace the alternative economies of desire inhabited by "impossible subjects" (Gopinath 2005), who, erased in single-issue mobilizing,
formulate socialities that open worlds beyond diasporic respectability,
heteronormative nationalism, and homonormative identity politics.
These writers have given us sophisticated insights into artistic and
activist acts whose "structures of feeling" are based on "dis/identifi-
cation" rather than narrow, identitarian notions of belonging (Muñoz
2000). Their insights have wider purchase in a context of neo-liberal
restructuring that "scripts its beneficiaries as worthy multicultural
global citizens and its losers as doomed by their own monoculturalism-
ism, deviance, inflexibility, criminality, and other attributes" (Melamed
2011, 87). They shed light on past and present modes of power and
control that vitalize and universalize the gender and sexual ontologies
of dominant subjects, while criminalizing and pathologizing the gender

expressions of racialized and colonized populations (Cohen 2010–11; Haritaworn 2015; Puar 2007; Reddy 2011). *Queering Urban Justice* adds to these debates a consideration of the city, and of urban space, as a crucial site of power and resistance.

Space is a central theme in this collection due to its importance in settler-colonial, anti-Black, racist, and imperialist processes of displacement and dispossession.[3] As Sherene Razack (2002) shows, the removal of Indigenous peoples from the land follows a logic of "white settler innocence." In this script, European settlers are invited to fantasize themselves as the only subjects capable of working, clearing, cultivating, and therefore owning the land (ibid., 5). Indigenous bodies, meanwhile, are segregated on the least valuable lands, thus demarcating space as respectable (white) or degenerate (Indigenous). As Razack puts it, place thus becomes race.

At the heart of this process is what Denise da Silva (2007) describes as the colonial distinction of "universal" subjects from "affectable" non-subjects. The former's proper genders and sexualities – both cis-heteropatriarchal and homo- and transnormative – are linked with their proper use of space and land. In contrast, the latter lacks proper distinctions between genders and sexualities as well as between human beings and non-human beings, including the land, which is treated as an agentic being (Smith 2005). Leanne Simpson (2014) sums this up succinctly.

You use gender violence to remove Indigenous peoples and their descendants from the land, you remove agency from the plant and animal worlds and you reposition aki (the land) as "natural resources" for the use and betterment of white people. (n.p.)

Refusing a view of colonialism as in the past, Indigenous writers have shown how land theft has always gone hand in hand with an evolving regime of gender and sexual violence, including successive reservation, residential school, adoption, and foster care systems, as well as the epidemic rape and murder of Indigenous women, Two Spirit, and LGBT people, which is enabled rather than interrupted by a prison industrial complex that similarly works to consolidate colonialism (Finley 2014; Native Youth Sexual Health Network 2014). A central aspect of

---

3 The following theoretical framework is based on Haritaworn's (2015) discussion of queer regeneration and queer of colour formations in Berlin.

land defence has been the rejection of settler identities (including queer, LGBT, and, at times, queer of colour) and the active engagement with traditional gender relations (see Ware's interview with Tabobondung in chapter 11).

In cities like Toronto, urban development occurs in the "architecture" (Thobani 2014) of settler colonialism as well as of anti-blackness. Katherine McKittrick (2006) observes that "black geographies in Canada are produced [through] narratives of erasure: concealing black places, demolishing 'unfit' communities, re-memorializing bloodless, black-less, roads" (27). Helping us understand settler colonialism and anti-blackness as mutually constitutive and symbiotic rather than additive, Tiffany Lethabo King (2013) describes the "settlement/plantation" as the paradigmatic space on Turtle Island. According to King, Black female bodies are the basic units of production and reproduction of the spaces within which white subjectivities have been able to expand. In the terms of King's evocative dissertation title, Black bodies *clear* Indigenous lands whose "cultivation" white settlers then claim as their "work."

In this architecture, white and middle-class people mark the valuable and accessible lands that have come under their control as respectable areas reserved for respectable bodies, uses and socialities, while "degenerate populations" are segregated in infertile, inaccessible, and badly serviced rural and urban areas that are deemed worthless and uninhabitable. This designation shifts, however, when degenerate lands gain value and are flipped for "regeneration," as is currently happening in the Downtown East of Toronto, home to the already gentrified Gay Village around Church and Wellesley. Not incidentally, the Downtown East also contains Regent Park, one of the most significant Black neighbourhoods in the country and on whose razed ground the city's condominium boom is mushrooming, alongside other neighbourhoods long inhabited by Indigenous, Black, and immigrant populations, like Moss Park and Jamestown. The close proximity of the Village and its spill into these areas brings acutely home how queer space on Turtle Island is formed within a racial and colonial logic of space that systematically displaces and erases racialized and colonized communities to reinscribe the grounds thus cleared for white and middle-class ownership and governance, including gendered governance, both heteronormative and queer.

What do QTBIPOC have to contribute to understanding these processes? McKittrick (2006) urges us to consider subaltern subjects as "geographic subjects," whose cognitive maps might advance "alternative geographic formulations of subaltern" that can "incite new, or different, and perhaps not just, more just, geographic stories" (xix). Similarly, Bacchetta, El-Tayeb, and Haritaworn (2015) note that queer of colour accounts of the city give rise to important theorizations that help us understand how racial and colonial capitalism organizes the world through gender and sexual violence (see also Million 2013). In this collection, we revalue the knowledge of those who have been pushed out of urban spaces to ask, Who is made to be absent in urban development? Who is excessive to, and whose removal is constitutive of, the Gay Village and other spaces designated as "gay," "queer," or "LGBT"? What does centring QTBIPOC reveal about space in the neo-liberal city? What would it take to queer urban justice? What alternative ways of living with each other and the world do the cognitive maps of QTBIPOC orient us towards?

The counter-narratives assembled here take issue with dominant queer maps and historiographies. They describe the city as a site where some bodies, acts, and socialities are exhaustively documented, while others barely register as subjects and events. Indeed, wider (whiter) queer spaces and histories in Toronto are increasingly well mapped and archived. There is now a plethora of LGBT maps of the city that assemble particular events considered important to local (white) LGBT history, from the bathhouse raids to the progressive spread of LGBT businesses and organizations.[4] Of note are FunMaps' (2013) *Toronto FunMap*, which maps gay sites of interest in Toronto and other southern Ontario cities, and the Queerstory App (http://www.queerstory.ca/), a community-history digital arts project telling Toronto-based queer stories that reinforce the "gay and trans rights forerunner" image of Toronto. *Queeropolis: Toronto 1972–2008* is a further example. This short film, commissioned by Pride Toronto, features a map of the city that is progressively filled with colourful pins marking the locations of LGBT establishments founded in the thirty-six-year period to the sound of audio clips of proud community members sharing personal experiences of queer Toronto (Foster and Mitchell 2008). It tells a tale of queer entrepreneurialism, progress, and arrival that, not incidentally, ends with an image of a city that is covered in cheerful, gay colours. Progress

---

4 The following discussion of queer maps and the Toronto village draws on Río Rodríguez (2016), which was written in direct conversation with this book.

is visualized here temporally as well as spatially: as queer fecundity and expansion, as homonormative control over land and real estate.

These and other mapping projects tend to represent some areas as "queer spaces," especially the Gay Village, but increasingly also the "Queer West" (Toronto's west end) (see Nash 2013). Celebratory and nostalgic narratives compete in these maps. While the Village is often described as a successful "gaybourhood," it has also been pronounced "in decline" since the late 2000s. The moral panic over the Village-in-decline provoked a series of studies on the "state of the Village," town hall meetings, online calls for support for the LGBTQ Village, and a series of articles about the "changing nature of the Gay Village" in the local gay community paper, *Xtra* (e.g., Houston 2013; Madi et al. 2014). What both celebratory and nostalgic cartographies of the Village have in common is that they foreground bodies, subjects, and identities that are most often imagined as white. They also dodge the important question of whom the establishments and areas featured in these maps actually belong to and serve. Furthermore, they are easily incorporated into a homonationalist and gay-imperialist view of an exceptionally LGBT-friendly Canada, whose claims to be a world leader and beacon of LGBT progress have their spatial reflections in a village and a Toronto where LGBT people have the longest history, the largest space, and the greatest rights (see Haritaworn 2015; Puar 2007). The city's status as a global trendsetter in LGBT activism is mirrored internationally. For example, the Gay and Lesbian Travel section of the *Guardian* (2015) lists Toronto at the top of "great destinations" and describes it as "one of the most queer-friendly cities on the planet" (n.p.).

In contrast, we ask how the "gay" geography of the Village is simultaneously a white geography in Razack's, King's, and McKittrick's sense, which expands settler moulds of gender, sexuality, consumption, and land use while erasing racialized and Indigenous urban life. As Río Rodríguez (2016) shows, the Village has been consistently experienced as an unwelcoming zone for trans women of colour, sex workers, street-involved queers, and others on the margins. Examples of this include the displacement of trans sex workers from the Village onto Homewood Avenue by neighbourhood associations, the painting over of a trans memorial in Barbara Hall Park as part of the ongoing gentrification of the area, and the ban on Black and Caribbean music by bars on Church Street. These erasures are commonplace. They serve to exclude histories of organizing by those most affected by systemic violence, upon whose backs change has been fought and won.

This chimes with Haritaworn's (2015) argument that queer-space debates often reify a capitalist paradigm of space whose basic tenets, beyond just being neo-liberal, are more appropriately traced back to the long *durée* of racial (Robinson 1983) and colonial (Coulthard 2014) capitalism. There are a growing number of critiques of the homonormativity of the neo-liberal city. Authors have variously foregrounded the palatability of themed village spaces to global city agendas of touristification and consumer capitalism, the assimilability of certain gay subjects as consumer citizens and urban entrepreneurs, and the displacement of "transgressive" practices and identities, particularly around cruising and bondage, domination, subordination, and masochism (BDSM), from, and the transgressiveness of, "mixed" multiracial neighbourhoods *versus* the homogeneous village (e.g., Bell and Binnie 2004; Doan and Higgins 2011; Nash 2013; Oswin 2015; Schulman 2012).

There have been few interrogations to date of how Black people, Indigenous people, and people of colour figure in formations of queer space. Even writers on gay gentrification have rarely considered the impacts of gentrification on QTBIPOC (e.g., Knopp 1990; see also chap. 1). However, as shown by the famous case of the Christopher Street piers in New York, which gained international attention as a result of queer of colour youth organizing for their right to the city, the effects of gentrification and policing are most keenly felt on the intersections. There, police, private security, and residents' associations collaborated in displacing low-income queer of colour youth from the piers so that the "waterfront" could be developed into prime real estate for affluent gay and straight consumption (FIERCE 2008; Hanhardt 2013; Manalansan 2005).

More often, however, non-white bodies and communities are treated as constitutive background figures, or absent presences, in discussions of queer space. Haritaworn (2015) traces this tendency back to the early accounts of queer space, such as those by Gayle Rubin (1984) and Manuel Castells (1983), where affectable Others figure in passing as a dangerous threat to lesbian and gay migrants from the province or as a degenerative influence on inner-city architectures that are being regenerated through the creative touch of risk-taking gays. Interestingly, these accounts foreshadow today's moral panics over hate crimes committed by people of colour, which ideologically pave the way for queer gentrification. Indeed, Haritaworn (2015) argues that Castells's passionate account of enterprising gay men who save dilapidated houses from the degenerative influence of working-class people and people of colour contains some of the key ingredients of the neo-liberal city's creative class, whose much-critiqued proponent, Richard Florida (2002), is, not incidentally, Toronto-based.

The figure of the enterprising gay who takes good risks is the finance-capitalist reformulation of the "gay pioneer," who ventures into degenerate areas that white, straight people are not (yet) willing to enter. It reverberates through both Castells and Florida and is repeatedly cited in the Toronto villagescape, sometimes literally. At the heart of the Village, at Church and Alexander, the city and the business association in 2005 built a pompous statue to commemorate Alexander Wood, a white settler from Scotland, who is thought to have spent time in that area in the early nineteenth century and whom they refer to as a "gay pioneer" and "forefather" of the Village (see Rodríguez 2016).

This theme highlights the need to understand queer gentrification and territorialization as a logical outflow of settler colonialism. Glen Coulthard (2014) proposes the term *"urbs nullius"* to make sense of the gentrification of inner-city areas such as the Downtown Eastside in Vancouver, where Indigenous peoples, who were once forced off their lands and onto reserves, and then from their remaining land bases into the cities, are now facing further eviction alongside poor Chinese and other surplus populations (see also Lawrence 2004). Coulthard explains the finance-capitalist treatment of the inner city as an uninhabited *urbs nullius* as the latest outflow of *terra nullius*, the colonial ideology of the empty land that awaits clearing. Building on this argument, we observe that spatial moulds and practices in contemporary Canada – including the forms of emplacement and displacement discussed in this book – occur in the architecture of settler colonialism (Thobani 2014).

In this inner-city landscape, the queer subject becomes an "exalted subject" in Sunera Thobani's (2007) sense, one who performs hir right to citizenship through hir settlement and cultivation of degenerate lands that must be saved from idle decay at the hands of poor Black, Indigenous, and racialized populations. The superior land use of LGBT subjects, who improve the building stock of the inner city rather than letting it go to waste, has become a theme in urban policy discourses transnationally. As Christina Hanhardt (2013) shows, gay villages are now celebrated as the successful territorialization and securitization of inner-city space. As the contributors to this anthology show, queer space formation in the Village and elsewhere has gone hand in hand with the displacement, through policing and gentrification, of queer youth; sex workers; trans women of colour; users of addiction, mental health, and homelessness services; and other populations deemed disposable. The gentrification project in Toronto's Gay Village involves, for instance, the displacement of low-income and homeless people through the replacement of a drop-in community centre and park with an LGBT sports centre that is supported and co-funded by the City of Toronto and private donors. Further, the notorious project to revive another community centre, The 519, has meant that drop-in programs and lobby seating have been replaced by upscale social events and bank machines. In these examples, race, access, and neo-liberal subjecthood coalesce to make space for the celebration of gay upper-class interests through the physical removal of racialized, disabled, and low-income populations, who are considered deficient "liabilities" (Hanhardt 2008, 64) unfit for neo-liberal citizenship.

In contrast, *Queering Urban Justice* foregrounds visions of urban justice that are disloyal to racial and colonial capitalism. The authors featured here ask, What does it take to unmap dominant LGBT cartographies? What would it mean to map space in ways that address very real histories of displacement and erasure? What would a paradigm of sharing space look like that interrupts these ongoing histories and takes a different course? What would it mean to take seriously QTBI-POC as geographic subjects who model different ways of inhabiting and sharing space?

The book complicates existing archives of queer space, which selectively "include" contributions by non-white people to diversify geographies that nevertheless reinscribe the city as a whitened space. Our contributors profoundly reframe who deserves to take up space, who deserves to be remembered, and what spatial and temporal acts and uses are considered worthwhile (see also Bacchetta, El-Tayeb, and Haritaworn 2015). The acts foregrounded here go beyond the "holy trinity" (Nair 2008) of gay marriage, hate crime, and gays in the military, which has come to characterize the white LGBT movement post-Stonewall. They force us to interrogate how spaces of celebration are often forged out of dislocation. They suggest new ways of living, working, playing, and being beyond white moulds of gender and space. These narratives talk directly back at violence, including interpersonal as well as institutional violence at the hands of the state, the LGBT establishment, and the market. They forge new theories, and build new spaces to think and act, beyond the narrow confines of rights, visibility, and recognition. They radically redefine what is a "queer" issue – from borders and prisons to urban justice, to Black and disabled liberation, to the decolonization of Turtle Island and of Palestine – and offer new directions to all who are interested in acting on the intersections of social, racial, economic, urban, migrant, and disability justice. The authors gathered in this book have a lot to teach. They prefigure the world we want to live in.

Mapping Queer Urban Justice

> So I am scouring maps of all kinds, the way that some fictions do, dis-cursively, elliptically, trying to locate their own transferred selves. (Brand 2001, 18–19)

This collection is divided into two sections: I: "Mapping Community" and II: "Cartographies of Resistance." Together, they draw the contours of historical and contemporary spaces in which QTBIPOC subjects in Toronto have built community, resisted various forms of oppression, and proposed new ways of thinking, healing, dreaming, and forming alliances. In this sense, the collection is a scholarly archival project of the spaces that have shaped – and been shaped by – QTBIPOC.

The first section, "Mapping Community," assembles histories that have been told repeatedly, but so far exist mainly in the oral rather than the written form. The contributions move back and forth through time from the 1970s to the present day. These individual and collective mind maps, or "sense of place maps" (Ingram, Boutillette, and Retter 1997), bring to the fore places and histories that are important in the formation of QTBIPOC communities in Toronto. Here, contributors document HIV/ AIDS organizing, a rich history of queer of colour creative resistance, an important genealogy of Black queer and trans community-building, and pivotal Two Spirited, queer, and trans folks of colour alliances in the face of settler-colonial, gendered, and racial oppression. The section thus assembles writings that intervene in dominant ways of archiving and mapping urban space as white and heteronormative.

The first chapter introduces QTBIPOC as subjects of urban justice, those who have made important, albeit largely unrecognized, contribu-tions to this movement since at least the 1960s. "'Our Study Is Sabo-tage': Queering Urban Justice, from Toronto to New York," a roundtable by Jin Haritaworn with Che Gossett, Río Rodríguez, and Syrus Marcus Ware, describes the right to the city as always already intersecting with racial, economic, gender, and disability justice. The chapter responds to the absence of queer of colour and other intersectional approaches from dominant accounts of the city by detailing several decades of interventions in some of the classic areas of urban justice, including gentrification, police violence, and queer and trans of colour community-building in neo-liberal cityscapes that are largely reserved for capitalist productivity and consumer citizenship. The authors propose that these missing contributions are essential to understanding who pays for and who benefits from urban development. In this transnational take on QTBIPOC and urban justice, events in Toronto such as the bathhouse raids and the struggle against gentrification and displacement in the Village are read alongside better-known examples in transnational urban justice discussions, including the struggle to reclaim the Christopher Street piers in New York and the *Move Along* report (Alliance for a Safe & Diverse DC, 2008), the community-based study to sabotage the prostitution-free zones in Washington, DC.

This historiography of queer of colour space-making is continued in John Paul Catungal's "'We Had to Take Space, We Had to Create Space': Locating Queer of Colour Politics in 1980s Toronto." The chapter revisits local queer of colour politics in 1980s Toronto – in particular, HIV/AIDS organizing – focusing on the work of the Asian Community AIDS Services and the Black Coalition for AIDS Prevention and their respective predecessors, Gay Asians Toronto and Zami. These organizations emerged out of a need for ethno-specific, culturally appropriate, and community-based support for sexual minorities of colour, particularly those affected by HIV/AIDS, who were being marginalized by mainstream gay and lesbian and AIDS organizations. Together, these organizations created local ecologies of ethno-specificity in otherwise "race-neutral" organizing contexts. At the same time, they were situated in extra-local networks of learning, inspiration, and emulation. They drew from US-based political organizing and knowledge production about queers of colour, particularly by Black feminists such as Audre Lorde, and from sexual health workers and organizers in US cities with substantial Asian and Black communities, whose experiences had informed some of their own efforts at local ethno-specific responses to HIV/AIDS in Toronto. The chapter concludes that local queer of colour politics in 1980s Toronto demanded an approach that treated the "local" not as bounded by the city, but as constituted by a broader trans-local geography of queer of colour networks.

OmiSoore H. Dryden's "'Má-ka Juk Yuh: A Genealogy of Black Queer Liveability in Toronto" similarly revalues local histories by offering up a thus far unpublished archive of thirty-five years of Black queer activism. For this chapter, Dryden and Debbie Douglas, co-editor of the seminal

1997 Black queer diasporic collection after which the chapter is named, gathered a group of eight Black queer diasporic elders around a kitchen table to recount, remember, and recall Black queer community-making in Toronto since the early 1980s. The conversants are key figures who have helped to create spaces for Black LGBTQ people in Toronto and innovated interlocking frameworks of racism, homophobia, and sexism that have produced indispensable lessons for wider social movements in Toronto. These elders look back on numerous important sites and moments, including Sister Vision: Black Women and Women of Colour Press (1984), Black and West Indian Gays (1983–4), Black Women's Collective (1984), Sisters Café (1991), and Black Coalition for Aids Prevention (1987). They reflect on difficult topics that are rarely talked about, such as BDSM, they call into space activists who have left or died, and they comment on historic moments such as the HIV/AIDS epidemic, apartheid, and #BlackLivesMatter. The chapter thereby also facilitates an exploration of how home, belonging, community, and family have been constructed and how these formations inform contemporary Black diasporic queer and trans organizing in the city. It serves as both a reminder (for some) and a schooling (for others) that there was and is a vibrant Black and queer "elsewhereness." This place and space of elsewhereness is one in which Black queer and trans diasporic lives always already exist, thus making visible a different reading of LGBTQ activism in Canada.

Building on the theme that specific queer diasporic entry points are valuable, Robert Diaz, Marissa Largo, and Fritz Luther Pino subsequently discuss "Diasporic Intimacies: Queer Filipinos/as and Canadian Imaginaries." The chapter is named after a series of events of the same name, which the authors organized at the Ontario College of Art and Design in 2015. Highlighting how artists, scholars, and community members have animated several decades of Filipino/a organizing, the authors describe artistic, academic, and community-based perspectives as entwined, in ways that intervene in and necessarily go beyond the academic institution. The queer Filipino/a Canadian critique expressed in these modalities encourages us to render our pain and survival through multiple forms of expression, without turning to the overwrought and often delegitimizing ruses of multicultural inclusion, belonging, and citizenship circulated by the state.

Commenting on a more recent chapter of queer and trans people of colour (QTPOC) history, Matthew Chin closes this section of the book with his chapter "On 'Gaymousness' and 'Calling Out': Affect,

Violence, and Humanity in Queer of Colour Politics." In the 2000s Toronto that Chin describes, QTPOC gained a critical mass of often arts-based and multiracial spaces, where tools inherited from earlier generations, such as intersectionality, community accountability, and transformative justice were actively put to use. Far from being either celebratory or nostalgic, Chin describes the task of formulating alternatives to the white-supremacist, cis-heteropatriarchal status quo as one that is as critical as it is unfinished. Drawing on his large-scale, qualitative research project with QTPOC organizers, Chin engages in critical reflexivity by drawing our attention to the emergence of regulatory ideals of anti-oppression that have become part of many organizers' community practice. Chin interprets this enactment as a form of discipline that produces a particular kind of political personhood and participates in cultures of fear and shame. Thus, the QTPOC whom he interviewed often found themselves evaluated on the basis of their politics and either elevated to the status of celebrity or "called out" in a form of public castigation – a process that many of his interviewees related in terms of (de)humanization. The chapter concludes by describing how many QTPOC are now attempting to build, in place of this punitive and hierarchical model, more sustainable models of community practice that prefigure the world we want to live in.

While the first section of this book foregrounds spaces where QTBIPOC have come together to organize, the second section, "Cartographies of Resistance," explores the possibilities and limits of transforming institutionalized spaces like the LGBT community and the academy. Traditionally hailed as progressive, these spaces are nevertheless reproductive of the very interlocking regimes of oppression that are at the basis of anti-blackness, settler colonialism, and border imperialism. The authors in this section document interventions that permit us to rethink how the chances of life and death are unevenly distributed in these sites. They outline, for instance, how the spaces of the academic and the prison industrial complex intersect with and are animated by anti-Black racism, processes of gentrification, epistemic violence, and neo-liberal solidarity. Our communities' survival is necessarily negotiated in tension with these systems, rendering QTBIPOC excessive to normative spatial and institutional citizenship.

Nwadiogo Ejiogu and Syrus Marcus Ware's chapter, "Calling a Shrimp a Shrimp: A Black Queer Intervention in Disability Studies," considers the university as one such site. The chapter is a reworking of Ejiogu and Ware's widely cited, taught, and circulated paper "How

Disability Studies Stays White, and What Kind of White It Stays," and here it appears in print for the first time. Reflecting on their time as graduate students in the field of disability studies, the authors explore how single-identity theories and politics leave out and hurt QTBIPOC. Using a close analysis of a disability studies classroom at a well-known Toronto university, they describe the lack of space given to discussions about race and intersectionality. Even though disability studies has emerged from the on-the-ground work of disability movements, much of the scholarship in this promising field has proceeded to erase how disability is mutually constituted by, with, and from racial, sexual, class-based, and gendered categories and colonial legacies. To fill this gap, Ejiogu and Ware chronicle some of the organic perspectives that have emerged out of Toronto-based disability justice activism, often led by queers of colour (see also Piepzna-Samarasinha, forthcoming). Stepping into a long tradition of women, queer, and trans of colour storytelling that makes one's own body available as a bridge that translates between movements and epistemologies, the authors draw on their own Black queer lives to show how disability, racialization, homophobia, class, and gender intersect in the spaces we are all trying to make sense of.

Elaborating further on the boundless potential of intersectional Black queer activism to effect large-scale transformation, the next chapter, "Black Lives Matter Toronto Teach-In," by Janaya Khan and LeRoi Newbold, co-founders of Black Lives Matter Toronto (BLM-TO), recounts one of the most successful local initiatives to combat anti-Black racism in recent years. In their historic teach-in held at a Black-owned bookshop in Toronto in 2015, which is here published for the first time, Khan and Newbold lay out the guiding principles of the movement and introduce local campaigns such as Take Back the Night and Freedom School, each of which has centred Black trans, queer, and female lives. They introduce Black Lives Matter as a unique contribution to resisting the extrajudicial killings of Black people by police and vigilantes that have long accompanied life in North American cities. This movement is always already queer and trans in that it goes beyond the narrow nationalism that can be prevalent in some Black communities, which merely calls on Black people to love Black, live Black, and buy Black, thereby keeping straight, cis Black men in the front of the movement. Sisters, queer and trans, and disabled folk, meanwhile, take up roles in the background or not at all. In contrast, Black Lives Matter affirms the lives of Black queer and trans folks, disabled folks, Black-undocumented folks, folks with records, women, and all Black lives along the gender spectrum. It both centres those that have been marginalized within Black liberation movements and names their leadership as a key tactic in (re)building these movements to prepare for the revolutionary leap it will take to break free.

The importance of this queer- and trans-led movement for Black lives is further highlighted in Tara Atluri's chapter, "Black Picket Signs/ White Picket Fences: Racism, Space, and Solidarity." The chapter presents a different temporal snapshot of the movement by paying tribute to the remarkable courage and inspiring tenacity of BLM-TO activists a few months after the teach-in that forms the basis of Khan and Newbold's chapter. In spring 2016, BLM-TO activists, remarkably, remapped and remade space by occupying the square in front of the police headquarters in Toronto for over two weeks. They established a tent city in this most lethal of architectures to protest the state-led harassment and murder of Black people, and they did so in ways that centred the lives and leadership of queer and trans Black folk. Atluri explores the queer possibilities of this intervention to argue that the matter of bodies, of embodied and phenomenological experiences of racism that live on and in the skin, are matters of spatial politics, structured by white-settler-colonial cartographies. Contrasting the intersectional visions of BLM-TO with the homonationalist figuration of Kathleen Wynne – the province's out lesbian premier who famously "met" the group during the tent city – Atluri shows how Black protest disrupts white-settler geographies. The landmarks of insurrectionary Black politics highlighted in this chapter could not be further removed from the white-queer politics of respectability that Wynne and her partner came to represent in media reports of the tent city.

Nayrouz Abu Hatoum and Ghaida Moussa's chapter, "Becoming through Others: Western Queer Self-Fashioning and Solidarity with Queer Palestine," similarly points to the limits of a white-queer politics that seeks to incorporate Others for its own agenda, this time in the name of allyship rather than policing. Written in the hopes of encouraging better ways of relating with and supporting those with whom we are in solidarity, their chapter provides a theoretical engagement with recent trajectories in the debate about queer solidarity with Palestine. By interrogating Western queer interest in the "Palestinian queer," the authors attempt to explore what makes dominant subjects turn to Others as a political cause. Abu Hatoum and Moussa offer a framework for thinking through Western queer solidarity with Palestinian queers that goes beyond a saviour mission directed towards the Arab world. Instead, by turning their gaze outwards, they seek to understand the work that the Palestinian queer does in the Western queer imagination. They ask, How are Palestinian queers mobilized at the service of a new brand of self-fashioned, radical-queer subjectivity in North America?

Azar Masoumi's chapter, "Compulsory Coming Out and Agentic Negotiations: Toronto QTPOC Narratives," is another critique of Western-imposed ways of being queer. The chapter builds on the author's interviews with twelve first- and second-generation immigrant queer women and trans Black and people of colour in Toronto to interrogate "coming out" as a compulsory step and *the* marker of queer and trans subjecthood. Drawing on queer of colour scholars and respondents' narratives, Azar Masoumi argues that coming out is a highly racialized narrative that posits non-white people as underdeveloped, backward subjects in need of rescue and liberation. For many participants, the centrality of racialization to their subjectivities and everyday lives means that living openly as subjects that are primarily or exclusively defined by their non-conforming genders and sexualities is not an option. Rather, participants' negotiations are complicated but also laden with agency: they simultaneously comply with, creatively reshape, and resist the dominant terms of compulsory coming out.

The last contribution to this anthology, "The Sacred Uprising: Indigenous Creative Activisms," is Syrus Marcus Ware's interview with Rebeka Tabobondung, the influential media activist whose impact on Toronto social movements is considerable. The chapter looks back on two decades of QTBIPOC coalition-building in Toronto, including the mobilization of specifically Indigenous counter-knowledge to the colonial gender binary in the campaign to make gendered spaces, such as the Centre for Women and Trans People at the University of Toronto, trans-inclusive. Tabobondung reflects on the development of Two Spirit–based artistic activisms in her home communities of Wasauksing First Nation and Tkaronto. This includes the creation of *MUSKRAT Magazine* and Maaiingan Productions, which have become key archives of Indigenous arts and culture. Considering the story of the muskrat as a root for her work, Tabobondung revisits the intense learning that happened among the QTBIPOC from Toronto who formed a contingent to join the protests against the Free Trade Area of the Americas (FTAA) in Quebec City in 2001. Two-spirited, queer, and trans folks of colour worked together to document activist responses to the FTAA gathering, act as street medics, and create communities of resistance that

Tabobondung subsequently termed the "sacred uprising" in her well-known film about that experience. Reflecting on these collaborations, which made bigger waves in both Quebec City and Toronto, Tabobondung shows how anti-colonial struggles are foundational to questions of gender, sexuality, and racialization on Turtle Island.

Taken together, these chapters offer an indispensable account of QTBIPOC spaces in Toronto and beyond. At the same time, they witness and participate in the historical moments of our times, including the momentous rise of Black Lives Matter, queer solidarity with Palestine, and trans and queer of colour resistance against gentrification. They interrogate the forces that have made it possible for QTBIPOC to be imagined as absent from, or newcomers to, the very spaces they have long invested in: from the erasure of queer, racialized bodies from the academic knowledge formations that they have innovated to the violent displacement of poor, disabled, racialized, and sex-working bodies from the Village and from Pride. As Jin Haritaworn argues in the epilogue to this book, QTBIPOC communities prefigure alternative futures and propose alternative models for sharing space that seek to leave no one behind. They offer visionary projects to transform the city, including imagining new ways of building communities of care, re-evaluating the role of feeling in alliance-building and settler-colonial projects, queering urban justice, and locating home at the complicated intersections of longing and violence. Besides insisting on remembering (as) those who were never meant to survive (Lorde 1978), they challenge a queer nostalgia (Haritaworn 2015), which selectively incorporates non-white queers into a dominant historiography that seeks to prolong the radical moment in a way benefiting not subaltern subjects, but a white-queer subject, who can afford to remain oblivious to the unequal terms under which some queers get to live, while others continue to die.

As editors and authors of this book, we offer up the following pages as catalytic moments that open up a different set of ancestries, genealogies, and futures. May they inspire a permanent readiness for the marvellous. May they help us imagine otherwise.

References

Alexander, M. Jacqui. 2005. *Pedagogies of Crossing: Meditations on Feminism, Sexual Politics, Memory, and the Sacred.* Durham, NC: Duke University Press. https://doi.org/10.1215/9780822386988.

Alliance for a Safe & Diverse DC. 2008. *Move Along: Policing Sex Work in Washington, D.C.* Washington, DC: Different Avenues. Accessed 28 December 2015. https://dctranscoalition.files.wordpress.com/2010/05/movealongreport.pdf.

Bacchetta, Paola. 2009. "Dyketactics! Notes towards an Un-silencing." In *Smash the Church, Smash the State: The Early Years of Gay Liberation*, edited by Tommi Avicolli Mecca, 218–31. San Francisco: City Light Books.

Bacchetta, Paola, Fatima El-Tayeb, and Jin Haritaworn. 2015. "Queer of Colour Formations and Translocal Spaces in Europe." *Environment and Planning D: Society and Space* 33 (5): 769–78. https://doi.org/10.1177/0263775815608712.

Bell, David, and Jon Binnie. 2004. "Authenticating Queer Space: Citizenship, Urbanism and Governance." *Urban Studies* 41 (9): 1807–20. https://doi.org/10.1080/0042098042000243165.

Brand, Dionne. 2001. *A Map to the Door of No Return.* Toronto: Doubleday.

Castells, Manuel. 1983. *The City and the Grassroots: A Cross-Cultural Theory of Urban Social Movements.* Berkeley: University of California Press.

Césaire, Aimé. 2000. *Discourse on Colonialism.* New York: New York University Press.

Cohen, Cathy. 2010–11. "Death and Rebirth of a Movement: Queering Critical Ethnic Studies." Special Issue, *Social Justice* (Community Accountability: Emerging Movements to Transform Violence) 37 (4): 126–32.

Coulthard, Glen Sean. 2014. *Red Skin, White Masks: Rejecting the Colonial Politics of Recognition.* Minneapolis: University of Minnesota Press. https://doi.org/10.5749/minnesota/9780816679645.001.0001.

da Silva, Denise Ferreira. 2007. *Toward a Global Idea of Race.* Minneapolis: University of Minnesota Press.

Derrida, Jacques, and Eric Prenowitz. 1995. "Archive Fever: A Freudian Impression." *Diacritics* 25 (2): 9–63. https://doi.org/10.2307/465144.

Doan, Petra L., and Harrison Higgins. 2011. "The Demise of Queer Space?" *Journal of Planning Education and Research* 31 (1): 6–25. https://doi.org/10.1177/0739456X10391266.

Douglas, Debbie, Courtnay McFarlane, Makeda Silvera, and Douglas Stewart, eds. 1997. *Má-ka: Diasporic Juks – Contemporary Writing by Queers of African Descent.* Toronto: Sister Vision.

El-Tayeb, Fatima. 2012. "'Gays Who Cannot Properly Be Gay': Queer Muslims in the Neoliberal European City." *European Journal of Women's Studies* 19 (1): 79–95. https://doi.org/10.1177/1350506811426388.

Ferguson, Roderick. 2004. *Aberrations in Black: Toward a Queer of Color Critique.* Minneapolis: University of Minnesota Press.

FIERCE. 2008. "LGBTQ Youth Fight for a S.P.O.T. on Pier 40." Press release (15 September). http://fiercenyc.org/media/docs/3202_PublicHearing PressRelease.

Finley, C. 2014. "Gay Marriage and Indigenous Sovereignty: Making Queer Love Legit and Fun in the Colville Nation." Paper presented at the Annual Meeting of the American Studies Association, Los Angeles, 5–9 November.

Florida, Richard. 2002. *The Rise of the Creative Class*. New York: Basic Books.

Foster, Tori, and Alexis Mitchell. 2008. *Queeropolis: Toronto 1972–2008*. Accessed 1 December 2016. http://www.alexismitchell.com/queeropolis/.

FunMaps. 2013. *Toronto FunMap: Including Ottawa, Niagara and the Thousand Islands*. Accessed 1 December 2016. https://issuu.com/funmaps/docs/toronto-funmap-2013-issuu.

Gopinath, Gayatri. 2005. *Impossible Desires: Queer Diasporas and South Asian Public Cultures*. Durham, NC: Duke University Press. https://doi.org/10.1215/9780822386537.

Guardian. 2015. "LGBT-Friendly Cities, Hotels, Restaurants and Clubs: Readers' Travel Tips." International edition. 15 October. Accessed 1 December 2016. https://www.theguardian.com/travel/2015/oct/15/lgbt-lesbian-gay-travel-tips.

Hanhardt, Christina B. 2008. "Butterflies, Whistles, and Fists: Gay Safe Street Patrols and the New Gay Ghetto, 1976–1981." *Radical History Review* 100 (Winter 2008): 61–85. https://doi.org/10.1215/01636545-2007-022.

– 2013. *Safe Space: Gay Neighborhood History and the Politics of Violence*. Durham, NC: Duke University Press. https://doi.org/10.1215/9780822378860.

Haritaworn, Jin. 2015. *Queer Lovers and Hateful Others*. London: Pluto. https://doi.org/10.2307/j.ctt183p5vv.

Houston, Andrea. 2013. "Keep the Village Queer: Study Participants." *Xtra*. 20 May. Accessed 1 December 2016. http://www.dailyxtra.com/toronto/news-and-ideas/news/keep-the-village-queer-study-participants-61939.

Hull, Akasha (Gloria T.), Patricia B. Scott, and Barbara Smith, eds. 1982. *But Some of Us Are Brave: All the Women Are White, All the Blacks Are Men – Black Women's Studies*. New York: Feminist Press.

Ingram, Gordon Brent, Anne-Marie Boutillette, and Yolanda Retter, eds. 1997. *Queers in Space: Communities, Public Places, Sites of Resistance*. Seattle: Bay Press.

King, Tiffany Lethabo. 2013. "In the Clearing: Black Female Bodies, Space and Settler Colonial Landscapes." Unpublished PhD diss., Department of American Studies, University of Maryland, Baltimore.

Knopp, Lawrence. 1990. "Some Theoretical Implications of Gay Involvement in an Urban Land Market." *Political Geography Quarterly* 9 (4): 337–52. https://doi.org/10.1016/0260-9827(90)90033-7.

Lawrence, Bonita. 2004. *"Real" Indians and Others: Mixed-Blood Urban Native Peoples and Indigenous Nationhood*. Lincoln: University of Nebraska Press.

Lorde, Audre. 1978. *The Black Unicorn: Poems*. New York: Norton.

Madi, Harold, et al. 2014. *Phase Two Report: State of the Village Report*. Toronto: Planning Partnership.

Manalansan, Martin F., IV. 2005. "Race, Violence, and Neoliberal Spatial Politics in the Global City." *Social Text* 23 (3–4): 141–55. https://doi.org/10.1215/01642472-23-3-4_84-85-141.

McKittrick, Katherine. 2006. *Demonic Grounds: Black Women and the Cartographies of Struggle*. Minneapolis: University of Minnesota Press.

Melamed, Jodi. 2011. "Reading Tehran in *Lolita*: Making Racialized and Gendered Difference Work for Neoliberal Multiculturalism." In *Strange Affinities: The Gender and Sexual Politics of Comparative Racialization*, edited by Grace Kyungwon Hong and Roderick A. Ferguson, 76–121. Durham, NC: Duke University Press. https://doi.org/10.1215/9780822394075-004.

Million, Dian. 2013. *Therapeutic Nations: Healing in an Age of Indigenous Human Rights*. Tucson: University of Arizona Press.

Moraga, Cherrie, and Gloria E. Anzaldúa, eds. 1981. *This Bridge Called My Back: Writings by Radical Women of Colour*. Watertown, MA. Persephone Press.

Muñoz, José. 2000. "Feeling Brown: Ethnicity and Affect in Ricardo Bracho's *The Sweetest Hangover (and Other STDs)*." *Theatre Journal* 52 (1): 67–79. https://doi.org/10.1353/tj.2000.0020.

Nair, Yasmin. 2008. "Why I Won't Come Out on National Coming Out Day." Blog entry, 9 October. Accessed 1 December 2016. www.yasminnair.net/content/why-i-won%E2%80%99t-come-out-national-coming-out-day-9-october-2008.

Nash, Catherine. 2013. "Queering Neighbourhoods: Politics and Practice in Toronto." *ACME: An International E-Journal for Critical Geographies* 12 (2): 193–219.

Native Youth Sexual Health Network. 2014. "Supporting the Resurgence of Community-Based Responses to Violence: Collaborative Statement and Resources with Families of Sisters in Spirit and No More Silence." Press release. 14 March. Accessed 1 August 2014. www.nativeyouthsexualhealth.com/march142014.pdf.

Oswin, Natalie. 2015. "World, City, Queer." *Antipode* 47 (3): 557–65. https://doi.org/10.1111/anti.12142.

Piepzna-Samarasinha, Leah Lakshmi. Forthcoming. "Toronto Crip City: A Not So Brief, Incomplete Personal History of Disabled QTPOC Cultural Activism in Toronto, 1997–2015." In *Marvellous Grounds*, edited by Jin

Haritaworn, Ghaida Moussa, and Syrus Marcus Ware. Toronto: Marvellous Grounds.

Puar, Jasbir. 2007. *Terrorist Assemblages: Homonationalism in Queer Times.* Durham, NC: Duke University Press. https://doi.org/10.1215/9780822390442.

Razack, Sherene H. 2002. "When Place Becomes Race." In *Race, Space, and the Law: Unmapping a White Settler Society*, edited by Sherene H. Razack, 1–20. Toronto: Between the Lines.

Reddy, Chandan. 2011. *Freedom with Violence: Race, Sexuality, and the US State.* Durham, NC: Duke University Press. https://doi.org/10.1215/9780822394648.

Robinson, Cedric. 1983. *Black Marxism: The Making of the Black Radical Tradition.* Chapel Hill: University of North Carolina Press.

Rodríguez, Río. 2016. "Mapping QTBIPOC Toronto." A major portfolio submitted in partial fulfilment of a master's degree in environmental studies, York University, Toronto.

Rodríguez, Río, and Amandeep Kaur Panag, eds. 2016. "QTBIPOC Space: Remapping Belonging in Toronto." *Marvellous Grounds* (website), no. 1. Accessed 1 December 2016. http://marvellousgrounds.com/blog/special-issue-1-qtbipoc-space/.

Rubin, Gayle S. 1984. "Thinking Sex: Notes for a Radical Theory of the Politics of Sexuality." In *Pleasure and Danger: Exploring Female Sexuality*, edited by Carole S. Vance, 143–78. Boston: Routledge and Kegan Paul.

Schulman, Sara. 2012. *The Gentrification of the Mind: Witness to a Lost Imagination.* Berkeley: University of California Press.

Silvera, Makeda, ed. 1991. *Piece of My Heart: A Lesbian of Colour Anthology.* Toronto: Sister Vision.

Simpson, Leanne Betasamosake. 2014. "Not Murdered, Not Missing: Rebelling against Colonial Gender Violence." Blog post, 8 March. Accessed 30 December 2016. http://leannesimpson.ca/not-murdered-not-missing/.

Smith, Andrea. 2005. *Conquest: Sexual Violence and American Indian Genocide.* Boston: South End Press.

Taylor, Diana. 2003. *The Archive and the Repertoire: Performing Cultural Memory in the Americas.* Durham, NC: Duke University Press. https://doi.org/10.1215/9780822385318.

Thobani, Sunera. 2007. *Exalted Subject: Studies in the Making of Race and Nation in Canada.* Toronto: University of Toronto Press.

– 2014. Prologue to *Queer Necropolitics*, edited by Jin Haritaworn, Adi Kuntsman, and Silvia Posocco, xv–xviii. London: Routledge.

Tinsley, Omise'eke Natasha. 2008. "Black Atlantic, Queer Atlantic: Queer Imaginings of the Middle Passage." *GLQ – A Journal of Lesbian and Gay Studies* 14 (2–3): 191–215. https://doi.org/10.1215/10642684-2007-030.

Walcott, Rinaldo. 2006. "Black Men in Frocks: Sexing Race in a Gay Ghetto (Toronto)." In *Claiming Space: Racialization in Canadian Cities*, edited by Cheryl Teelucksingh, 121–33. Waterloo, ON: Wilfrid Laurier University Press.

Walia, Harsha. 2013. *Undoing Border Imperialism*. Oakland, CA: AK Press.

PART ONE

Mapping Community

1 "Our Study Is Sabotage": Queering Urban Justice, from Toronto to New York

A ROUNDTABLE BY JIN HARITAWORN,
WITH CHE GOSSETT, RÍO RODRÍGUEZ,
AND SYRUS MARCUS WARE[1]

We organized this roundtable at the Faculty of Environmental Studies at York University, Toronto, as part of the faculty's seminar series.
The series has often presented an alternative curriculum, which is put
together collaboratively by activist students and faculty with a personal
and political investment in anti-racist and anti-colonial, and at times
queer and feminist, art, activism, and scholarship. Discussing queer of
colour politics in Toronto in a transnational context, alongside the better-
known struggle for the Christopher Street piers in New York and against
police violence in Philadelphia, the speakers responded to the absence
of queer of colour and other intersectional approaches from dominant
accounts of the city and of urban and environmental justice. They
proposed that trans and queer Black people and people of colour had
engaged in important struggles around AIDS activism, Black liberation,
prison abolition, disability arts, sexual health, and community-based
education, all of which were central to understanding the costs of urban
development and to formulating alternatives to the neo-liberal city.

JIN HARITAWORN: I'm excited to have this panel here at the Faculty of Environmental Studies. There's a lot of people here who
are doing urban studies and interested in urban justice, but who
do not generally consider queers of colour as protagonists in these
struggles. What does urban justice mean to you? What would it
mean, to invoke Katherine McKittrick,[2] to treat queers of colour as
geographic subjects?

---

1 We thank Chantal Persad for transcribing this roundtable.
2 Katherine McKittrick, *Demonic Grounds: Black Women and the Cartographies of Struggle*
(Minneapolis: University of Minnesota Press, 2006), xix.

CHE GOSSETT: Urban justice has really been on my mind because of all the systemic changes that are happening in Philadelphia, where I'm currently living, and in so many other cities across the US. A huge phenomenon right now is neo-liberal restructuring: the decimation of the educational institutions, the massive closing of schools, while prisons are being built, the school-to-prison pipeline. Urban justice really asks the question, "Whose city is it?" It pushes back against the idea that the city is the privilege and the territory for wealthy folks and that they get to determine the landscape. Black feminist, queer, and trans politics have always been urban justice. When I think of urban justice, I think of Stonewall fighters Sylvia Rivera and Marsha P. Johnson. The group that they founded in New York City in 1970, STAR [Street Transvestite Action Revolutionaries],[3] did a lot of amazing work to combat homelessness of queer youth and to take up and make space where the state [had] abandoned queer and trans people of colour. I think of June Jordan, who did a lot of work around urban planning.[4] Of the Combahee River Collective, the Black lesbian feminist group that was active from 1974 to 1980 in Chicago, and their visions around a political horizon that is very different than the capitalist one we're being offered.[5] I think that those legacies have a lot of resonance now and we can continue to build on them while recognizing that urban justice, like so much, is inseparable from Black feminist and trans feminist legacies of resistance and resilience and creating different spaces. I also think about the AIDS activist movement and moment, which in Philadelphia is still happening and is a huge force in the city. ACT UP Philadelphia was started by a lot of folks who were of colour, homeless, actively involved in doing sex work, and making demands for housing for folks living with HIV/AIDS.

SYRUS MARCUS WARE: When I think of urban justice, I'm thinking about the relationships among prisoners' justice, disability justice,

---

3 Leslie Feinberg, interview by Sylvia Rivera, "I'm Glad I Was in the Stonewall Riot," *Workers World*, 1998, accessed 1 December 2016, https://www.workers.org/ww/1998/sylvia0702.php.
4 Cheryl Fish, "Place, Emotion, and Environmental Justice in Harlem: June Jordan and Buckminster Fuller's 1965 'Architextual Collaboration,'" *Discourse* 29, no. 2 (2007): 330–45.
5 Combahee River Collective, *A Black Feminist Statement* (New York: Kitchen Table: Women of Color Press, 1985).

and gentrification. One of the sites where we have organized around prison abolition in Toronto is the Don Jail. We would come to the Don Jail every year on 10 August to mark Prisoners' Justice Day. It's a very unique thing to have a prison right in the centre of the city. Part of the reason why they move prisons outside of the city is to separate prisoners from family and community who might provide access and support. They also move them "away" so that we can't witness the atrocious things that happen in prisons.

One of the things we're seeing in Toronto right now is the physical and symbolic gentrification of the area around the Don Jail. They've moved all the prisoners out to suburban areas, taking the conversation about prison abolition outside of the downtown core. They've renamed the street where the Don is located Jack Layton Way, after the former Toronto mayor remembered for championing progressive causes. Meanwhile, the physical site of the Don Jail has become part of Bridgepoint Health, a mental health facility – a transition that brings home the close overlaps between the prison and psychiatry, and the PIC [Prison Industrial Complex] and the medical industrial complex.

I'm thinking about the microcosms of organizing in the city, including independent networks of people doing community accountability, in trying to deal with conflict in their communities, and people organizing around social change, whether through groups like the Black queer and trans arts/activist collective Blackness Yes! or the migration/border activist movement No One Is Illegal. I'm also just thinking about the possibilities. I read a lot of Octavia Butler, and I'm kinda obsessed with the idea that given that things are about to change in a very dramatic way – that there's this polar vortex, and climate change is on the precipice – we're going to be in a situation, where we have to be able to be together in a really different way than we're used to. There's a sense that relying on other people for some sense of community built on social justice is going to be so much more urgent. And I think that being in a condensed environment like downtown Toronto demands of us that we start trying to imagine how we're going to live together – I don't know, in close proximity in a bunker.

RÍO RODRÍGUEZ: I host radical-queer walking tours of Church-Wellesley, Toronto's Gay Village. The tours attempt to introduce mostly young people to local urban histories and themes and concepts such as sex work, gentrification, policing, and community

organizing. Urban justice essentially speaks to who has the ownership over and power to exist in the city, to define themselves and
exert their rights to safety, belonging, and representation in urban
spaces.

Many of you have heard of the brilliant Allied Media Conference, which happens in Detroit every year. In 2014, they had a
track called creative place-making. And I really liked how they defined this creative place-making as the opposite of gentrification,
as that which is outside of gentrification. They ask us what the role
of creativity is in achieving that thing for which we have no word
and how we can keep and honour the existing creativity and identity of a place. Roberto Bedoya calls this the swelling conversation
between the politics of belonging and dis-belonging.[6] Who has the
power to make a place their own, and who does not? Who has
the power to have their own history reflected in a neighbourhood?
These questions definitely play out in the Church-Wellesley area.

Our tour explores stumblings of urban justice based on single-
issue identities. It attempts to make space for us to talk about the
ways that urban discourses that incorporate gay people – but don't
attend to intersectionalities of race and class – have failed us. For
example, the tour takes a spot at George Hislop Park. George Hislop is widely known as one of the Canadian gay activists who filed
the federal lawsuit that won equal benefits for the surviving same-
sex partners of deceased pensioners. So, essentially, they named
this park after him as a way to reflect and celebrate the gay presence in Canada. So it's a place where we stop and talk about what
naming means, who gets to name what, and which bodies get reflected in urban space. We also stop at Maitland and Homewood,
which is this famous strip just east of the Village where residents
began organizing in 2008 to resist the presence of trans sex workers and push them out of the neighbourhood. The city responded
by instituting policies that further displaced the sex workers – they
now have signs where you cannot stop a car between certain hours,
to prevent sex workers from meeting clients.[7]

---

6 Roberto Bedoya, "Placemaking and the Politics of Belonging and Dis-belonging," *GIA
Reader* 24, no. 1 (2013): 20–1.
7 For a deeper discussion of these events, see Gabriela Rodríguez, "Mapping QTBIPOC
Toronto" (a major portfolio submitted in partial fulfilment of a master's degree in
environmental studies, York University, Toronto, 2016).

So our tour explores how the successes of white-dominated LGBT activism to claim the right to define the city have fallen short of really achieving urban justice. When gay figures find reflection in the cityscape, it's often at the expense of other queer and trans bodies that have traditionally been excluded on the basis of racism, classism, and transphobia.

JIN: It's interesting to listen for transnational resonances in your responses. While capital travels – all these evil ways to keep sex workers out, poor people out, are happening in a lot of places at the same time – resistance to it doesn't travel as easily, right? It's also really good to hear your unapologetically multi-issue perspectives on urban struggles. As Río says, the kind of equity-and-diversity perspectives that have been mainstreamed so far – where we can apparently only "do" one difference at a time – do not amount to urban justice. They do amount to gay gentrification. I think all of you have brought home how queer and trans people of colour are affected by urban injustices. Can you talk about how they have contributed to struggles against policing, incarceration, and gentrification?

CHE: I have archive fever to channel Derrida and his book of that same name.[8] I'm a fan of archives, especially queer and trans and AIDS archives. I really like, Río, how you were talking about excavating hidden geographies of the city, queer geographies, queer and trans people of colour geographies of the city. As someone who lives in Philadelphia, I oftentimes feel really fond of local history, herstory, theirstory, hirstory. It's close to my heart; I'm fascinated by it. I think there's a lot of resonance today with the ways in which queer and trans folks of colour were resisting gentrification, incarceration, policing, and criminalization in Philadelphia in the 1970s.

In 1970, there was this amazing moment that feels really emblematic of that for me. The Black Panther Party had a big convention at Philadelphia Temple University called the People's Revolutionary Constitutional Convention.[9] This constitution is a people's

---

8 Jacques Derrida, *Archive Fever: A Freudian Impression* (Chicago: University of Chicago Press, 1996).
9 See Leslie Feinberg, "Early Left-Wing Liberation: 'Unity with All the Oppressed,'" *Workers World*, 5 October 2006, accessed 1 December 2016, https://www.workers.org/2006/us/lavender-red-75/.

constitution, not the settler-colonial, state-slavery one. Hundreds of people came. It's where Huey Newton met Sylvia Rivera, for instance. Also, Afeni Shakur came. It was this unique site of convergence, and there's a lot of continuity from that moment until now. I don't know if folks have seen films like *United in Anger* or *How to Survive a Plague*.[10] Both films profile ACT UP, and there's a person who appears in both who is a gay or queer Black man, amazing anti-war activist, who died in the 1990s – Oretz Alderson. He was also at this convention and brought hundreds of queer people of colour there.

A week before the convention, Frank Rizzo, the notorious fascist mayor, had the Panthers strip at the local Black Panther Party office before cameras, in a moment of police terrorism and white supremacy. So there's an archive of conversations and convergences between Black liberationist politics, queer liberationist politics, trans liberationist politics that is really powerful. This archive shows how queer and trans of colour organizers have always been working in prison-abolitionist ways, even if they didn't name themselves such. It meant that you didn't call the police to solve violence. It meant that when Sylvia Rivera spoke at the 1973 Pride march in New York City, she talked about getting letters from people in prison every week, about being a survivor of sexual violence and formerly incarcerated, about centring incarcerated trans people in our movements.[11] This is in continuity with Cece Mc-Donald's recent statements that prisons are not safe, no matter if they're men's or women's prisons.[12] So anti-policing and decriminalization has always been at the heart of our movement – it's not necessarily a new thing. Considering that the scale of mass incarceration would have been unimaginable in 1970, Rivera's words are even more crucial today.

---

10 Jim Hubbard, *United in Anger: A History of ACT UP*, 2014; David France, *How to Survive a Plague*, 2012.

11 See Reina Gossett's important archive on Sylvia Rivera at http://thespiritwas. tumblr.com/post/28415757544/ten-posts-for-sylvia-riveras-ten-year-memorial, accessed 1 December 2016.

12 Andrea Abikaram, "There Is No Such Thing as Prison Reform: An Interview with Cece MacDonald," *Transformation*, 2012, accessed 1 December 2016, https://www. opendemocracy.net/transformation/andrea-abikaram/there-is-no-such-thing-as-prison-reform-interview-with-cece-mcdonald.

SYRUS: I'm also fascinated by that convention. They had all of these different subgroups from key communities writing sections of this constitution that was, like, by the people for the people. One of the demands or tenets was the right to be gay anytime any place, and the right to sex change on demand. As a trans person, I'm like, "Yes – this is 1970! Crucial." A few years ago, I was speaking at the Society for Disabilities conference in New York, and there was somebody in the audience who told this story about being in San Francisco in the early 1970s. There were all these activists organizing to get wheel cuts in the sidewalk just so you could physically move through your city. They had taken over city hall and had barricaded themselves in. There weren't any food supplies, there wasn't attendant care … it was really stressful. And she told this story about how the Black Panther Party came and stood at the door, armed at the ready, and brought food. So there's many examples of how we were always already connected, always already supporting each other's movements. We must trouble the idea that we were separate until now.

In Canada, there's traditionally been a high representation of trans folks of colour in prison-abolition work in Toronto. I can't really tell you why, but I can tell you the what. One of the first groups that was organizing around prisoners with HIV and AIDS was the Prisoners HIV/AIDS Support Action Network (PASAN). They started in 1991, and I worked there for a couple of years in the early 2000s. From the outset, there were always trans people involved. In fact, Viviane Namaste wrote PASAN's trans brief, a key document about the experiences of trans prisoners in Canada, in 1999. Certainly trans people of colour, who are tremendously over-incarcerated, were accessing resources from the agency, and so it was sort of built in. I think it's really significant that one of the largest prisoner-focused AIDS service organizations in the country was founded on trans people's voices.

I'm also thinking of the large uprising for the FTAA – the Free Trade Area of the Americas – in Quebec City in 2001. There was this open call for activists. "We need street medics because there's gonna be tear gas" or "We need people at the wall." And you just had to go because it was this major thing. But there was no analysis around how our bodies would experience that kind of confrontation differently depending on where we were located. So a group of us organized what we at the time called the queer and trans people of colour contingent. We decided that we wanted to go, but we didn't want to be the shield for white activists, which is what would have happened if we hadn't planned. We organized this bus to go to Quebec together. There were seventy-five of us; some had training to be street medics, some didn't. We connected together, and we stayed in two different locations; one was in a literacy centre, and one was a house. It was really significant to me that we had this intervention in an intervention. You can imagine the sort of things that played out in the marches and demonstrations. White activists were telling activists of colour, "Take out your earrings; that's dangerous," policing our bodies in the middle of it. We were so over their contributing to the policing of our bodies in this space. We were doing work on the front lines at street medics. It was really exciting, but it was not unnoticed by the state. One of the locations that we were staying at was not located in the red zone but in the green zone, so away from the FTAA, and it had a gas bomb dropped onto it in the middle of the night. It was really impactful to have such a toxic substance dropped on you while you're sleeping. It was not an accident.

I'm also thinking of the organizing that we did through the Prisoners Justice Action Committee. We had been doing organizing around Prisoners' Justice Day, which is 10 August. A lot of us were questioning the implicit racism that was built into even a lot of prison-abolition movements. We started organizing as PJAC, and together we created Canada's first Prisoners' Justice Film Festival and ran the 81 Reasons Campaign, a campaign aimed at stopping the building of a youth superjail in Brampton (the Roy McMurtry Centre). We really centred the idea that talking about disability, talking about transphobia, talking about all of these things together made the prison-abolition work that we were doing stronger. Because if we're trying to build community that is truly grounded in social justice, but we're not having these conversations from the beginning, then you know what are we actually doing?

RÍO: I really like this question because having a historicized understanding of systems of policing and incarceration really opens the floodgates to having these really brilliant conversations about cissexism and colonial violence and why we need movements that are anti-racist, anti-classist, anti-ableist, and abolitionist. I think that queer people of colour have been a part of and held down those movements everywhere and have really centred the need for an intersectional analysis. The question of whose bodies continue to be pushed out and told that they don't belong is very present in all kinds of community organizing in Toronto.

Someone whom I really admire is Monica Forrester, a long-time local organizer for trans women and sex workers, low-income women, specifically in the realm of housing. She has this incredible library of knowledge, of lived experience, of history. There's an ongoing history of trans women being pushed out of the Village, but also organizing and supporting each other. I really appreciate this work as someone who is trying to document unwritten histories. It can be frustrating because they're often so difficult to find. There's so many publications and well-known narratives that centre white gay stories about gay liberation in Toronto. Events like Operation Soap, the bathhouse raids, which was the largest mass arrest in Canadian history, are commonly told as white narratives that omit the presence and roles of people of colour in these events.

Something I want to invest more time in, that I've heard referenced in passing, and that like the examples given by Che and Syrus is rooted in queer of colour organizing and in alternatives to mainstream justice, was a street-based safety project called Operation Jack o'Lantern. The name refers to Halloween, which in Toronto was a really dangerous time in the 1960s and 1970s. Halloween was a time of drag celebration, but it also became an informal invitation to bash people. Homophobes would come out just to assault and show hatred. Jack o'Lantern was organized by a network of people protecting each other on Halloween. These alternative sorts of networks and histories so often go unspoken, it's something I'm interested in archiving.

JIN: It's great to talk about the alternative forms of place-making that exist in trans and queer of colour communities. Wider struggles and theories can clearly learn from these, however resistant to this they are – or amnesiac, as you say. Could you talk about other examples that you've come across?

CHE: There's a group in New York City, FIERCE, that does a lot of wonderful campaigns, like against the gentrification of the Christopher Street piers, where low-income queers of colour met for decades until luxury-home owners, police, and private security pushed them out. There's a great film that the organization put together to document this struggle, called *Fenced Out*.[13] I lived in Washington, DC, for a short while and got involved in a campaign against prostitution-free zones that resonates with what Río was talking about, including signs to drivers that you can't stop here. DC put up signs that had the same continuity of carceral logic, which polices poor, Black communities, as the drug-free zone or the gang-free zone. Like Jin was saying, we see the same methodology in so many places at the same time. Except this was a prostitution-free zone, so it meant that trans women of colour, whether they were sex workers or not, were profiled and stopped by the cops for walking while trans of colour.

Out of that reality a campaign evolved, which is really powerful and, to me, illustrates how people can create campaigns for de-criminalization. The collective of service providers, academics, and sex workers put together a participatory action report called The Move Along Report about this struggle.[14] But it's also a demand for a different paradigm of space, where people can walk and not be policed, not be profiled by the cops. The campaign was horizontal: it wasn't dictated by one non-profit's agenda, for instance. I think that's really important, that we think about power and ways to horizontalize and empower relationships.

SYRUS: One example I would reference is Blackness Yes!, which is a group that began in Toronto in 1998. It was started by the same loose group of people who had until then done a lot of informal or-ganizing of the Black queer community, including Black CAP, the Black Coalition for AIDS Prevention founded in 1987. They were frustrated that going to Toronto's Pride Festival every year had be-come like going to an all-white homonormative festival. There was really nothing that was culturally specific. They felt, in fact, that their presence in the space, in the mini-city that is this festival, was constantly questioned. "Why are you here?" They couldn't possi-bly also be coming to celebrate; they couldn't possibly also be part of this community.

---

13 Gabriel Martinez, Paper Tiger Television Collective, New Neutral Zone, and FIERCE Entertainment, *Fenced Out*, 2001, DVD.

14 Alliance for a Safe & Diverse DC, *Move Along: Policing Sex Work in Washington, D.C.* (Washington, DC: Different Avenues, 2010), accessed 28 December 2015, https:// dctranscoalition.files.wordpress.com/2010/05/movealongreport.pdf.

So they started this group called Blackness Yes! The idea was to get a float and march in the Pride Parade to have visibility of Black queer and trans voices in the city, not only for people who were at the festival but also for those who would be watching – because, at the time, they were starting to televise the festival. They wanted somebody who might be watching in Brampton, or other racialized suburbs of Toronto, to get the message that there were other people and a community. That's how it began.

There's always been a lot of tension between Pride Toronto and Blackness Yes! That year the response was, "It's too late to add a float, but you can have this little parking lot, this tiny little strip of it; you could do programming there." And the Blackness Yes! organizers planned a day of DJs and programming and called it Blockorama, which is built on the Trinidadian tradition of blockos, which are street parties. It's now in its eighteenth year. It's the largest stage at Pride, and it's really one of the best places to go to. We've really created a space, a site, that is absolutely about queer and trans people of colour but is also deeply rooted in a radically intersectional agenda. One of the successes of Blockorama is that we've been one of the first stages to have ASL [American Sign Language] interpretation throughout the entire day. This didn't just happen but was the result of fighting actively with the institution the whole way. There was a lot of active work to make sure that trans women, Black trans women, were featured very heavily in the program and in the programming decisions.

When there was a highly divisive controversy in Pride 2010 around the right of Queers Against Israeli Apartheid to be in the march, even some of the more progressive groups sidestepped away from taking a stance. Blockorama really came out and vocally supported QuAIA. We drew attention to the ways that Pride Toronto continues to uphold a whitewashed definition of the LGBTQ community in Toronto. This is again a transnational phenomenon. That same year, Blackness Yes! wrote a solidarity statement for queers of colour in Berlin, who were protesting against the homonationalism and gay imperialism of the local Pride there.[15] So

---

15 See SUSPECT, "Where Now? From Pride Scandal to Transnational Movement," *Bully Bloggers*, 26 June 2010, accessed 23 August 2016, https://bullybloggers.wordpress.com/2010/06/26/where-now-from-pride-scandal-to-transnational-movement/.

Blockorama is an example of actively, physically making a space, but also of the plant on top of the much deeper root system of Black queer and trans organizing in the city.

It's funny that, after eighteen years, the same questions have come up in relation to the participation of Black Lives Matter Toronto (BLM-TO) in Toronto Pride in 2016.[16] BLM-TO was Pride's honoured group, and still people were asking, "Why are you here?" and "Why aren't you at Caribana instead?," referring to the large Caribbean festival in the city – a festival that does have a huge black queer presence and that has been actively "queered" by Blackness Yes! for six years. BLM-TO took up the demands of Black community groups like Blackness Yes! and Black Queer Youth and made them central to a large-scale sit-in that they staged in the middle of the Pride Parade. In this way, the timeline seems to expand and contract. What is different now from 1998 for Black queer and trans folks? Why are we still fighting for the same presence, support, and visibility within the white-supremacist LGBT-TI2QQA [lesbian, gay, bisexual, trans, intersexed, queer, questioning, and asexual] communities in Toronto?

RÍO: These are exciting examples. I think it can feel overwhelming to look at the city and the Village and feel like there's this assimilation and homogenization of bodies and places. The ways that we claim and create new urban spaces can be exclusionary and problematic given our settler-colonial context. But I think there's a lot to learn from the queer place-making that people of colour do in this city. Some examples that I'm personally really excited [about] from Toronto local history are the ethno-specific AIDS and HIV services that exist in the city, which were born out of the white-supremacist HIV/AIDS movement. A lot of place-making happens outside of big non-profits, health services, and agencies. Queer people of colour create alternative spaces – for example, through performance, cabaret, and other forms of community art. There's groups like Colour Me Dragg and Unapologetic Burlesque, which are queer of colour performance companies that build physical spaces where queers of colour can gather, to celebrate our collective brilliance and cultural and gender expressions, in a way that builds community and furthers the careers and economic survival of community

---

16 See chapter 7 by Khan and Newbold.

artists. In addition, the digital world has become an incredible opportunity for queer people of colour to create community, connect with each other, blog, and represent themselves. I'm also thinking of alternative forms of organizing that are rooted in transformative justice, prison abolition, decolonization, and the sort of analysis that centres queer of colour and other intersectional experiences. This, too, is something that many broader urban struggles can learn from.

JIN: Why do you think this learning is not really happening right now? With everything that queer of colour activism has to offer, what are some of the resistances to incorporating these gifts and methodologies of urban justice, and where are they coming from?

RÍO: I think it's definitely true that a lot of the resistance we see stems from white gay fears that their histories are being pushed out, sometimes manifested as ideas about "reverse racism." To return to my example of Maitland and Homewood, the residents there resist the presence of sex workers because they feel that it makes them "unsafe." The steps in front of the Second Cup on Church Street is another really famous site in the Village. The steps are right in front of where Ginger, [a location] of the Southeast Asian restaurant chain, is now and a twenty-four-hour Second Cup coffee shop once was. This space was really important, similar to what the piers meant to queer of colour youth in New York. Because the Village is a place where you have to have ID – [a] particular kind of ID; they might not like you if you have international ID. You have to be of age, you have to have the money to get into the dance club/party, there might be steps and other barriers to get into the club. In contrast, the steps outside of this Second Cup were a public meeting space where people of all ages could go. They were later removed. There's a lot of different stories about why that happened, including statements by city councillors about why they didn't want those bodies there in public sight – you know, young people, people of colour, people who were street-involved or users, sex workers, immigrants. So that resistance comes from conceptions about who owns the city and who deserves to be there.

There's other exciting examples of how we've chosen to deal with this resistance. Something that I always found so fascinating happened in 2011, with the case of Alvaro Orozco, a young Nicaraguan person who was claiming refugee status in Canada because he was facing violence and discrimination [in his home country] as a young gay man.[17] His refugee claim was denied because he failed to answer a bunch of questions around Pride and his sexual history. They told him that they didn't believe he was gay. What was fascinating about this case was the huge public outcry, as a result of which Alvaro was able to stay on humanitarian and compassionate grounds. People subverted the state's resistance in really creative ways. The campaign was fascinating; it was incredibly creative arts–based. It consisted in a bunch of queer people of colour playing into this nationalist resistance and making some really deliberate and strategic choices to subvert that. It was so funny to watch people I knew take off their QPOC anarchist hats, look into a camera, and say, "I think Alvaro Orozco would be a wonderful Canadian citizen and contribute to this nation in such a positive way."

SYRUS: I think a lot of the resistance to Blockorama subscribes to this idea that if we inscribe our narratives into history, or into the collective memory of what's happened here, that white subjects and white stories will be decentred. There's a real resistance by the white gay, homonormative establishment to even naming Sylvia Rivera or Marsha P. Johnson – to even talking about who was involved in the riots at the Stonewall bar. When I share stories about Sylvia Rivera saying, "I didn't throw the first Molotov cocktail/ beer bottle [while resisting arrest]; I threw the second [one at the cops]," I've had people say, "You know that's not true; the reason that happened was because people were upset about Judy Garland." They're resistant to the possibility that all of these things could be happening at the same time. By telling our stories, we're necessarily erasing the dominant narrative. But while there's resistance to the work that we're doing, there's also resistance to the resistance and some tremendously creative ways of turning the dominant narrative on its head.

To return to Río's example, Operation Soap, contrary to the dominant white gay archive, included queer of colour subjects. One of the stories that brings this home [is] what happened during the trial, when each of the "found-ins" – what people who were "found in" the bathhouse raids were called – were brought into the courtroom, where police had to identify them before they could be charged. So this group of East Asian activists, some of whom later

---

17 See "Canada Let Alvaro Stay," Alvaro official blog, accessed 1 December 2016, http://canada-let-alvaro-stay.blogspot.ca/.

founded Gay Asians of Toronto, turned state racism on itself. When it was time for this East Asian man to come into the courtroom to be identified by the police officer, they all stood together. They all went in the courtroom and stood beside him. So when the officer was asked, "Can you point at the man?" there was a whole row of East Asians, and he said, "I can't" because, of course, there's this idea that all Asians look the same. I always thought that was brilliant. It illustrates our creativity in turning these things on their head.

CHE: I think that there's multiple forms of resistance. I'm thinking of the ways that racism invisibilizes Black queer and trans people within communities that are being gentrified. This even happens in critiques of queer gentrification themselves. For example, *Flag Wars*, the widely viewed documentary about gay gentrification in Columbus, Ohio, reproduces a binary view of gays (white) and Blacks (straight).[18] There's not a lot of spaces where Black queer and trans people can even exist – with such constraints on liveable life, having to struggle against both gentrification and the invisibilization of our identities.

I also wonder, how do we define anti-gentrification? Anti-gentrification is about more than people's homes. It's about people who are homeless and live and work on the streets, including sex workers, and it's also about abolition as spatial justice. How do we build coalitions that broaden the idea of gentrification beyond homonationalist and racial-capitalist investment in financial speculation and property ownership? The [New York–based] organization Queers for Economic Justice [QEJ] did phenomenal work on issues of urban justice and welfare access for queer and/or trans people of colour. Here I'm thinking of the work of my sister Reina Gossett, who worked at QEJ, and the Welfare Warriors Research Collaborative, who met for three years and collectively authored the brilliant QEJ report about the struggle to win access to welfare in the face of the anti-trans institutional violence that was happening at the welfare office for trans folks, mostly people of colour, in NYC.[19] This shows queer and trans of colour theory, knowledge,

18 Linda Goode Bryant and Laura Poitras, *Flag Wars*, 2003, 86 min.
19 Welfare Warriors Research Collaborative, *A Fabulous Attitude: Low Income LGBTGNC People Surviving and Thriving on Love, Shelter, and Knowledge* (New York: Queers for Economic Justice, 2010), accessed 1 December 2016, https://www.issuelab.org/resource/a_fabulous_attitude_low_income_lgbtgnc_people_surviving_and_thriving_on_love_shelter_and_knowledge.

and power – how poor and low-income queer and trans people of colour are theorizing activism and producing knowledge but in ways that are part of *study*. As Fred Moten and Stephano Harney remind us, "And we have a word for the *sabotage* of information, and that word is *study*."[20] Our study is sabotage, and [it] is also about repurposing and prefigurative politics. It redistributes power via the theory and knowledge that we produce in urban space as we navigate and challenge the institutional arrangements and orchestration of power.

---

20 Stefano Harney and Fred Moten, "From Cooperation to Black Operation: A Conversation with Stefano Harney and Fred Moten on *The Undercommons*," *Transversal Texts* (blog), April 2016, accessed 1 December 2016, http://transversal.at/blog/From-cooperation-to-black-operation.

2 "We Had to Take Space, We Had to Create Space": Locating Queer of Colour Politics in 1980s Toronto

JOHN PAUL CATUNGAL

Toronto in the 1980s was a site of political uncertainty and changing priorities in the scene of queer activism, resulting partly from the epidemic of HIV/AIDS, which severely ravaged huge portions of queer and other communities. In various geographical contexts, scholars have documented the ways that the AIDS crisis of the 1980s influenced some forms of gay and lesbian organizing to reroute political energies towards creating alternative and community-based health and social care structures, especially in contexts where government action was absent (Rayside and Lindquist 1992; Schulman 2012). In Toronto, despite the fact that the municipal Board of Health supported community-based responses to HIV/AIDS, profound medical uncertainty coupled with homophobia, AIDS-phobia, and the adoption of one-size-fits-all approaches to social service delivery led to a landscape of access that was unevenly distributed by race and ethnicity (Catungal 2013). Thanks to the leadership of queer of colour activists, who had already made space for anti-racist organizing through broader interventions in the queer political scene, alternative ethno-specific approaches to HIV/AIDS support services and prevention initiatives emerged and became part of the broader social ecosystem of local responses to HIV/AIDS (ibid.). Many of these organizations continue their work to this day.

Organizations founded for and by members of queer of colour communities were a vibrant, if sometimes neglected, part of this recent queer history. In the 1980s, organizations like Zami and Gay Asians Toronto (GAT) emerged from the leadership and desire of local queers of colour to create spaces for themselves apart from the mainstream (read: white-stream) queer scene and apart from the seemingly "everywhere" undercurrent of homophobia and heteronormativity that permeated most of society, including racialized communities. These organizations, founded upon a "for us, by us" ethos that centred queer bodies of colour as well as their needs, desires, and capacities, challenged the racial status quo of queer community-building and activism in Toronto, but not without experiencing roadblocks and difficulties.

These genealogies are one main focus of this chapter. In what follows, I tell the origin stories of two ethno-specific AIDS service organizations (e-ASOs) – the Black Coalition for AIDS Prevention (Black CAP) and the Asian Community AIDS Services (ACAS) – and trace, in the process, the centrality and leadership of queer of colour activists and collectivities to their reshaping of local responses to HIV/AIDS in Toronto. In so doing, I also make the point that queer of colour organizing before and during the AIDS epidemic was located in and plugged into political networks that extended beyond the city. In other words, while there is no denying that these organizations were situated in place, they were (as they still are now) part of a broader, transnational network of struggle for anti-oppressive politics. Queer of colour leaders drew inspiration and influence from global anti-racist and feminist activist formations, especially those situated in the United States, and they were engaged in conversation with cognate political formations within and beyond the city.

Thus, this chapter also offers a glimpse into the more than local geography of this queer of colour organizing. Inspired by recent scholarly arguments for considering local politics as "purposive assemblages of parts of here and elsewhere" (McCann 2011, 145), I draw on secondary sources and semi-structured interviews[1] conducted between 2010 and 2013 to point out that Toronto's e-ASOs and the queer of colour organizations that preceded them are a product as much of local political context and leadership as they are of transnational linkages and entanglements with social formations and movements elsewhere. In this light, queer of colour Toronto in the 1980s could usefully be thought of as a node in the urban-global nexus of queer and anti-racist politics, its political geographies of organizing simultaneously local and transnational.

---

1 Interview transcripts are excerpted here verbatim in recognition of the multiplicity of Englishes spoken by the interviewees. This is in keeping with their critique of the subtle and overt policing of language in mainstream organizations as a practice of ethno-racial exclusion (see Catungal 2013).

The chapter proceeds with an account of origin stories: those of Black CAP and ACAS as well as those of Zami and GAT, which were central to the eventual formation of Black CAP and ACAS, respectively. I point both to the local exigencies of racial inequality that necessitated their formation and to the extra-local linkages they forged as they drew on, were inspired by, and affected queer politics in other places. Finally, I conclude with some thoughts on the theoretical and political implications of paying attention to the urban-global nexus as a lens through which to tell the histories and geographies of local queer of colour politics.

"God, the Reason That We Were Created Was a Political Act Itself": E-ASO Origin Stories

As I have argued elsewhere (Catungal 2013), the Toronto-based e-ASOs ACAS and Black CAP emerged in a context of institutionalized racial neglect on the part of mainstream AIDS organizations and the local state, whose one-size-fits-all approaches were unable to account, in culturally and linguistically appropriate ways, for the needs of folks of colour during the mounting crisis of HIV in 1980s Toronto.[2] The quote in this subsection's title, which is drawn from an interview with an e-ASO worker, offers a sense of this fraught context.

Already existing queer of colour networks, especially in the form of queer of colour organizations, were key to the formation of e-ASOs as queer spaces of anti-racism. These groups were formed just before or around the beginning of the AIDS crisis in Toronto, and their goals and activities were both social and political in nature. Many of these groups' members went on to become – and continue to be – key figures in local queer politics and in the AIDS sector, with several playing important roles in very public debates about racism in the gay and lesbian movement at the time. For instance, Richard Fung, co-founder of GAT and current faculty member at Toronto's OCAD University, was publicly vocal in his critique of a notorious racist advertisement for a "Black

---

2 ACAS and Black CAP are part of a larger set of ethno-specific organizations in Toronto's AIDS sector. While this chapter focuses on these two organizations largely due to space constraints, the larger research on which this chapter is drawn also examines the emergence, evolution, and socio-spatial practices of the Alliance for South Asian AIDS Prevention (see Catungal 2013, 2014).

houseboy" that was published in April 1985 by Toronto-based *The Body Politic* (TBP), "one of the most important, not to mention politically engaged and intellectually sophisticated, lesbian and gay periodicals in North America" in the 1970s and 1980s (Churchill 2003, 115). Fung wrote in 1985 the following in a letter to the TBP editorial collective: "To champion the cause of uninhibited desire without addressing the impact of racism and sexism in the sexual arena is to call for the entrenchment of white male privilege" (quoted in Warner 2002, 318–19). Similarly, Doug Stewart, eventual founding executive director of Black CAP and then-member of Zami, wrote in 1985 that such racism "forces gay men like me to prioritize my concerns" (quoted in ibid., 318). Writing for the fifth-anniversary publication of ACAS, Dr. Alan Li elaborated on this point, noting how multiple embodied oppressions – in this case, queer Asians with HIV – were also erased in the AIDS sector. "In effect, our triple status (Asian, gay & HIV+) translated us into being a 'non-entity' when it came to getting services" (ACAS 1999, n.p.).

The persistence and institutionalization of racism in gay and lesbian politics in the 1980s meant that the presence of groups for gays and lesbians of colour in this field was fraught. Nevertheless, such groups became ready and visible resources in local responses to HIV/AIDS, at least once certain members of the mainstream sector had recognized the issues that had arisen from these organizations' centring of gay white men as central subjects of caregiving and social service provision. As the narratives below show, these groups were, in many cases, contacted by concerned workers at mainstream AIDS organizations – particularly Doug Stewart – in severe cases in which people of colour with AIDS were already incredibly ill and/or close to dying. It is worth noting at the outset that the interviewees understand the inability of mainstream AIDS organizations like the AIDS Committee of Toronto to provide culturally appropriate services to be an effect of the normalization of whiteness in these organizations. Hence, in their work to provide culturally appropriate services to people of colour with HIV/AIDS, groups for gays and lesbians of colour became precursors to what eventually became e-ASOs, their members early iterations of e-ASO workers.

Zami and the Black Coalition for AIDS Prevention

Black CAP was formed in 1987 out of the efforts of various members of Toronto's Black communities, with the goal of generating awareness and education about HIV transmission and prevention. Its history, like that of the other e-ASOs that I describe below, is one of neglect and erasure from mainstream organizations, and its emergence as an ethno-specific organization can be traced to the incapability and, arguably, refusal of mainstream AIDS organizations to provide services and support structures that name, recognize, and appreciate the importance of racialization and racial and ethnic identifications to sexual health. However, its emergence as an organization needs to be traced to a precursor organization called Zami.

In 1984, Doug Stewart co-founded Zami with Derych Gordon, Sylmadel Coke, Debbie Douglas, and Carol Allen (Warner 2002, 185). He was also the eventual first executive director of Black CAP. Doug[3] recalls his involvement in Zami, focusing on lived experiences of erasure and the collective organizing that emerged as a result of the realization of their shared experiences.

Zami came out of a group of us sitting around the table at somebody's home one night and talking about all the different things that were not available for Black queer folk. As we're talking, somebody had the idea that we should start our own organization. We should do something about it [the general lack of services for Black queer folk]. As was the case of the 1980s, it felt like anyway, we had an idea and we just did it. Let's plan a party. Let's do a demo.

The organizing that was born of this evening spoke against whiteness in many institutions, including in local gay and lesbian social movements. Hence, as Doug explains, Zami drew its inspiration and political energy not necessarily from the histories of mainstream gay liberation movements, but from the work of civil rights and feminist activist groups, some of which he was plugged into. "That was the energy at the time. That was an energy framed by the civil rights movement,

---

3 Three attribution conventions are used in this chapter. Names without asterisks (e.g., Doug) are used in instances where the interviewees agreed to have quotes attributed directly to them. Names with asterisks (e.g., Robert*) are pseudonyms. Some quotes are attributed only to "Interviewee" at the request of the research participants. The last two modes of attribution offer slightly different degrees of confidentiality because, while a pseudonym always provides confidentiality, "Interviewee" indicates that, for this specific quote, the participant wishes to remain anonymous; other quotes in this publication may be attributed to them.

women's movement – a very active feminist movement. I was also in an environment with feminists who were doing a lot of work at the time."

The use of more established social movements as inspirations and models for gay and lesbian organizing that the quote above alludes to has also been documented in the contexts of San Francisco (Armstrong 2002, chap. 3) and New York (Bernstein 1997). Similarly, Harris (1996) identifies more generally the influences of Black feminist thought and organizing on Black queer theorizing and activism.

The desire to create institutions and services geared specifically for Black people, especially Black queer people, was born out of Zami members' shared realization that their erasure from mainstream institutions could not be boiled down to a singular functional explanation, but that their critique demanded a political ethos that was informed by an intersectional approach, which recognized and named the multiplicity of Black people's identities. This was also influenced by their positions as racialized and immigrant peoples in the Canadian white-settler nation, a geopolitical context wherein multiculturalism demanded of racialized subjects docility and gratefulness. Doug notes his dissatisfaction with this demand for a particular form of racialized citizenship.

A number of us who had either come as young people, as immigrants, were starting to find our footing in Canada and actually began to question and challenge the status quo of what was. I think more of us were starting to gain voice around not just being grateful for being allowed to come to Canada, to settle in Canada, that we at least had a better life than somewhere else, that we got to assimilate. More of us were getting a sense of, "Wait a minute, why do I have to give in to the status quo? Why not assert who I am in different ways?" I mean, racially, also in terms of gender, also in terms of sexual orientation. While we were asserting our racial identities, we were also asserting intersectionality and the complexity of what that might mean in a much more assertive way than what historically happened. It was a time a lot of that converged. It was an opportunity to have that conversation.

For Doug, the lived and embodied experience of multiple oppressions demanded a space for community-building and affirmation. To him, Zami provided exactly that space. "Zami was a place that a number of us who were Black and queer, we needed some place, something that can begin to create a space and have that very visible and named, and create some cohesion for us where we can continue to strengthen our voices." Not surprisingly, this desire for affirming space was part of a broader critique of the whiteness of mainstream institutions that was brewing in Toronto's larger queer of colour scene in the 1980s. An interviewee situates Zami in this broader collective struggle.

> There was Gay Asians Toronto that had been formed. There was also Khush, which was for South Asian gay men. There were a couple of organizations for women. There was a Black lesbian group. There was ALOT, Asian Lesbians of Toronto. There were a few things that started. We started around the same time. We said, hey, there hasn't been space in the larger community, so we had to take space, we had to create space. Because when we were in those spaces trying to name our experiences, we were not having them resonate or having a certain patience or openness to those experiences that varied from dominant cultural norms, which was urban, middle class, European historical backgrounds.

As a support counsellor for the AIDS Committee of Toronto (ACT) in the 1980s, Doug Stewart was one of the very few racialized employees who worked in a mainstream organization. He brought with him to his work his embodied experience and knowledge of racialized queerness, which was useful for his line of work. "Because of me being one of a few racialized people in that work, I was used as a resource to consult around education programs, outreach, and anything else. I brought a lens, something to think about. I had a role in multiple ways. That was the link."

Eventually, however, it became very clear that individuals within ACT were not enough and that a different organizational approach and ethos were needed, one that recognized that, according to an anonymous interviewee, "one of the things that was missing – one of the gaps in the services – was the need for culturally specific services that took into account their needs." He continues, "We had people external to the organization saying what they needed and what it should be." In articulating their desires and needs for appropriate services, people also voiced their understanding and lived experiences of erasure in mainstream organizations. As Robert* notes, "It was clear to me even then, even at the time that I got involved, that what you refer to as mainstream organizations did not have the same involvement with Black people's health and well-being as an organization as Black CAP or as any organization that was formed from or within our own communities."

As part of one of the only organized groups dealing specifically with the intersection of Blackness and queer sexuality, some Zami members were called upon in the mid-1980s to help with what an interviewee calls "complicated cases," which mainstream organizations like ACT had no capacity to deal with. These complicated cases were those that involved HIV+ people of colour, including both Black heterosexuals and gay men, some of whom, at the time of contact with members of groups for gays and lesbians of colour, were already quite ill and/or dying.

Black CAP was officially formed in 1987 out of the initiative of Black community leaders, who, according to Doug Stewart (1992, 12) in a column for the Ontario Council of Agencies Serving Immigrants (OCASI) Newsletter, "were concerned about the numbers of people who were trying to access services and were not getting competent care and services in the health care system." An interviewee expands on this narrative, noting,

> So, Black CAP was created ... by a group of, I guess, concerned members of the community who were Black African and Caribbean, who really saw, you know, they saw ACT, they saw Toronto People with AIDS Foundation, but there was no organization that specifically addressed or reflected their issues as Black, predominantly gay, people, or let's just say queer people at that time. You know, recognizing at that time that there were a lot of Black gay men who were dying of HIV disease – lots of white gay men dying as well, by the way, but again, no kind of space or a home for those Black gay men to come together to get support, to connect with others, and also no organization doing education in Black communities around what was really going to be an emerging, significant issue in the Black communities of Toronto.

The stories of Black gay men (and other racialized people) with AIDS, as so-called complicated cases, revealed the limits of mainstream AIDS organizations like ACT. These cases were important to the formation of e-ASOs like Black CAP because they showed that "ACT couldn't do all of that in the way it was structured and the staff it had. ... It made sense, just politically and strategically, to have some of those [ethno-specific] organizations formed" (Interviewee).

Gay Asians Toronto and Asian Community AIDS Services

ACAS was formed with the amalgamation of three HIV/AIDS projects that were geared to Asian communities in Toronto. These were the Vietnamese AIDS Project, the Toronto Chinese Health Education

Committee, and the Gay Asian AIDS Project (GAAP). GAAP was started by a group called GAT, which was founded in 1980 by four gay Asian men: Richard Fung, Tony Souza, Nito Marquez, and Gerald Chen. According to an interviewee, "The Gay Asian AIDS project stem[med] from the same root of activism and the same group of people that formed Gay Asians Toronto."

Richard Fung traces the emergence of GAT to a conference that he attended in Washington, DC.

> In October 1979, I drove to the first National March on Washington for Lesbian and Gay Rights with my partner, Tim McCaskell, and our friend Tony Souza. We arrived a day early so Tony and I could attend the first Third World conference, which brought together hundreds of Black, Latino/a, and Asian-American lesbians and gays. (2012, n.p.)

Ghaziani (2008) calls the 1979 National March on Washington the "birth of a national [American] movement" (42) as it brought together gay and lesbian organizations that were, at that point, mostly localized in their respective activist foci. The desire to scale up to the "national" level with a march in Washington was, by that time, seen as "an established element in the New Left repertoire" (ibid., 43; see also Berlant 1997). Organizers strategically evoked other marches on Washington, especially those that were part of the civil rights movement, to draw parallels between the successes of that movement and the desire of gay and lesbian organizers for the same (Ghaziani 2008, 43). Cognizant of the politics of racial difference in gay-rights organizing, delegates who were involved in organizing the National March chose to create an advisory committee involving "groups experiencing special oppression within the gay community"; this included "Third World people" (ibid., 57). They also organized to ensure that the first National Third World Lesbian and Gay Conference, which Fung mentioned above, happened on the same weekend as the National March (ibid., 58). At the Third World conference, Fung became part of a group of gay Asians that sought to march as a group.

> Coming from Toronto, where on any given night in a gay bar you could count the number of Asians – or any people of colour – on one hand, I was stunned but exhilarated when, on entering the building, I was scooped up by a cluster of women and men to form an Asian caucus. Over that weekend, we listened to speeches by leaders like Audre Lorde, and we talked

to delicious exhaustion. The Asian caucus fashioned a banner proclaiming "Asian Gay and Proud," which we paraded through the streets of Washington. (2012, n.p.)

In this narrative, it becomes clear that the reach and influence of the National March actually breached the national scale, at least to the extent that it directly affected local organizing in a Canadian city.

Fung's telling of the history of GAT traces a multi-sited and multiracial history, and it emphasizes how this history was born out of a transnational gathering of queer people of colour and inspired partly by US Black, lesbian, feminist thought and activism. Energized by "the high that was Washington, the first time that my intersecting ethnic and sexual identities found a space to come together," Fung sought to create a similar space specifically in Toronto.

I put a personal ad in *The Body Politic*, and soon Tony and I met Nito Marquez and Gerald Chan, who had written a landmark article in *The Asianadian* magazine about being gay and Asian. We met with writer Suniti Namjoshi and the couple of Asian lesbians we knew in the Toronto scene, but they felt that a mixed gender group wasn't feasible at that time. In the end, the four of us launched Gay Asians Toronto in 1980. (2012, n.p.)

In *Never Going Back,* a broad chronicle of the history of queer activism in Canada, Tom Warner (2002) writes that GAT was founded with the following goals in mind: "promoting unity and mutual support among Asians; organizing social, cultural, educational and recreational activities for its members; providing culturally sensitive social and support services; and advocating on issues relevant to the community's concerns" (185).

Although GAT was an ethno-specific group, its work was often decidedly broader than its target community, and its activities often breached the boundaries of ethno-racial identification. For example, one interviewee, an active member of GAT, recalls the group's involvement in fundraising for the Right to Privacy Committee, which was embroiled in a legal battle that had arisen from the fallout of the bathhouse raids in Toronto in 1981.[4] "The first event that I went to was a fundraiser variety

---

4 In 1981, the police forces conducted Operation Soap, a coordinated series of raids of four Toronto bathhouses using laws defining bawdy houses as "any place where 'indecent' acts took place" (see Thomas [2011, n.p.]) for a fuller account).

show put together by Gay Asians Toronto to raise money for the Right to Privacy Committee, which was the community coalition fighting the bath raids." Similarly, GAT was involved in early HIV/AIDS organizing from the beginning, even before ACAS or GAAP had been dreamed up by its founders. "We were one of the first groups to raise money for HIV, I think back in '83. ... And also had, in terms of HIV – we were organizing educational workshops on HIV prevention" (Interviewee).

One of GAT's main targets for activism was racism in the mainstream gay community. On this work, it partnered with other organizations for gays and lesbians of colour in the city. An interviewee, who was involved in local queer politics at the time, recalls, for example, the collaborative, cross-group work that GAT members did on the relationship between racism and gay and lesbian organizing in the city.

> [GAT] also worked with other queer groups of colour on mostly anti-racism issues because ... in the early days, there was a huge controversy about *The Body Politic* printing a classified ad, calling for Black houseboys, and also that communities were having a huge debate and fights about whether sexual liberation is the ultimate goal and the be-all for everything or whether that still needs to be in the context of, you know, the social reality of power and oppression and how does that affect the marginalized communities and all that stuff. ... So – so [they] did work together on some issues, and so that's how I got to know Doug [Stewart] and some of the other people.

No doubt due to his active involvement and leadership in GAT, and perhaps also partly because he was in the field of medicine, Alan Li was contacted by Doug Stewart, who was working at the time as a support counsellor at ACT, to deal with one of those complicated cases that was mentioned above. Li recalls during our interview,

> The first person with AIDS I came into contact with was referred by Doug Stewart, a case worker/counsellor at the AIDS Committee of Toronto, way back when I was a medical student. He called me up because he has a Vietnamese client that has a lot of language barriers, who was very sick and doesn't have support and was very isolated. And so I volunteered to be a buddy for him, and that was in the early days, when there was very little treatment available, and so we were trying to get him aerosolized pentamadine because he already had PCP (Pneumocystis pneumonia, which was the biggest killer for PHAs [people with HIV/AIDS] at that time),

and lot of the doctors were really ignorant. … He went to a doctor in Chinatown who doesn't know anything about HIV, and he is too intimidated to raise questions or to advocate for treatments. Most of those treatment drugs were experimental at the time. So we tried to get him information, we tried to help communicate with his doctors, but of course, that didn't really go very well, and he died very quickly.

In his 1993 work, "Life of GAAP," Li talked about how the experience of this Vietnamese client "spoke to … cultural-specific or language-specific support that are needed," an experience that was shared by others who faced "problems accessing services that would understand Asians' special needs, including how to deal with the impact of AIDS on one's family, acceptance in the Asian community and strong ethnic ties" (quoted in Warner 2002, 256). Indeed, in addition to the lack of capacity and "huge distrust and fear of mistreatment of the mainstream ethno-racial services," including among medical professionals in ethno-racial communities, another interviewee names the "lack of capacity and cultural sensitivity that people experienced in the mainstream AIDS services." The interviewee continues, "That person [the Vietnamese client] is actually somewhat fortunate because Doug actually go out of his way to look for additional support for him, recognizing within the then current ACT structure that there wasn't any resources to support that man."

In crediting Doug Stewart for his individual initiative and naming ACT's structural incapability, this interviewee echoes the critiques, mentioned above, about how ACT's approach to providing HIV/AIDS social services was steeped in whiteness in the form of its one-size-fits-all model.

There wasn't really that diversity of staff within the organization. And … it's hard for them to really have that expertise to address the … needs of the persons affected, and a lot of times, it's not just the person affected, it's more their families and their loved ones, right? And especially for Asian families, there was huge issues that was really difficult to deal with, and – and most of the time, it also has language issues. So it really was a big challenge for – for organizations such as ACT to deal with it. It's not necessarily they were just arrogant and just doesn't wanna deal with it. They just don't have the capacity to deal with it. So that was – I think that was a huge issue.

In the mid-1980s, the city of Toronto began to make funding available for HIV/AIDS prevention work at the community level, and two ethno-specific projects emerged from what an interviewee interestingly calls the "Asian mainstream community" – *mainstream* referring to the fact that they did not do prevention work specifically with *gay* Asian communities. These were the Toronto Chinese Health Education Committee and the Vietnamese AIDS Project; both were initiated by health care and social service providers from these ethno-racial communities. An interviewee, who was involved with the Toronto Chinese Health Education Committee, elaborates on the limits of this Asian mainstream approach.

> Basically what happened is that after six to eight months of really trying hard to work with them, including helping to write a whole script for the slideshow they were trying to put together, trying to personalize the issues and make it more human and incorporate beyond just how to put on a condom, you know, which is basically what they wanted to do. They don't want to address sexuality. They don't want to address the human, more emotional aspect of HIV. And so, you know, it just became quite clear that ... they're not gonna reach out to the gay community. They're not gonna want to do work that relates to supporting people with HIV and the communities that's affected.

The combination of these experiences led GAT leaders to realize that they "had to develop something for our own community because there is no ... safe house" for gay Asians in either mainstream ethno-racial or mainstream HIV/AIDS social service spaces. This realization was also informed by their membership in a cross-continental network of gay Asian organizations, particularly those who were involved in doing HIV/AIDS work with Asian North American communities.

> Actually, also in that particular history, similar groups in Boston, New York, and San Francisco – the gay Asian groups in there – they're all kind of formed around the same time, early '80s, and they're all also organizing around HIV towards the end of the '80s. So we all communicated with each other, and – and we have a little bit of a peer network, and we learn from each other's experiences. And actually, we [in Toronto] have very similar struggles with San Francisco, except they're much bigger in terms of [the Asian] population. ... But they were trying to work with the mainstream Asian counterparts as well, and they're running into the same kind of struggles and stuff. (Interviewee)

This inter-urban network facilitated the sharing of similar experiences across locales, and GAT members – eventual GAAP founders – thought that the experiences of gay Asian organizations in other cities resonated with their local experiences. An interviewee expands on this argument, noting,

> There's no safe space in the mainstream ethno-racial communities for us. And I think we felt closer alliance to the mainstream HIV community, but ... I think that we still feel that we were being treated as an after-thought. And there's no cultural-specific attention to a lot of the issues that are beyond just health. ... At that particular time, what we decided we needed to do was to form the Gay Asian AIDS Project.

At a time when most HIV/AIDS funding was geared to prevention work, GAAP found a way to combine both prevention and support. It eventually acquired funding for support services from the provincial Ministry of Health. In the early 1990s, three HIV/AIDS projects coexisted, with GAAP being the only one targeting gay Asian populations and the two others targeting Chinese and Vietnamese populations specifically. Some activists thought that these three projects, and the energies of the people who were involved in all of them, were spread too thin. An interviewee, for example, noted that he "really pushed for an effort to look at merging those organizations" because it "just seems really duplicating and taxing to manage and support all these different efforts and not have those work together and synergize and support each other." On World AIDS Day 1994, the three projects officially merged, signing a partnership agreement, and ACAS was born.

Queer of Colour Toronto as a Node in Global Queer of Colour Politics

Ethno-specific AIDS service organizations arrived late on the scene of local responses to HIV/AIDS, but the political conditions for their emergence were being established well before their formal founding. In this light, e-ASOs were not so much "latecomers" to the scene of HIV/AIDS service provision, at least not in the modernist sense of a linear progression that identifies white gay activists as pioneer subjects. As the above origin stories show, the existence of several political structures locally and internationally – for example, queer of colour organizations, cognate political movements such as feminist and civil rights organizing – were central to the emergent anti-racist sexual politics of e-ASOs.

As I have noted in earlier work (Catungal 2013, 2014) and expanded on above, e-ASOs emerged in response to the racial erasures, with deadly consequences, engendered by mainstream responses to HIV/ AIDS in the 1980s. However, their emergence was not only a reaction to racial erasures but also a testament to the political presence, savvy, and activism of already existing local organizations for queers of colour. The presence of organizations like Zami and GAT in the local queer scene made them available resources at a time when cracks in the idea that "one size fits all" started showing in the form of bodies of colour dying from AIDS in that decade. Not incidentally, individual queer people of colour like Doug Stewart, who managed to be part of mainstream AIDS organizations despite their institutional whiteness, became key actors in the formation of e-ASOs as alternative, "for us, by us" approaches. This is, no doubt, because of their embeddedness in anti-racist queer of colour organizing and their embodied intersectional experiences of race and sexuality. The stories above also suggest that ethno-specific organizations were part of a loose network of queer of colour organizing that served not only as each other's inspiration but also as each other's occasional collaborators – relations that continue today.

Beyond these local geographies of action, inspiration, and collaboration, queer of colour Toronto in the 1980s was also embedded in extralocal networks of anti-racist queer activism. To a certain degree, what was happening was, at least in part, one local instantiation of globalizing types of queer of colour politics. Indeed, as the origin stories above show, participation in a continental network of activism and organizing was important to the capacity of queer of colour organizations and e-ASOs to organize and act locally. Queer of colour activists, many of whom also became anti-racist HIV/AIDS activists, tapped into, learned from, and sometimes inspired others in this transnational assemblage of queer of colour activisms. The circulation of newsletters to other parts of the diaspora, communication with e-ASOs in other locales, and learning from globally circulating perspectives offered by Audre Lorde and others became important components of the political arsenal of local queer of colour and HIV/AIDS activists. These practices of extra-local entanglement ensured that queer of colour organizing in Toronto was a local hub in a global network of similar political struggles. At this urban-global nexus, being inspired by, and learning from, international gatherings (as in the case of Richard Fung) are part of the story of the genesis of local queer of colour politics. Thus, in locating the "local" within such a trans-local network, this paper suggests that queer of colour and anti-racist HIV/AIDS activisms in 1980s Toronto were shaped by both endogenous and exogenous political energies and practices.

There are several possible implications of this argument for how we might understand the marvellous grounds of queer of colour Toronto, but space constraints permit only one important implication to be singled out for extended discussion. It is that such an argument offers us an entry point into theorizing the solidarities, connections, and other relationships that link differently situated political formations together. Such a task is even more paramount at a time when homonormative and homonationalist forms of queer politics continue to circulate globally through well-worn and overlapping circuits of empire and capital. By paying attention to the anti-racist challenges issued by queer of colour activists as well as to the local and extra-local practices through which they enact and materialize their politics, queer of colour scholars can highlight the idea that local struggles *connect with* broader struggles in other places, sometimes through the very forging of interconnections by queer of colour activists.

As the stories above show, local queer of colour politics in 1980s Toronto was constituted by "parts of here and elsewhere," to borrow McCann's (2011, 145) memorable phrase, assembled from the visions, experiences, and activisms of local queers of colour and those from "elsewhere" that they drew on, learned from, and contributed to. Paying attention to both local embeddedness and extra-local entanglements is one way of unpacking the genealogies and geographies of local iterations of queer of colour politics. Doing so allows us not only to trace the urban-global nexus within which the marvellous grounds of queer of colour activisms in 1980s Toronto were forged but also to highlight political possibilities for learning, inspiration, and solidarity across issues and across spaces.

References

ACAS (Asian Community AIDS Services). 1999. "Fifth Anniversary." Toronto: Asian Community AIDS Services.

Armstrong, Elizabeth A. 2002. *Forging Gay Identities: Organizing Sexuality in San Francisco, 1950–1994*. Chicago: University of Chicago Press.

Berlant, Lauren. 1997. *The Queen of America Goes to Washington City: Essays on Sex and Citizenship*. Durham, NC: Duke University Press.

Bernstein, Mary. 1997. "Celebration and Suppression: The Strategic Uses of Identity by the Lesbian and Gay Movement." *American Journal of Sociology* 103 (3): 531–65. https://doi.org/10.1086/231250.

Catungal, John Paul. 2013. "Ethno-Specific Safe Houses in the Liberal Contact Zone: Race Politics, Place-Making and the Genealogies of the AIDS Sector in Global-Multicultural Toronto." *ACME: An International E-Journal for Critical Geographies* 12 (2): 250–78.

– 2014. "For Us, by Us: Political Geographies of Race, Sexuality and Health in the Work of Ethno-Specific AIDS Service Organizations in Global-Multicultural Toronto." Unpublished PhD diss., University of Toronto.

Churchill, David S. 2003. "Personal Ad Politics: Race, Sexuality and Power at the Body Politic." *Left History* 8 (2): 114–34.

Fung, Richard. 2012. "Gay Asians of Toronto." Profile of organization. Canadian Lesbian and Gay Archives. 15 November. Accessed 14 July 2013. http://www.clga.ca/gay-asians-toronto.

Ghaziani, Amin. 2008. *The Dividends of Dissent: How Conflict and Culture Work in Lesbian and Gay Marches on Washington.* Chicago: University of Chicago Press.

Harris, Laura Alexandra. 1996. "Black Queer Feminism: The Pleasure Principle." *Feminist Review* 54 (1): 3–30. https://doi.org/10.1057/fr.1996.31.

McCann, Eugene. 2011. "Veritable Inventions: Cities, Policies and Assemblage." *Area* 43 (2): 143–7. https://doi.org/10.1111/j.1475-4762.2011.01011.x.

Rayside, David M., and Evert A. Lindquist. 1992. "AIDS Activism and the State in Canada." *Studies in Political Economy* 39 (1): 37–76. https://doi.org/10.1080/19187033.1992.11675417.

Schulman, Sara. 2012. *The Gentrification of the Mind: Witness to a Lost Imagination.* Berkeley: University of California Press.

Stewart, Douglas. 1992. "Black Coalition for AIDS Prevention." OCASI Newsletter. May: 15–16.

Thomas, Nicki. 2011. "Thirty Years after the Bathhouse Raids." *Toronto Star,* 4 February. Accessed 1 December 2016. https://www.thestar.com/news/gta/2011/02/04/thirty_years_after_the_bathhouse_raids.html.

Warner, Tom. 2002. *Never Going Back: A History of Queer Activism in Canada.* Toronto: University of Toronto Press.

3 Má-ka Juk Yuh: A Genealogy of Black Queer Liveability in Toronto

OMISOORE H. DRYDEN[1]

We are sodomites and man-royals, gays and lesbians, zamis, battyboys, dykes and fags: homosexuals. We are Black, African, Jamaican, Grenadian, Caribbean, Canadian – African. We are hyphenated. We are critical thinkers. We are feminist and activists. We are rebels.

> – Debbie Douglas, *Má-ka: Diasporic Juks*[2]

During the 2016 Pride Month in Toronto, a human rights panel on "Blackness and Queer Politics" was held at The 519.[3] According to the Pride Guide, this panel would discuss "the systemic and daily oppression faced by Black queer and trans communities, highlighting the ways that anti-blackness is present in LGBTQ spaces."[4] With the bifurcation of race from sexuality, understood as two separate yet perhaps similar identities/positions/schools of thought, the relationship between

---

1 We thank Amandeep Kaur Panag for transcribing this interview. The interview was significantly shortened by the editors.
2 In Debbie Douglas, Courtnay McFarlane, Makeda Silvera, and Douglas Stewart, eds., *Má-ka: Diasporic Juks – Contemporary Writing by Queers of African Descent* (Toronto: Sister Vision: Black Women and Women of Colour Press, 1997), x. The collection compiles the essays, poetry, and testimonies of queers of African descent, with contributors from North America, Europe, and Africa – an anthology of writing by women and men who live with shifting identities (social, cultural, and sexual).
3 The 519 is a community centre providing services to lesbian, gay, bisexual, and transgender people in Toronto, located at 519 Church Street.
4 Visit https://www.evensi.ca/human-rights-panel-blackness-and-queer-politics-the-519/179401158.

LGBTQ and blackness often renders blackness external to LGBTQ organizing, politics, and community-making; and LGBTQ lives and issues external to Black organizing, politics, and community-making. As can be expected at such panels, there were lively debates surrounding the limits, conditions, and politics of belonging, not only to the normative LGBTQ community but also within/of Canada.

The conversations also included explorations and contemplation of space, place, and belonging. Panellists spoke about searching for, building, and finding community. Thus, it was no surprise that the evening was filled with sounds of laughter and rage, feelings of love, regret, loss, and longing. One young Black gay man asked others in attendance (specifically other Black queer and trans people) the following question: "Where are you?" He declared that it was fantastic to see everyone who came to the panel, but wondered why he did not see more Black queer and trans people on and around Church Street.[5] It was a thought-provoking question – one that served as both a reminder (for some) and a schooling (for others) that there was and is a vibrant "elsewhereness." This elsewhereness is not a place (outside) from which blackness must be brought into LGBTQ organizing and community. Instead, this place and space of elsewhereness is one in which Black queer and trans diasporic lives always already exist, thus providing a different reading of LGBTQ activism in Canada. We came into our queered sexualities in different spaces, places, locations, and time. We came into our queered sexualities within the Black, African, and Caribbean diasporic communities in Toronto. I hope that the stories below demonstrate the fecundity of a Black and queer elsewhereness.

One of the panellists asked us to remember and think through the strategies of "Black feminisms" of the 1970s and 1980s, specifically to how they relate to the anti-Black racism and queer and trans political work of today and tomorrow. Indeed, there is a (re)turn to Sister Vision: Black Women and Women of Colour Press in current discussions in Toronto. Sister Vision was co-founded in 1985 by Makeda Silvera and Stephanie Martin. The creation of this press was a seminal moment in Black feminism and Black queer activism in Toronto, giving rise to such important books as the 1997 *Má-ka: Diasporic Juks – Contemporary Writing by Queers of African Descent*, edited by Debbie Douglas, Courtnay

---

5 As discussed in the Introduction, Church Street is considered to be Toronto's Gay Village.

McFarlane, Makeda Silvera, and Douglas Stewart, in honour of which this chapter is named.

On 26 June 2016, I had the opportunity to speak with eight Black lesbian, gay, bisexual, and queer folks to explore the question, What were some of the politics and practices that helped to create spaces for Black LGBTQ people in Toronto – spaces that were created to address the interlocking frameworks of racism, homophobia, and sexism? Beverly Bains, Carol Camper, Dionne Falconer, Junior Harrison, Courtnay McFarlane, Philip Pike, Carol Thames, and I met at the home of Debbie Douglas, not only for food and drinks but also to explore some of the Black queer spaces that have been created over the past thirty-five years. In other words, I wanted to hear and record their stories and experiences. I wanted to be reminded of and schooled in their legacies as individuals, as a group/community, and of blackness-queerness in Toronto. The questions I constructed were designed to elicit a variety of memories. The guidance and direction of Debbie Douglas and Beverly Bains in the construction of these questions, I firmly believe, allowed for the vibrant, rich, and layered conversation. Topics included the motivations for creating space, the language used to speak about Black sex and sexualities, past and present methods of sharing information, and the presence of children, Caribbean food, and #BlackLivesMatterTO.[6]

As an entrance into the discussions on activism and community organizing, we began with a moment of reflection about the Black queer and trans people who have died. Names were called, including Sherona Hall, Garfield, and Sumaya Delmar – may they continue to *Walk Good*.

OMISOORE DRYDEN: Why Black queer community-making?
DEBBIE DOUGLAS: We were determined that we were going to live in Black community and take up space in Black community.
COURTNAY MCFARLANE: We were also confronting the racism we felt from the white community, including the lesbian and gay community.
DEBBIE: This community-making began for me at 101 Dewson, in the early 1980s. It was Makeda Silvera and Steph Martin's home, and they turned it into a collective. It became a place of living,

---

6 Many notable and significant people were missing from this conversation. As the majority of people could attend on a specific day, we decided to go ahead. As it was, on the day of the gathering another three very significant people were unable to attend.

organizing, partying, and arguing and coming into our own. It was a place where my feminism blossomed. It was also a place where my daughter was nurtured as a young baby.

OMISOORE: Were children always part of the activism and the organizing? [All agree.]

DEBBIE: There were always children. Many of the women had children, were mothers; Makeda had children, I had Siobhan. At the kitchen table, we would come together and do a lot of the organizing for events and actions that happened in Toronto. We came up with ideas and started and ended groups. We would debate and decide what we were going to call ourselves. And sometimes we formed a group just to name ourselves, and then the group ended. [Whole room laughs.]

COURTNAY: 101, as we called it, was like the Black queer 519. It was a place we would go – both a collective and a home. You know how you said, Debbie, this was where you came to feminism? This was where I went as a teenager; this was a Black queer home. I remember we had Zami parties there, and we organized ILGAPOC, the International Lesbian and Gay People of Colour conference, in 1988. I was just thinking about planning for that conference and remembered all the organizers posing on the back deck so we could get our picture taken. So many things I remember. When we couldn't find space for dances or for parties, we would have them at 101 Dewson. We had Zami's Colour Purple party there. [All agree.]

OMISOORE: How did you get involved in doing politics?

BEVERLY BAINS: I came into my politics on campus at the University of Toronto [U of T] in the early and mid-1970s. As an activist, and a young undergraduate, I started with African Caribbean Students' Association, which was just beginning. My introduction to politics and activism was through Marxism, through the International African Liberation struggle. That was my introduction on campus. And then I joined the Communist Party and subsequently became a member. I started with the big battles around the role of women and issues of race. I wondered, where do I really fit in, in these struggles around international politics? And revolutionary politics? I'm a Black woman. In that moment, I found the Communist Party to be very reductionist, with everything reduced to class. Women and race were subsumed under a reductionist class analysis. There was no room for conversations around racism.

I also started to be involved in feminist activism, and this is when I became connected with the Black Women's Collective [BWC]. I was looking for something else, something with a larger and more complicated class analysis – for conversations about Black women's lives, and a political analysis around issues of race, class, and gender, as places we occupied simultaneously. This is how I came into my feminism.

CAROL CAMPER: One thing I remember about the period 1988 to 1989, in white women's organizing around International Women's Day and other events, is that there would sometimes be a single Black woman in those groups. Her role, it seemed, was to perform something that the white women needed. It was as if white women felt they could not possibly be racist because of their proximity to this single Black woman. The Black woman was to be "proof" to the rest of us that all of our critiques were invalid. I observe this as someone who, a very long time ago, was almost pulled into that sort of thing myself. I was adopted by a white family, grew up in a white community, usually the only non-white person in my school. My white friends would say that I was cool or that I wasn't like other Black people. I remember being in lesbian bars and white women telling me I must be able to sing. [Whole group laughs.] I married a white man who was sort of my ally until he wasn't. To a certain degree, I was comfortable. However, when I dug down, I realized that this was not comfortable, and I decided I'm not doing that. I've had a lifetime of trying to be like everyone else, and it failed. And I'm glad that it did fail.

But I continue to wonder about that lone Black woman and the role that you are asked to perform. Being the solitary Black person, you become very isolated. I came from that isolation, which is why I sought out the BWC. I first connected because of the connection between race and politics, not even around sexuality. The sexuality was a bonus! [All laugh.]

DIONNE FALCONER: I remember coming out as bi, and this was not easy. And I think it was the perception of heterosexual privilege. "Yes, but you have heterosexual privilege." But the conversation is a bit more complex than that. Sometimes things would get drawn as if they're black and white, when they're not. Our sexuality isn't, and notions of gender change over time.

COURTNAY: I was a teenager growing up in Scarborough, and I knew from grade 6 that I was attracted to guys. And you know,

I'd go to Cedarbrae Public Library and find all kinds of things: Jean Genet novels, Masters and Johnson's texts; anything with homosexuality in it, I would find it. I found the *Body Politic*. All of these texts were accessible at Cedarbrae Library. I had this whole sense of gay life outside of Lawrence and Scarborough Golf Club Road.

I remember I got to high school, and back then the newspapers had personal ads, and you would look at them. I'm convinced it was in the *Toronto Star* that I saw an ad for a group for Black and West Indian lesbians and gays. The meeting was at The 519, and I ended up going. Remember the Pine Room? I think we were there downstairs.

PHILIP PIKE: My entry point into the community was through Black CAP [Black Coalition for AIDS Prevention]. I tend to be a very methodical person, so it was a very conscious, deliberate step on my part. I was a late bloomer in many ways; I didn't come out until I was about twenty-two. From the time I had come to Canada, at the age of nine, until my early thirties, my world, with the exception of my family, was a very white world. So there came a point – I had just turned thirty, I had been out for about eight years, and I just felt a need to connect more fully to my Black identity. I was at work one day – I remember this as if it was yesterday – and I picked up *Share* magazine, and there was an ad for volunteer board members for Black CAP. I responded, and was interviewed, and joined. It was a conscious step: I had read about the organization, I knew it was a Black queer – to use the present word – space. It was a very wonderful experience.

It is often said that girls who go to all-female schools have a certain kind of self-affirmation and come out of that experience very affirmed and confident. Black CAP felt like that for me in terms of my Black and queer identity: two things coming together. But above that identity piece, these were also just wonderfully talented people. They were writers, poets, artists, and filmmakers – the whole gamut. It was just a huge privilege to be in that group. It was, for me, a second kind of schooling – or graduation.

CAROL THAMES: It's interesting listening to the stories because I came out in 1981. And when I came out, it was more in the party scene. In the late 1980s, far more people came out; a certain level of consciousness came with that new-found group with its sexual identity, which formed a different kind of community.

Coming out as a Black queer youth in the city was about surviving and creating an identity because you're dealing with two folds:
racism and sexual identity. If you were estranged from your family,
you may have entered a community that isolated you as a Black
person. I remember coming out at that time, I was twenty-one. My
then partner and I were standing in a bar and were the only two
Black women in there. I thought, "Oh my God, if a fight breaks
out, what will happen?" Not to mention the type of pushback I
received for being dressed up and wearing lipstick and makeup. I
was called a "faghag."

DEBBIE: The first thing we did when we started Zami, being young
and brave, was we marched off to *Contrast* magazine because we
were going to put an ad in this Black community newspaper to an-
nounce the formation of this wonderful group and call out all the
Black gays and lesbians to come to a meeting. We walked into the
newspaper and introduced ourselves, and the receptionist said,
"You're what?!" We said, "We're gay and lesbian, we have an ad
that we would like published in the Community Events section.
We would like it to be run once an issue." She asked us to wait and
went to get the publisher. [Laughter.] When the publisher comes
out, we repeat our spiel. "We're Zami. We think it's important for
folks in the community to know we are meeting." And he said,
"We don't do that here." [Laughter.] So we said, "OK, we'll pay
for the ad." And he stated he didn't want our money, claiming
this was a "family newspaper." As we walked out of there, down
Bathurst Street [where *Contrast* was located], we look back, and we
can see the whole office had come out to the street and watched us
four gay people walking away. They just watched us walk down
the street. [Laughter.] In the end, we decided we'd have to put ads
in the gay newspapers and mainstream papers, such as *Now* and
the *Toronto Star*.

COURTNAY: We used flyers, phone calls, call trees, word of mouth to
get the word out. …

DEBBIE: … phone trees …

CAROL T: … out-of-pocket potlucks, parties …

DIONNE: All of this work was self-funded through fundraising and
membership fees.

COURTNAY: At Zami, we used to work the Gay Community Dance
Committee [GCDC]. They used to have these dances at the Ma-
sonic Temple. Members of groups would volunteer to work the

coat check, and we'd get a percentage of the door. This would pay for our snacks at meetings, printing of flyers, photocopying. The GCDC evolved to give small grants and eventually into the Lesbian and Gay Community Appeal. We did grant proposals, like with Toronto Arts Council. Through AYA,[7] we would connect with different organizations and festivals, especially if there was an out-of-town artist brought in to speak or show their work. We could organize something at a local bar. It would be a slow money day, so it became a way to gather without having to pay out cash. Overall, we did things that cost little or no money.

DEBBIE: Douglas Stewart and I were roommates/housemates at Dewson. We knew we weren't the only Black queers around. And while we felt comfortable in white spaces, we were very clear that they were *white* spaces. In the Black community, political organizing was at its height, and many of us were absent from this work. Sherona Hall was very much engaged, yet for the most part, she remained discreet about her sexuality. Makeda Silvera was a journalist writing for community newspapers. People would drive by and throw eggs at her house! So we felt we needed to create a political space, one that centred homosexuality in the Black community, a space where we could talk and plan. With my then partner, and Douglas's then partner, the four of us thought, "Let's create this group." We came up with the name Zami, from Audre Lorde's work. Also, I'm Grenadian, and *zami* is one of the words used for lesbian sex in the eastern Caribbean, including Trinidad.

COURTNAY: Use it in a sentence.

DEBBIE: "Gurl, you like to zami, ehh?" [Whole room laughs.]

COURTNAY: Zami started as a Caribbean group …

DIONNE: No, West Indian!

COURTNAY: Yes, West Indian! Not even Caribbean … we were West Indian, that's right. We had South Asian and East Asian men who identified as West Indian who were part of the group. I remember this classified ad placed in *Body Politic* in 1985, by a white gay man looking for a "Black houseboy." Just the everyday racism that was part of white gay media. A group of us came together, including Gay Asians of Toronto with Richard Fung, to challenge this. We

---

7 This is the Black gay men's group founded in 1994 (see below for more details). AYA is a fern, taken from Akan symbols.

wrote a piece on lesbians, gays, and race. We created our own panels and forums.

JUNIOR: When I saw that ad for Zami, perhaps in *Now*, I went to a place of profound fear. I thought, I cannot go to this group. Someone will know my mother! The West Indian community is a small community. So my reaction was, "Absolutely not." Instead, I decided that I needed to avoid this, disappear, and meld into a big sea of gay. And then we created AYA. AYA would meet every third Sunday at The 519. It was an incredible, pivotal point in my life. It allowed me to learn how blackness exists in larger LGBT space. We would come and do our thing. It was a Black queer–only space. Non-Black people would push their head in the door; all of us in the room would turn around and look at them, and it was very clear, we were unapologetic about our Black-only space. Later on, other groups, like the Asian Men's group, Gay Asians of Toronto, would ask us how we keep our meetings Black-only. In these groups, white partners of gay Asian men would show up, ready to contribute and serve on committees, and ultimately take up a lot of space. So for me, it was one of the moments I realized it is OK to have our space. We need to come together and work on our own stuff alone, and then later come together with other groups in coalition. It didn't need to be all together, all the time. This gave me even more confidence to go into larger communities and do what was needed. I realized that I had worth. I'm tearing up. I had worth, not because a white man smiles at me. No. I *have* worth.

COURTNAY: We were pretty hardened and militant around that piece. There were also members who had white partners, but it was very much a *Black gay men's* space.

JUNIOR: I remember that a meeting would happen, but honestly, I heard a meeting for "iron men." It was a meeting of gay men, but I heard it as "iron men" and thought, "Oooo, I should go!!"

COURTNAY: Oh, it was AYA!

JUNIOR: Yes, AYA men, but I heard "iron men." [Laughter.] I remember Mabinti walking around and handing out flyers for Sepia.[8] She would approach you and say, "Forgive me for presuming. ..." [Laughter.]

---

8 This is an organization created for Black lesbian women in the city of Toronto.

COURTNAY: AYA organized events through Sepia. When the women would come out, they were happy, usually, to see the men who attended. However, when the men came out, they would see the women, wonder why women were there, and then leave.

JUNIOR: And then they would come back later to see if the women left.

COURTNAY: We were at a retreat, there were about nine or ten of us, and we did an exercise around masculinity. It was important to have this conversation with men about sexist language and its prevalence in our conversations, in gay culture. We did body movement exercises and talked about our experience of gender. We needed to explore masculinity as something that not everyone claimed easily or comfortably. I remember positioning myself outside of this whole thing called masculinity, and some of the men wanted to pull me in!

DIONNE: I remember the Black Women's Collective. When I was introduced to the BWC in 1988, it was expanding and had just started to recruit new members. At this time, the BWC was bringing Angela Davis to speak.

CAROL C: I came in after the Angela Davis event because I was trying to find community. I was also coming out, but I needed a politicized Black women's community to be part of. I remember seeing posters up around the University of Toronto for this Angela Davis event and thinking, "If I can find one of those posters, there might be a contact number."

DIONNE: I came in from political feminist organizing, and at the BWC, there was this language of intersectionality – talking about race and gender, sexual orientation and class/socio-economic status. I think we actually [used] words like *intersectional* and *Aboriginal rights* in our constitution. The BWC also had a newspaper, *Our Lives*. And then there was Black CAP.[9] Black CAP began in 1987. Douglas Stewart was a counsellor at the AIDS Committee of Toronto, and he had witnessed Black people coming forward who were HIV-positive. So Douglas got together with Black folks who worked in different organizations, in health and social services. "We need to do something." This is the genesis of Black CAP. And

---

9 See also chapter 2 by John Paul Catungal, which draws on an interview with Douglas Stewart.

at the time, there was one other group [that] was trying to engage around HIV in the Black community, which was Combat. The difference between Combat and Black CAP was around sexuality. Combat was about straight Black people.

CAROL C: Combat was pretty anti-sex in general. It was very conservative and straight. They seemed very mad about people out here having sex, especially people of the same sex.

COURTNAY: Black CAP came into being because of the BWC and Zami and all those connected with these organizations.

DIONNE: The idea of coalition, specifically Black coalition, having different groups coming together, was embedded in the way that Black CAP was organized. This is how I got involved because they needed a representative from the BWC.

DEBBIE: Black CAP was one of the first spaces where you saw Black heterosexual women engaged with gay people.

COURTNAY: When I was involved with Black CAP, part of our outreach included doing anti-homophobia work. This was very much a part of what Black CAP was committed to.

DIONNE: Right! It's also a space where some Black people came out. If you're lesbian, gay, bi, trans, queer – whatever your identity – questioning, it's a space *for you.*

JUNIOR: I came into Black political consciousness when I discovered I was HIV-positive. There was something ignited in me. I needed to know where the other Black faces were who were also dealing with this thing. So I went on this search, and I went to the AIDS Committee of Toronto. The receptionist said, "I think there's this organization called Black CAP, and you should call them." No cell phone back in the 1990s. [All laugh.] I called the organization. "Hi, I'm Black, I'm gay, I'm positive, I'm looking for …"

OMISOORE: So many of us died in the 1980s and 1990s. …

JUNIOR: That's why I'm single. It's true, we talk about it all the time. My brothers. … There's a group, the AIDS generation, who would have been in their forties to fifties today, but they are gone. So when I go out, those few times I do, into Black gay spaces, I'm with men in their twenties and thirties, but not their forties or fifties.

DIONNE: In the early days, it was community that then took care of you; families were a complicated matter. There's the side where the family dismisses you and the side where you don't want your family to know. Some had never come out, so now they'd be coming out as HIV-positive as well as gay. But you know, there were also Black people doing different pieces, but in more isolated ways. Over time, Black people came together. More of us supporting each other, taking care of each other.

JUNIOR: Black CAP is an AIDS organization, but it had to become so much more for everyone. The mainstream agencies didn't feel it necessary to focus on race. My journey through Black CAP was eye-opening. Black CAP ignited my political passion. I chose at certain points to put myself at the forefront, going out and doing public speaking, because I felt it really necessary that somebody put a face onto this disease.

OMISOORE: Can we talk about Blackness Yes!/Blockorama? Blocko was and is so significant.

CAROL T: The thing for me is that concrete parking lot at Wellesley and Yonge. It was the Black community that brought it alive – actually the Black queer and trans community. There was a tiny little strip that they allowed us to spread out onto on Maitland Street. And people came and brought that space alive! It was awesome.

DIONNE: We went to Black Pride in Washington, DC, and that's where the idea of Blocko began to percolate.

JUNIOR: The whole Black Pride movement started to develop in the US, and DC was the biggest one. When was the Black Nation conference in New York?

COURTNAY: 1995. And the debate was whether or not Black people should call themselves "queer."

DIONNE: I remember Ruth Ellis[10] saying, "Ain't nothing queer about what I do!"

COURTNAY: This speaks to the inspiration that many of us got from being in Black queer spaces in the US and in the UK. For AYA, it was Gay Men of African Descent, and the woman who started Sepia had some American models, like Cinnamon Girls. There were always things that were organized in the Black community by queer folks, and we would attend and be part of it.

JUNIOR: And each time we came back feeling energized. I remember going to Toronto Pride and walking around and wondering,

---

10 Ruth Ellis was an African American woman who was also known for being the oldest living out lesbian. She was born in 1899 and died in her sleep on 5 October 2000. At the time of this conference, she was ninety-six years old. To learn more about Ruth Ellis, check out Yvonne Welbon's 1999 film, *Living with Pride: Ruth C. Ellis @ 100* (http://www.imdb.com/title/tt0216886/).

"Where are we?" I think it was Douglas who went to the UK to Nottingham Carnival. They had tents and DJs. So he went to Toronto Pride to say we wanted to do an event. "We are handing you your diversity on a platter, and we are not paying for anything. We are a coordinating committee. We will organize entertainment, and Pride is going to fund it."

DIONNE: We used loading crates for a stage ...

COURTNAY: ... and created a sort of amphitheatre, a circle of bodies at different levels in the parking lot.

JUNIOR: I remember, I'd get in the car and go into all the community centres, Driftwood, and drive down to Keele and Eglinton, and plaster the bus shelter, and of course advertise through word of mouth. And the next thing we knew, people showed up!

DEBBIE: We also had women in our community show up and sell food.

COURTNAY: As Douglas says, we brought cooked food to Pride! [All laugh.]

JUNIOR: We had a bit of entertainment, and the rest was for the crowd – to dance, see each other, and have a great time. I think for most of my stint with Blocko, I was the liaison/PR with the Pride organization. So I'd have to go to each meeting. We would be done with our planning by January – we'd have entertainment lined up, we had a system organized. So when we went to the first meeting in February, I'd say, "We are done and ready to go." So first I would have to remind them who I am. "I'm from Blackness Yes!; we're the Blockorama stage." They would usually respond, "Where? Oh, you people over there." So every year, I'd come with my fact sheet, and I would just put it on the table. Every year, I'd have to explain this is why we exist. And it's not like the Pride committee had new people on it – it was the same people! After Pride, at the community wrap-up, the Pride committee itself would be so aggravated with our success. "You people want to separate yourselves over there." "Yeah, we do! We don't need you."

DIONNE: And then they'd move us around, remember. ...

COURTNAY: Right. On the day of Blocko, we wouldn't get the things we requested, so we would have to scramble. That was actually an undervaluing of us and the community space we created.

JUNIOR: And I'd be running from Maitland and Yonge over to Church and Wellesley to say, "Well, it's three o'clock, four o'clock, five o'clock; we haven't received anything." They'd be like, "Where?

Who? *Blacko*? What?" Then we'd be setting up, and the police would come over and ask us ...

WHOLE GROUP: ... "What are you doing?"

COURTNAY: Exactly, because we *couldn't* be part of Pride.

JUNIOR: One of the biggest fights we had was, *we never wanted alcohol in our space!*

COURTNAY: So they needed to justify our presence and profit from us. But we recognized the place of alcohol, and we felt it was important and vital to have alcohol-free spaces. The people who came to that space included grannies, children, people with substance-abuse issues, and we wanted them to feel comfortable in that space. And when you look at those early photographs, you see the kind of diversity of folks in that space. Every year, in spite of Pride Toronto and the shitty way they treated us, we would leave feeling exhausted but full, because of the joy that we felt creating space for Black folks – diverse Black folks. It was also our experience of being part of community organizing: groups start, do their thing, and then they end. Sometimes it ends well, and sometimes it's acrimony, and you can't even look at the person for ten years, and we still carry stuff around. To look at Blocko, it's going to be eighteen this year, and I think about Douglas's modelling. We created this thing, we did this thing, and then we can leave this thing now to the next group. This is really a model of transitioning: succession planning. I think that Blockorama is almost twenty years old and is now an institution. I think it's part of how it became us. It wasn't just mine, it was ours!

DIONNE: In Zami and the early days of Black CAP, it was men and women working together.

COURTNAY: So I remember a particular Angela Davis event. I think I have a T-shirt that was designed by Multicultural Women in Concert. The event stands out in my mind because there were four of us from Zami who did childcare for the event. Zami men did the childcare.

DEBBIE: That was always part of our organizing: we expected the men who are our allies to show support and solidarity.

JUNIOR: In Black CAP, we would go into communities, and we would feel untouchable. I remember speaking at a high school on Vaughan Road, and this young Black woman said, "So how'd you get it?" And I just said, "My dear, you know I don't have a vagina." It just popped into my head. And after [that] I thought, "Oh my God, I can't believe I said that." [All laugh and applaud.]

COURTNAY: I organized a cultural celebration with Black lesbians and gay men in the late 1980s. It was the first of its kind. We had visual artists, performers. … It was a coming together of Black queer artists and community. We had exhibits and a fashion show; it was a whole thing.

BEVERLY: Remember International Women's Day [IWD] events? Remember when we came up with the slogan "From Toronto to South Africa"? That was the big shift in IWD celebration. The BWC was instrumental in this shift and in how the women's movement actually functions. And I fought with my communist sisters, who believed that it was a problem that Black women, Indigenous women, and other racialized women would lead IWD. They argued it was like segregation, and I said, "It is not, absolutely not." That was my breaking point.

DEBBIE: That was part of the tension of IWD. We needed a different focus in reproductive rights conversations. For Black women and Indigenous women, especially, it wasn't about abortion.

BEVERLY: It was about forced sterilization and keeping your kids!

DEBBIE: The silver lining is, it created for the first time a close political relationship between Black women and Indigenous women. And then there are the academic institutions and our work there. I went to York, like many others, thinking that it was more politically active than other institutions. While at York, we created the York Women's Centre – Domenica DiLeo, Sil – I don't remember her last name – Brenda Clarke, and myself. Domenica DiLeo – you have to give her credit, our Italian sister, she had the idea. This was around 1984, 1985. She would walk up to any woman she saw and say we needed a women's centre. I remember I was hanging out on campus one day, and this white woman came up and said, "Hi, my name is Domenica, and I think we need to start a women's centre. I'm having a meeting this evening; would you like to come?" About thirty of us showed up, and about twenty of us came out! I went to school straight and came home a lesbian! [All laugh and clap.]

OMISOORE: As so many of us do! I thought that was the whole point of university.

DIONNE: Around 1986 or 1987, I met with Angela Robertson. Angela had started Black Women at York, and I wanted to start a Black Women at U of T and OISE [Ontario Institute for Studies in Education] with some other women.

DEBBIE: There were a lot of tensions around issues of sex and sexual behaviour, and a real policing (at times) around women's sexuality. Not always a very sex-positive space, right? We would now call this respectability politics. A lot of the organizing was happening in a very middle-class place, even though a lot of us identified as working-class women. But I remember when we used to have events, readings – remember the S&M night? – there were huge debates. There were debates about our own power.

DIONNE: ... and about bondage ...

DEBBIE: I think you got called out for just being involved in the scene. There was quite a debate in the Black lesbian, feminist community. It was anti-feminist. ... Who gets to decide? I think there are some women who would say they felt isolated from a sense of community, that they were not included, because their politics were questioned.

BEVERLY: That approach to our sexuality was very much a radical feminist approach that actually moved across race. As Black feminists, we were also caught within a respectability notion of how blackness is supposed to be.

CAROL T: There was this public-private thing. A lot of the sistahs were like, "We don't want you to talk about what you're doing. Just do it over there." There was this sense of secretiveness around it. I remember my partner at the time saying to me, "You gotta tone it down." But that's not fair because I came out as "x," and why do I need to tone it down and become "y"? And I didn't like the outfits of "y." Actually, that was my argument – I didn't like the outfits! As simple as that.

OMISOORE: So was it a form of slut shaming?

CAROL T: As a woman who experienced it, yes. I think there was a sense of honouring your braveness but not knowing how to step over that line. So your sister would look at you and say, "Wow you're brave, that's something. I wouldn't do it, but you're brave." I'm sitting here, and I feel sad. There's like a post-traumatic stress. There are many people in this room that I fought with, that I ignored for many years, part of it around my children – because both my children are interracial and were born in a lesbian relationship – part of it involved my sexual practice, and so it feels – whole to be here. [Cries softly.]

CAROL C: I felt quite policed, actually, in the Black lesbian community around my sexuality. I certainly felt I was too much – too sexy. One time I was told, "She's too young for you, and she's too innocent." The woman was in her thirties! And they talked like she was a teenager. I'm glad I didn't heed the warning. But it was years after that I finally decided, "I want this, so I'm going for it. And she wants it too, so there you go!" But the thing that was weird for me was that I came out into a community of Black women who were political radicals. However, on many levels, they were culturally and sexually conservative. And it took me years to get that, but it was always like, "What is it that's so bad about being *me*? I'm not taking anyone against their will. I'm not breaking up families. ..." [All laugh.]

OMISOORE: What were the experiences like with Black men?

JUNIOR: SLUT!!! [Puts his hands up and waves. All laugh.]

DEBBIE: We have to talk about Wong's Jamaican Chinese food restaurant.

OMISOORE: What is Wong's?

COURTNAY: Wong's was a Jamaican Chinese restaurant on Bathurst Street. It was an institution.

DEBBIE: Wong's was a place of political debate.

COURTNAY: It was a space where you could see all these worlds colliding. We'd go to Wong's and make lots of noise and have red bean soup. We made sure to take up space in Black community. Wong's was near Third World Art and Books, another space that had vibrant and critical political discussions.

DEBBIE: We used to have huge debates at Wong's with other customers about homosexuality, about women's rights. ... And they would be like, "Eat your food!"

DIONNE: And how these collective activisms have continued. So much activism now – like #BlackLivesMatterTO.[11] I think those women and trans people are incredible. I think they are absolutely phenomenal – in just the way they have been able to organize and stay focused, and just get stuff done and just be up in people's faces and *not* get dissuaded by the bullshit that comes at them, the anger that comes at them, the violence that comes at them, the state that comes at them. I just think that they're absolutely incredible!

DEBBIE: And I think it's important for them to know that they are supported – and that they *will be* supported even when we disagree

---

11 See also chapter 7, "Black Lives Matter Toronto Teach-In," by Janaya Khan and LeRoi Newbold.

with their tactics. They have raised a conversation about blackness and the city of Toronto in a way that hasn't been raised in a very long time.

COURTNAY: Since the 1970s and 1980s.

DEBBIE: And I think those opportunities will come. You have to keep reaching out to them. I think it was important when they were camped out in front of the police station, and during the day one of us would show up. So they knew that we were watching, that we had their backs. Because I really do feel a sense – and I don't want to be ageist – *I really do feel a sense of responsibility for their well-being.* I think they are brave, I think they are smart, and I think they are fearless.

CAROL T: One of the things I think is wonderful, watching what they've done, is they've taken the history of what Black people have been doing for the past four hundred years in order to survive the design of this society. So that's what they've done. And they've identified to the state that we are aware that this is not by accident: society is created this way.

COURTNAY: It speaks to that history, that connection between Black queer and broader communities across the Canadian and American divide.

BEVERLY: Can I say one more thing … and thank you, OmiSoore, for this process; I think this is a really amazing process. But I want to say something connected to Black Lives Matter. *I think they are amazing, and I think that we gave them something.* And I don't think that we ourselves actually acknowledge how much groundwork we have laid. They are brave because we were brave, too. We were brave at a time when there was no Twitter, no Facebook; no one would see us getting beat down. And I will tell you, I absolutely am proud of them. And I know for a fact, we could not have gotten away with having a barricade in the same way without losing our lives. Because there was nobody there to see that. Nobody would have paid attention.

CAROL T: And some of us died. We took the risk no matter what. But more of us would have died in the moment.

BEVERLY: Also, living in a very different period. There's so much surveillance and regulation today. There's also, as Simone Brown says, a lot of "sousveillance."[12] We, ourselves, can actually turn

---

12 Simone Browne, *Dark Matters: On the Surveillance of Blackness* (Durham, NC: Duke University Press, 2015).

the camera on them (motherfuckers) and create a different kind of public opinion or bring the city to favour us in that moment. I agree with you that we *have* to keep supporting Black Lives Matter. They have actually taken up the mantle. They're doing it similarly, but differently, *and* they have to. Right!

DEBBIE: And it's theirs.

BEVERLY: It's theirs. It's absolutely theirs And, I think, that's the connection we need to keep bridging with them and us.

OMISOORE: Any advice for your former selves?

JUNIOR: I don't know about former selves. We're still in it. That's the tough part to realize; it has been ten, fifteen, twenty, thirty years, and we're still in it.

DEBBIE: So maybe that's the advice we would give, right? That the struggle will continue. You will change, your politics will change, and you'll have a different relationship to it. People come in and out, and give you things, and you give them things, and that shapes how you respond politically or not. It's OK to be fearless!

DIONNE: And that you will change. That the same eighteen-year-old Dionne is not the same forty-plus-year-old Dionne. The kind of energy, the kind of fire ... some situations that were considered black and white. ... The certainty of these things will shift and change. Be freer on some things. Don't hold it so tight. You can hold it, but not so tight! There's different ways of looking at things, and it's OK. It's absolutely OK. To be joyous. And, you know, to fuck more, right? [All laugh and clap.]

PHILIP: That's a tricky piece because our journey makes us who we are, so all those mistakes, all those "too much holding," all those "not enough fucking" – all those things contribute to who we are in this moment. It's an accumulation of all those things, so time travel is a tricky thing. If you go back and change one thing, it changes who we have now become.

BEVERLY: One thing I would change is, I felt pretty lonely in the work that I was doing. Because I was simultaneously in various movements all at once, but somehow I felt I was alone. Because there's something about being in numerous movements all at once, but not having a solid grounding. That's the thing: when you extend yourself across movements and across struggles, you end up somehow without an actual community, without an ongoing affinity you can fall back on. I was unable to sustain ongoing support, so I felt very lonely at times. I was constantly knocking up against various barriers. For example, in the National Action Committee [on] the Status of Women [NAC], I fought hard for a woman of colour to be president and to change the dynamics of NAC as an organization that would actually reflect the lives of women of colour. And that did happen; but then something else happened: we were forced to, and took on, a narrative that we can only organize around race. Therefore, there was no room to talk about sexuality, especially for those of us who were racialized and those of us who were transitioning. There was no room for us. So I ended up fighting with all the women of colour and losing any support whatsoever. Then having the white women come after me because they saw me as their enemy anyway. I guess one thing that would have been helpful while I was in NAC is to have a support base outside of NAC and not leave my entire self inside, with no support outside.

COURTNAY: I'm thinking about that young man, and I want to look at him and say, "Wow, you were courageous." In the moment, it didn't feel that way. You were just doing what you need to do for yourself; things were interesting, you felt supported and safe. But thinking about some of the things he did, spaces he was in. ... Wow. *I thank him.*

DEBBIE: I don't think we did a very good job of caring for ourselves. I don't think we ever talked about it. I think it was somehow seen as part and parcel of the political work, to withdraw. And I think we lost lots of sisters and brothers along the way because of that. We could be really harsh with each other.

JUNIOR: Part of my survival has always been about self-care. You always need to step away, you determine the length, and I think it's really good on all levels – mental, physical, what have you. Black CAP is my home forever, but I have had to make the decision to give it breathing room; let it breathe while I'm not there. I'm not saying I'll never go back, but I think it's important always to have some step-away time.

BEVERLY: Many of us have stepped away in different ways. We've gone into academia; I would call that stepping away. But you step into a different battle. Some of us have stepped into working in organizations after we come from the ground. So you're stepping away, but also into something.

COURTNAY: There are things you're carrying from those previous places into our current space.

CAROL T: I've had battles in the queer community with my brothers and sisters who look like me, but one of the things I can be sure of is that if something was happening to me on the street, they would never walk by; they would stop and say, "Are you OK?" And I would do the same. And that's always been my safety net, in a weird unspoken/spoken way, that you'd know that these are the people I grew up with, came into community and grew into adulthood with. So there's a comfort level. It's like a family.

MÁ-KA JUKS: **A Conclusion of Sorts**

So many wonderful stories were shared that afternoon. And from these stories, we see an early Black queer diasporic analytic forming – one that is even better established in the current moment. What I learned and was reminded of are the ways in which Black queer folks situated Black queerness in this geographical space of Toronto. Claiming Toronto as a home space/place, Black lesbians, gay men, and bisexual people acknowledged how simultaneous conditions framed and informed not only their identities but also how they built community and engaged in political actions.

To read through this dialogue, one begins to experience the roots and routes to contemporary Black queered diasporic identities and engagements begun by radical Black feminists. The ways in which community was formed and re-formed emerged out of knowledge produced by the interstices of violence, silence, in(hyper)visibility. No longer "outside" children to LGBTQ spaces/places, these activists, scholars, and workers turned towards one another and created and claimed a centrality that insisted upon the interconnectedness of their blackness, sexuality, and gender.

This chapter captures a conversation (albeit a shortened version) among various participants who were at the forefront of this work and continue to be committed and engaged in this work today. We get a glimpse of how Black lesbians, gay men, and bisexual people collaborated to make home, (re)think belonging and community, while at the same time honour the various roots and routes that brought them (us) together. I return to the introduction of *Má-ka: Diasporic Juks* to reflect on the words of Douglas Stewart, another mentor who was unable to attend the gathering. He states,

Living in Canada … *searching for language* to describe our terrain … learning how to be resilient, how to endure. Má-ka anywhere out there. Only a matter of time before yuh feel it. ... Má-ka blooms in celebration. People try to chop-slash-mash má-ka down. But má-ka juk back, claiming the terrain, reshaping it. Yu nuh feel it?[13]

And yes, it did indeed *juk*. As the conversation clearly outlined, Black queers have been claiming space, place, and reshaping how we think of blackness and queerness. The purpose of this gathering was quite layered. In one moment, it is to document the work of Black queer activism in Canada. In another moment, this is a reflection on Black queer space/place/home in Toronto – how it is imaged, created, shared, and held, disrupting colonial practices of anti-Black racism and homophobia.

The time ran out before the stories did. There is a lot more to say about the vibrant histories of Black queer diasporic activism in Toronto, and I hope this offering (incomplete as it is) holds a space in this tapestry of Black liveability – a space we refuse to relinquish or to give up on.

---

13 Douglas Stewart, introduction to *Má-ka: Diasporic Juks*, by Douglas et al., x; emphasis added; see also note 2 above.

4 Diasporic Intimacies: Queer Filipinos/as and Canadian Imaginaries

ROBERT DIAZ, MARISSA LARGO,
AND FRITZ LUTHER PINO

On 23 January 2015, Casey Mecija, the former lead singer of the band Ohbijou, gave an impromptu performance of her song "Balikbayan" to a transfixed audience made up primarily of Filipino/a artists, activists, scholars, and community members. Meaning "returnee," "Balikbayan" evoked the psychic ambivalences effected by diasporic returns. The song traced the movement of goods and bodies between the Global North and the Global South as it pondered the tense pull of belonging – often tenuous, painful, and unresolved – in spaces that could never fully signify "home." Mecija performed "Balikbayan" during "Diasporic Intimacies: Queer Filipinos/as and Canadian Imaginaries," a groundbreaking series of events that we co-organized and reflect upon in greater detail in this chapter. In what follows, we map out the critical contributions of this gathering, and we trace the possible interventions that queer Filipino/a histories can make in bringing together queer of colour, postcolonial, and Indigenous critique to bear on the multiple forms of marginalization that multiculturalism and settler colonialism often demand.

"Diasporic Intimacies" brought together Filipino/a artists, scholars, and community members as they shared stories that collectively embodied the vibrant contributions that sexually marginalized Filipinos/as have made to Canadian culture and society. This gathering was interdisciplinary in scope and focus. It comprised a full-day conference, a month-long art exhibit, an artist/community dialogue, and a movie screening. These events were held in three locations in Toronto: OCAD University, the Open Gallery at 41 Richmond Street, and The 519 (the Church Street community centre). We chose these spaces since they brought multiple constituencies into dialogue, while destabilizing the barriers that often exist among academic institutions, artistic galleries, and community organizations. In this regard, "Diasporic Intimacies" follows from and is indebted to similar gatherings in the past, which have served as models for ethical forms of knowledge production about marginalized communities, the most recent of which was a conference organized by the critic and scholar Andrea Fatona, called the "State of Blackness: From Production to Presentation," held in 2014. "State of Blackness" similarly placed established and emerging cultural practitioners in critical conversation so that they could interrogate, and find a means of challenging, the often stunting effects of anti-blackness in Canadian artistic and community settings.

That "Diasporic Intimacies" was held in Toronto holds immense political significance. Filipinos/as make up 4.2 per cent of the visible-minority population in the city. For the past few decades, Filipino/a activists and community members have challenged racist and anti-immigrant policies, which have targeted people of colour through inequitable employment policies, systemic de-skilling, and patriarchal labour-migration schemes. While acknowledging past social justice work, "Diasporic Intimacies" also sought to foreground the crucial role of sexually marginalized Filipinos/as in past, present, and future forms of social organizing. The event staked out a space and place for multiple members of the LGBTQ Filipino/a community to challenge their continued institutional and theoretical invisibility in mainstream Canadian queer history as well as their absence in the growing field of Filipino/a Canadian studies. The stories of non-normative sexualities, desires, and kinship bonds enlivened in this gathering offered compelling critiques of the fallacies of Canadian multiculturalism and settler colonialism, which often delineate difference through disciplinary manifestations of inclusion and cultural citizenship.

As many scholars have argued, multiculturalism has defined Canada's liberal and pluralist politics within and beyond the nation since its formation as a federal policy in 1971 and eventual entrenchment in the Canadian Charter of Rights and Freedoms in 1982 (Bannerji 2000; Thobani 2007). These scholars point out that, despite its refashioning as a celebration of racial and religious diversity, multiculturalism is unable to address the complex histories of settler colonialism, Indigenous sovereignty, racial oppression, and patriarchy that continue to affect marginalized communities (Bannerji 2000; Thobani 2007). By focusing on diverse forms of cultural expression, "Diasporic Intimacies" documented flashpoints that unsettled such seamless narratives of inclusion; it did this by highlighting histories of postcolonial violence, abjection, and alienation that refuse Canadian nationalism's integrationalist models for defining visibility. Using images of pain, pleasure, and perseverance, queer Filipinos/as deployed their diasporic histories anew, displaying new forms of knowledge and new forms of expression.

It was thus fitting that "Diasporic Intimacies" began with a performance of Mecija's "Balikbayan." This song symbolizes her personal and political journey as a community-engaged activist, artist, and scholar. It marked one of the first times that she has spoken directly to her identity as a lesbian and second-generation Filipina Canadian. "Balikbayan" evokes a queer ethos – not only because it was written and performed by a sexually marginalized *Pinay* but also because its queerness is rooted in its unsettling of archives and forms of knowledge that have traditionally mattered when indexing Filipina subjectivity in Canadian academic settings. Through its contradictory, affective registers and non-linear narrative, the song resists the tropes of racial authenticity that are often metaphorized through problematic visual cues (the folkloric Filipino body or images of the caring labourer). Instead, the song gestures to the longer *durée* of colonial relations that have affected Filipinos/as as a diasporic community, linking such histories to everyday struggles with migration and movement.

In "Balikbayan," Mecija channels the migrant subject's voice, despite being born in Canada. She thus disentangles the tropes that dictate what stories certain subjects can or should tell. She encourages us to enact what, in another context, Christine Balance calls "disobedient" forms of listening because they necessarily resist the pull of authenticity demanded from the diasporic and postcolonial performing body. The song queers the genres and narratives that have relayed our histories as subjects of imperial histories – through and in the queer subject's voice. At the same time, its ambivalent embrace of "home" lays bare how settler colonialism factors into how queer Filipinos/as in Canada seek more just futures. Such futures must take into account the reality that we continue to occupy land that cannot be "ours."

The feelings of loss and melancholy that "Balikbayan" conveys, then, serve as crucial counterpoints to the state-sanctioned forms of governmentality that sometimes eradicate the complex affinities that can exist among communities located across multiple geographies and positionalities. In its many rhythmic nuances, "Balikbayan" gestures to the unique political questions and multidisciplinary approaches that animated "Diasporic Intimacies" as a gathering of the intersectional experiences of queer, racialized, and postcolonial subjects.

"Diasporic Intimacies" mobilized the knowledge produced by LGBTQ Filipinos/as in Canada to build alliances, drawing on postcolonial histories to transform artistic production, art education, curatorial practice, socially inflected research, and front-line community engagement. Participants engaged with the challenges and opportunities that our growing community faces. These challenges covered a gamut of concerns, such as the representation of queer Filipinos/as in the visual arts; the effects of settlement and migration policy on the community; the nuances of multicultural notions of diversity; the need to document lesbian, trans, and female histories in queer-community organizing; the need to foreground Indigenous notions of sexual identity and collectivity; the role that performance plays in understanding queer Filipino/a sexuality; and the way that medical discourses affect HIV/AIDS intervention, transgender capacity-building, notions of aging, and continued mental health.

In the process, participants reanimated and de-territorialized queer of colour critique. As a political movement of critically engaged scholarship, queer of colour critique has revitalized crucial histories of racialization to centre sexuality's role in such histories. As a political project, queer of colour critique suggests that processes of racialization across the histories of colonialism, slavery, mass incarceration, and genocide often turn on, and depend on, the disciplining of non-normative sexualities and intimacies (Ferguson 2004). While it certainly applies outside the United States, this scholarship remains primarily US-centric, and, as a result, scholars have often criticized it for framing queerness through American racial formation.

"Diasporic Intimacies" moved beyond US-centric models of queer racialization to focus on the specificity of LGBTQ Filipino/a experiences as distinct from, although connected to, the experiences of other racially marginalized communities in Canada. During his welcoming remarks at the conference, the prolific artist and scholar Richard Fung suggested that while *Asian* served as a useful category for enacting multiple forms of coalition-building, it should "not be allowed to erase the questions of specificity, and the specific histories and identities that people who may fall out of that pan-ethnicity experience" (2015). In other words, *Asian* must not be deployed if there is a risk of creating pejorative categorizations, which occlude the distinct colonial, political, and migratory histories that many communities in Canada embody.

The turn to such specificity is particularly relevant when we consider how Canadian multiculturalism obfuscates the rich contradictions present within and across racialized and colonized communities in the Canadian context of settler colonialism and anti-blackness. While some expressions of racial and cultural Otherness are celebrated in the name of diversity, others are marked for policing (see chapter 7 by Janaya Khan and LeRoi Newbold, chapter 8 by Tara Atluri, and chapter 1 by Haritaworn, Gossett, Rodríguez, and Ware). Queer Filipinos/as must thus resist having their lives co-opted for the purposes of celebrating limited, and often violent, forms of inclusionary rhetoric.

In the process of providing specificity, "Diasporic Intimacies" also sought to shift the geopolitical routes of queer and Filipino studies. Over the past fifteen years, queer studies has broadened its scope by foregrounding the experiences of sexual minorities living outside the North American and European contexts (Luibhéid and Cantu 2005; Gopinath 2005; Puar 2007). Filipino studies has similarly reflected this transnational turn by examining sexual marginalization through global and diasporic frames. Despite the richness of such scholarship, however, the majority of research on LGBTQ Filipino/a lives continues to focus on the imperial routes between the Philippines and the United States (Manalansan 2003; Ponce 2012). Such a focus is perhaps unsurprising given the colonial history that both countries share and given the locations from which knowledge around Filipino/a lives continues to be circulated. Yet by foregrounding a reimagined queer of colour critique, "Diasporic Intimacies" insisted on examining the imbricated processes of racialization and sexualization that occur across multiple imperial histories and geographies – which include those of the Canadian nation state.

Accordingly, "Diasporic Intimacies" emphasized how Filipinos/as in Canada, as the product of multiple forms of colonialism, expand upon, and challenge, the ways in which forms of knowledge about queer Filipino/ as have been compartmentalized and archived in Filipino/a Canadian studies. As Robert Diaz suggests, the lack of queer analyses in the field "is rooted in theoretical approaches that symptomatically reify ethno and homo nationalistic ideals of gender, masculinity, citizenship, and cultural acceptance. Even though Filipino/a Canadian studies has been essential in exposing multiculturalism's many fallacies, it has been limited by a continued reliance on heteronormative ideations of family, kinship, religion, civil responsibility, and gendered Citizenship" (2016, 329).

Such an interdisciplinary approach was also proposed by Roland Coloma, one of the event's keynote speakers (2015). Coloma suggested that by focusing on queerness as presence, queerness as fantasy, and queerness as that which is "beyond" our horizon, we may begin to understand the political possibilities that queer studies offers Filipino/a Canadian studies in its current form. When queer histories do not exist, Coloma argued, fantasy – or the insertion of a queerness that is not there – becomes an essential tool for writing new histories and for imaging new forms of world-making that the archive in its current form often does not capture. In Coloma's view, fantasy thus resists the ruse of absence and instead understands queerness as a resistive act that always already insists on its existence amid loss, unintelligibility, and incomprehensibility.

On that note, Coloma suggested that any project of archival recovery needs to believe in what is possible and invest in a sense of futurity. As many have pointed out, artistic practice and cultural expression lend themselves especially well to such prefigurative possibilities. "Diasporic Intimacies" thus prioritized art and social activism produced by women and trans communities since these communities' efforts have not only been essential since the beginning of Filipino/a organizing in the city, but have also been at the forefront of re-imagining how queerness both fuels and unsettles rich forms of collectivity beyond the homonormative forms of sociality currently demanded of queer communities before they can be accepted by the state.

In this regard, a major component of "Diasporic Intimacies" was an art exhibit that Marissa Largo and Robert Diaz co-curated, entitled *Visualizing the Intimate in Filipino/a Lives*. This exhibit featured the work of eleven emerging Toronto-based artists – Maria Patricia Abuel, Jo SiMalaya Alcampo, Lexy Baluyot, Nicole Cajucom, Martie Hechanova, Marissa Largo, Tim Manalo, Julius Manapul, Blessie Maturan, Loisel Wilson Oñate, and Danelle Jane Tran – as well as the work of artists from two community-based organizations, Kapisanan Philippine Centre for Arts and Culture and the Magkaisa Centre.

By consolidating Filipino/a Canadian artists who embody various gendered, classed, and other subjectivities, we sought to unsettle the national borders and fixed identities often produced through dominant Canadian imaginaries – imaginaries that inevitably become uniformly produced in what counts as artistic work. The heterogeneity of the group and their complex concerns challenge the multiculturalist imperative of disciplining ethnic difference. It reflects the polymorphic nature of subject formation in the age of global migration, which the artists translated into diverse materials and techniques. At the same time, the exhibit presented an entangled archive of contemporary art that transgressed the dichotomies of "the West and the rest" (Hall 1992).

In Julius Manapul's contribution, for example, he examines his diasporic sexual and racial identity against both the heteronormative and the homonormative standards of Canadian society. He appropriates Western visual culture and juxtaposes its use with Filipino materiality. In the tableau he composed for the exhibit (see figure 4.1), Manapul reinterprets his past works on "queertopia" – a seemingly perfect abode for him and his queer family – in light of his recent divorce. Articles signifying unfulfilled promises, such as his marriage licence and the crib for his fictional child, created from *balikbayan* boxes (containers used by diasporic Filipinos to send goods "back home") and flanked by two of his "homonormative mannequins," point to his ongoing intimate struggles as a diasporic queer subject vis-à-vis Western normative ideals.

There is no "happily ever after," Manapul suggests in his animation *Kissing Utopia Good-Bye* (2012), only the constant recuperative acts of his diasporic queer identity. The artist conveys this reality in his playful and multilayered appropriation of Disney imagery and Western gay porn, which for him signify unattainable perfection. His *Queerious Butterflies* (2014) takes over the space, performing a transgressive act of embodying a subjectivity that cannot be pinned down by taxonomic classification or colonial imperatives. Instead, these butterflies become the fabric and backdrop for Manapul's fashions an unfurling subjectivity based on his own queer aesthetic.

Similarly, the artist's *Queerious Murses* (2015) are fabricated from intricate cut-outs that subvert dominant and oppressive queer representations. Embedded and hidden in the ornamentation are Tagalog words that have pejorative provenance, such as *bakla* and *bading* (terms that denote homosexuality, effeminacy, and related performances), or racialized and sexualized slurs, like *rice queen*. Like other diasporic queer Filipino men, Manapul has reclaimed these terms to disrupt static notions of queerness in favour of an emergent subjectivity that is remade through aesthetics. Much like a designer bag, queerness here becomes an approachable object, which one carries as one moves through the world, to craft a particular identity that externalizes one's desires for belonging. Manapul's visual strategy of subverting dominant and normative representations behoves viewers to question their assumptions of race, gender, and sexual identity in light of migration.

In her contribution, Jo SiMalaya Alcampo delves into the materiality of Indigenous Filipino culture and language in an exploration of her own diasporic, ethnic, and sexual identity in her video *SIYA: Beneath the Barong* (see figure 4.2). Much like Manapul's reconfiguration of

Figure 4.1 *Visualizing the Intimate*. Installation by Julius Poncelet Manapul, 2015.
Photo by M. Adia, 2015.

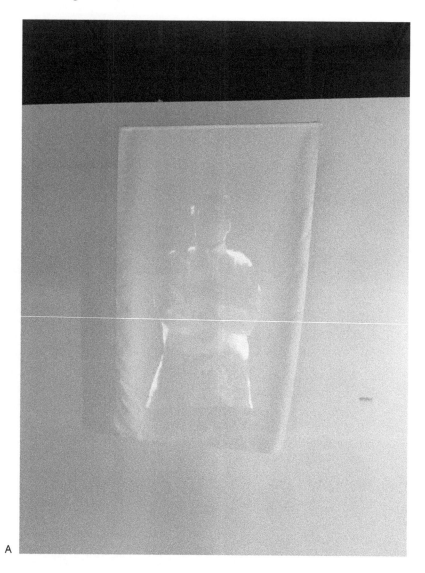

A

Figure 4.2 *SIYA: Beneath the Barong*. Video by Jo SiMalaya Alcampo.
Image courtesy of the artist.

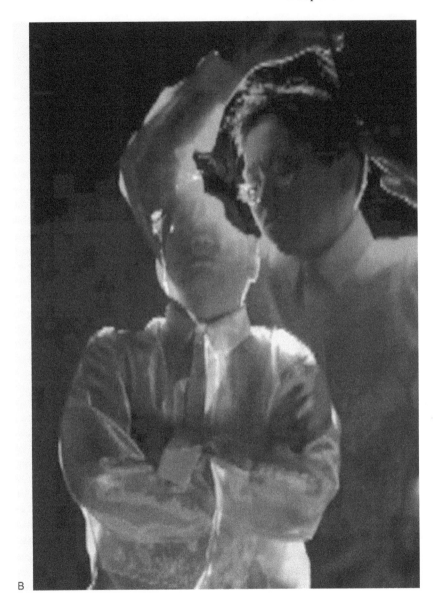

B

Figure 4.2 (Continued)

the terms *bakla* and *bading*, Alcampo's work plays with the fluidity of the term *siya* (which is pronounced "shah" and means "she," "he," or "they"), a genderless pronoun in the Filipino language. The single-channel video is projected onto a translucent fabric reminiscent of the Filipino Indigenous textile, piña – the same material that is traditionally used to construct the barong Tagalog (a formal Filipino men's attire), which Alcampo dons in the video. She performs "macho" poses of an Elvis impersonator, while her backlit barong reveals the contours of her breast. Alcampo subverts the colonial logics of gender binaries in her performance by whimsically embodying an emergent queer Filipino/a diasporic aesthetic.

Engaging similarly with feminist self-representation, Maria Patricia Abuel questions conservative gendered expectations with regard to the labour, notions of femininity, and moral behaviour to which Filipinas, both in the Philippines and in the diaspora, are held. Her series of digitally altered smartphone photos #*selfie* (2014) – *Babae, Diyos,* and *Trabaho* ("Woman," "God," and "Work") – is a set of ironic self-portraits, in which she renders herself as the archetypal fair, pious, and sacrificial Filipina. Recognition is often gained by looking into the other's eyes; however, in these renderings, Abuel denies the return of the gaze. We can never fully know the women in these photos as they are two-dimensional representations informed by colonial domination, neoliberal agendas, and religious doctrine. Abuel queers the normative and stereotypical expectations of Filipinas in her self-representations and puts forward her hybrid subjectivity, constructed from multiple and sometimes competing influences.

Adding nuance to such a queer reading of familial expectations, Lexy Baluyot's fascinating and grotesque sculptures, *Dissection and Decay of Your Flowery Bullshit* (2014), viscerally express her disdain for the gender-policing comments thrown at her as a child. Drawing on her training in prosthetic creation, Baluyot's sculptures defy that which is presented as natural, whether it be organic matter and flesh or socially constructed notions of gender, all of which pose intimate intrusions into her queer identity. "I visualized their targeted words, the rationalizations coming from their mouths as an ever-growing stream of flowers and twisting vines, strangling me," Baluyot muses (artist statement).

These examples from the *Visualizing the Intimate in Filipino/a Lives* exhibit demonstrate how artistic representations through a queer, diasporic, and racialized lens decentre Eurocentric, aesthetic values and destabilize the trope of the (cis-male) Filipino migrant labourer. Within the patriarchal, heteronormative, and colonial apparatus, the Filipina body in Canada has largely been imagined as engaged in domestic labour, in part due to the feminization of labour and migration encoded in the Live-in Caregiver Program (Coloma et al. 2012). At the same time, queerness in Canada is predominantly represented in white, androcentric terms. As an alternative to this, the queer representations of the artists in *Visualizing the Intimate in Filipino/a Lives* are the result of a creative labour that undermines the demands of capitalism and demonstrates an alternative to the heteronormative and homonormative imaginaries that are so intertwined with the imperatives of the nation state and the market. Art in this context enacts a rebellious denial of the globalizing desire to consolidate the difference enshrined in multiculturalism, immigration, and labour policies.

While not all artists in the exhibition identify as queer, all of them demonstrated what Marissa Largo (2015) calls a "queer decolonial aesthetic." Returning to the discussion of Casey Mecija, *queer*, as a verb, can be mobilized to denaturalize normative notions of place and space. This resonates with José Esteban Muñoz's (2009) proposition that queer aesthetic practices "attempt to call the natural into question" (138). In a similar spirit, the artists in the exhibition not only explored aspects of sexual and gender marginalization but also interrogated how their racialized and otherwise minoritized subjectivity *denaturalizes* their visibility in the colonial constructs of Canadian society and beyond. Through this queer de-colonial aesthetic, the cultural productions of these artists represent Filipinos/as in Canada as being engaged in acts of self-definition that reimagine the Filipino/a Canadian identity beyond the discourse of multiculturalism and the state, and they critique the sexualization of the Filipina body; gender dichotomies; the exoticization and fetishization of racial, ethnic, and sexual difference; and the neo-liberal policies that have placed these limits on Filipinos/as' visibility in Canada. Driven by a desire to see themselves as historical and cultural subjects, the cultural producers of the "Diasporic Intimacies" conference engaged in aesthetic and political practices of self-representation that claimed belonging – national and otherwise – on their own terms and radically reshaped the possibilities for embodying gender and sexuality beyond racist and colonial moulds (see also Haritaworn 2015).

It is also important to note that outside of the visual arts, "Diasporic Intimacies" sought to prioritize the diverse forms of community engagement – such as queer performance – that occur in everyday forms of activism. During a panel on queer female and transgender histories in Toronto, for example, Lisa Valencia-Svensson discussed the political value of donning various self-made and extravagant costumes as a means of political protest. Showcasing headdresses, scarves, shirts, and other paraphernalia to a rapt audience, Valencia-Svensson argued that she chose to wear these outlandish headdresses and signage on her body to critique the absence of queer Filipina women in mainstream activist dialogues in Toronto, while also strategically pointing out relevant issues of concern, such as the expansion of global capitalism, the harms of the military industrial complex, the demise of the social and welfare state, the denial of services to refugees and asylum claimers, and the rampant homophobia and racism of political leaders.

What was striking about Valencia-Svensson's artefacts is that they were not extravagant at all, in the sense that they were not made of expensive material. Rather, these objects exuded the DIY vibe of found objects. Yet in their simplicity, one found their political value. For example, Valencia-Svensson had created a bra, made out of Sachet packets, commonly found in Filipino/a "sari-sari stores" in Manila. Through this tongue-in-cheek use of objects meant for those Filipinos/as who are often most underprivileged in terms of class, Valencia-Svensson forced the viewer in Canada to witness a remnant of class inequity in the Philippines. She further drew attention to how such inequities are fuelled by the complex transnational processes that the Canadian state's labour policies have made possible, such as the continued remittance culture that many Filipinos/as in Canada must maintain to support their families in the Philippines.

Taken as a whole, the diverse archive of artistic expression and social engagement that "Diasporic Intimacies" documented embodied what Martin Manalansan in his keynote address referred to as the "fabulosity" of queer Filipino/a lives (2015). Discussing the various meanings of the word, Manalansan suggested that, despite its conflation with material excess and wealth (through the reality show genre, for instance), *fabulosity* at its core indexed the act of telling a story, fable, or tale. He traced the term to its etymological roots to suggest that it could serve as a way of imparting particular types of knowledge, even to an audience that was unwilling to witness it. It was a way of making one's mark. In this regard, then, fabulosity offers queer Filipinos/as a way to engage with a set of conditions and lived realities. Mobilizing this reading of fabulosity to examine the representations of queerness at "Diasporic Intimacies," Manalansan then suggested that the stories put forward during the space we had created were "fabulous" – not because they were filled with excessive displays of elite life but because they possessed "moments of exuberance, of joy, of pleasure, that robs against the frictive (in friction) relationship with pathos, with violence, with death" (ibid.) He noted that at "the heart of these fabulous narratives are its sensorial or visceral experiences that are messy, funky, and that which produce discomfort" (ibid.) In this regard, as both a quotidian and an extravagant example of queer Filipino/a embodiment, fabulosity interrupts the often facile ways in which the Canadian state disciplines and articulates difference by foregrounding intimacies and ways of being that often cannot be captured or easily deployed.

"Diasporic Intimacies" imagined a future where queer Filipinos/as would be a crucial component of critical analysis, historiography, and cultural production across and within various forms of knowledge production around race and sexuality in Canada. It interrogated the role of multiple stakeholders – such as art galleries, post-secondary institutions, and community organizations – in providing a capacious and in-depth picture of LGBTQ Filipino/a representation and cultural practices. In the process, it expanded scholarship and critical dialogues about Canadian racialization by emphasizing how diasporic forms of sexual identity influence the articulation of, and embodiment of, queerness in Canada. Refusing the guises of state inclusion that often reproduce the "good racial immigrant" through normalized understandings of family, community, and our social bonds, the stories shared in "Diasporic Intimacies" instead demanded that Filipinos/as in Canada build other networks outside the state so that they could pursue lasting and sustainable relationships with other people of colour, black, and Indigenous communities, who continue to experience displacement, incarceration, social death, and genocide.

In this regard, "Diasporic Intimacies" foregrounded the queer potentialities of intimacy. Discussing the meaning of *intimacy* in the context of colonial relations, feminist scholar Ann Stoler writes that the "intimate" can refer to relationships grounded in the "familiar and the essential" and relationships "grounded in sex" (2002). In colonial regimes, intimacy is a crucial instrument for operationalizing laws around domesticity and cohabitation. Expanding on such a definition, Lisa Lowe re-imagines colonial relations through "the circuits, connections, associations, and mixings of differentially laboring peoples, eclipsed by the operations that universalize the Anglo-American" subject (Lowe 2015, 21). For Lowe, intimacy can also serve as a hermeneutic that reveals the intricacies of proximity between marginalized peoples, which have often been seen as distinct (such as the figures of the "coolie" and the "black enslaved body") but which also produce necessary, and often transgressive, forms of contact and knowledge exchange.

Ultimately, the participants of the "Diasporic Intimacies" conference collectively animated Stoler's and Lowe's notions of intimacy. They imagined the personal and political implications of "the intimate" for queer Filipinos/as because they refuted, re-articulated, and re-signified their relationship to postcolonial histories and settler-colonial realities. For many queer Filipinos/as, the intimate marks our community's contradictory experiences with colonialism, migration, queerness, and dislocation. Intimacy lays bare the everyday manifestations of familial, cultural, and national tropes of sexual identity and their effects on our lived realities. We thus sought to push the boundaries of what the intimate can mean theoretically, politically, and socially and what role sexuality plays in shaping our everyday experiences. Queer Filipinos/as refused to be normalized – a process often reflected in discourses of successful integration, assimilation, or settlement, which delete or at least sanitize the specificity of our lives. At the same time, we sought to re-imagine our lives through the lens of other lives that had been dehumanized in ways that were sometimes transecting, sometimes different means, towards a hopeful, if cautious, future.

References

Bannerji, Himani. 2000. *The Dark Side of the Nation: Essays on Multiculturalism, Nationalism, and Gender*. Toronto: Canadian Scholars' Press.

Coloma, Roland S. 2015. "New Directions in Filipina/o Canadian Studies." Keynote address presented at the "Diasporic Intimacies: Queer Filipinos/ as and Canadian Imaginaries" conference, OCAD University, Toronto, 23 January.

Coloma, Roland Sintos, Bonnie S. McElhinny, Ethel Tungohan, John Paul C. Catungal, and Lisa M. Davidson, eds. 2012. *Filipinos in Canada: Disturbing Invisibility*. Toronto: University of Toronto Press.

Diaz, Robert. 2016. "Queer Unsettlements: Diasporic Filipinos in Canada's World Pride." *Journal of Asian American Studies* 19 (3): 327–50. https://doi .org/10.1353/jaas.2016.0030.

Ferguson, Roderick. 2004. *Aberrations in Black: Toward a Queer of Color Critique*. Minneapolis: University of Minnesota Press.

Fung, Robert. 2015. Welcome remarks delivered at the "Diasporic Intimacies: Queer Filipinos/as and Canadian Imaginaries" conference, OCAD University, Toronto, 23 January.

Gopinath, Gayatri. 2005. *Impossible Desires: Queer Diasporas and South Asian Public Cultures.* Durham, NC: Duke University Press. https://doi.org/10.1215/9780822386537.

Hall, Stuart. 1992. "The West and the Rest: Discourse and Power." In *Formations of Modernity,* edited by Stuart Hall and Bram Gieben, 275–331. Cambridge: Open University.

Haritaworn, Jin. 2015. *Queer Lovers and Hateful Others: Regenerating Violent Times and Places.* Chicago: University of Chicago Press. https://doi.org/10.2307/j.ctt183p5vv.

Largo, Marissa. 2015. "A Country That Does Not Exist: The Queer Decolonial Aesthetic of Julius Poncelet Manapul." *Asian Diasporic Visual Cultures and the Americas* 1 (1–2): 108–30. https://doi.org/10.1163/23523085-00101006.

Lowe, Lisa. 2015. *The Intimacies of Four Continents.* Durham, NC: Duke University Press.

Luibhéid, Eithne, and Lionel Cantú Jr., eds. 2005. *Queer Migrations: Sexuality, U.S. Citizenship, and Border Crossings.* Minneapolis: University of Minnesota Press.

Manalansan, Martin F., IV. 2003. *Global Divas: Filipino Gay Men in the Diaspora.* Durham, NC: Duke University Press. https://doi.org/10.1215/9780822385172.

– 2015. "Fabulosity and Queer Filipino Lives." Keynote address presented at the "Diasporic Intimacies: Queer Filipinos/as and Canadian Imaginaries" conference, OCAD University, Toronto, 23 January.

Muñoz, José Esteban. 2009. *Cruising Utopia: The Then and There of Queer Futurity.* New York: New York University Press.

Ponce, Martin Joseph. 2012. *Beyond the Nation: Diasporic Filipino Literature and Queer Reading.* New York: New York University Press. https://doi.org/10.18574/nyu/9780814768051.001.0001.

Puar, Jasbir K. 2007. *Terrorist Assemblages: Homonationalism in Queer Times.* Durham, NC: Duke University Press. https://doi.org/10.1215/9780822390442.

Stoler, Ann Laura. 2002. *Carnal Knowledge and Imperial Power: Race and the Intimate in Colonial Rule.* Berkeley: University of California Press.

Thobani, Sunera. 2007. *Exalted Subjects: Studies in the Making of Race and Nation in Canada.* Toronto: University of Toronto Press.

5 On "Gaymousness" and "Calling Out": Affect, Violence, and Humanity in Queer of Colour Politics

MATTHEW CHIN

I distinctly remember the first time I fell onto the wrong side of politics. It was the summer of 2008, and I had moved out of my parents' house in the suburbs to a place in the west end of downtown Toronto. I would later learn that this house had a reputation for being a hub of queer of colour radicalism. In speaking to politically active queer and trans folks of colour about where I lived, they would knowingly shake their heads with a smile and say something like, "Oh! You live in *that* house!"

That afternoon, I was riding the subway with my close friend and roommate, Patrick, who had recently started working as a settlement worker at a local community health centre. I was trying to make a joke about one of the subway posters, but Patrick wouldn't play along. I kept trying to point out one of the images, but he playfully pretended not to "see." I grew exasperated with his refusal to engage, and in a loud strident voice, I exclaimed, "It's right there! What are you, blind?!"

The change in atmosphere was immediate, and the jocular familiarity of the moment evaporated. Almost as soon as I uttered the words, I knew that I had made a mistake. Patrick let out a huge gasp and cut his eyes at me. Before he could say anything, I rushed to defend myself from the charge of ableism that I knew would be swift to come. I quickly tried to assure Patrick that this was just a slip of the tongue, that as a "good" (i.e., radical) queer person of colour, I would never use disability status as a pejorative descriptor. According to the anti-oppression politics that I was quickly coming to adopt, I knew that it was problematic to refer to negative things or situations using the terms associated with subordinated populations. I cared (and continue to care) about disability justice and the eradication of ableism. And I had made a mistake. Why was this mistake so serious, and why did I experience such a profound sense of shame in having committed it?

In this chapter, I seek to answer these questions by looking at how radicalism is mobilized in anti-oppression politics as a means of moral evaluation among queer and trans people of colour (QTPOC) in Toronto. Scholars have been keen to point out the utility of anti-oppressive approaches in describing social problems and political actions because of their structural orientation. For instance, instead of positing that marginalized populations, such as people living in poverty, are to blame for their situation (e.g., people are poor because they are lazy and do not want to work), anti-oppressive approaches examine the conditions under which people are made to be poor. While recognizing the benefits of such approaches in combatting mechanisms of exclusion, this chapter explores their shortcomings by detailing how anti-oppressive practice plays out in queer and trans of colour communities.

I suggest that the enactment of anti-oppression politics sets in motion centrifugal social forces such that those deemed to be insufficiently radical are subject to exclusion through a process referred to as "calling out," or publicly chastising, while those who are considered "radical" are venerated in an often uncomfortable form of celebritism. These social forces are intimately related to questions of affect, particularly shame and fear, which emerge as dominant feelings in high-stakes environments, where the evaluation of one's humanity is directly related to one's capacity for proper political practice. To take such affect seriously as an inherently social phenomenon, I treat shame and fear not as the property of individuals but as spaces that are subject to transformation. In acknowledging the problematic nature of how the workings of anti-oppression operate to hierarchize queer and trans of colour social relations, QTPOC organizers increasingly turn to transformative justice as a way of addressing the challenges that arise through the mobilization of radical politics. Yet while the principles of transformative justice counter the often-polarizing effects of anti-oppression practice, enacting these principles can prove to be challenging when the parties to a conflict do not consent to this mode of interaction.

The research for this chapter is drawn from a larger study (Chin 2016) that looked at art as a form of political practice among Toronto-based queer and trans of colour community organizations. In this study, I carried out sixty-three interviews with community organizers, program participants, and arts administrators and funders as well as two years of ethnographic fieldwork with grassroots QTPOC arts initiatives. I specifically chose Toronto as the site for this project because it functions as a uniquely apt space to investigate the cultural production of subjects constituted through modes of racialized, gendered, and sexualized difference. While hegemonic narratives might celebrate the city's embrace of diversity by highlighting its reputation as the most multicultural city in the world (Fajardo 2016) or by pointing out that Toronto was the location of North America's first same-sex marriage (Senger 2013), QTPOC have long experienced the ways in which Canada's unique brand of "democratic racism" (Henry and Tator 1994) has coloured the city's engagement with non-white sexual- and gender-minority subjects. For this reason, QTPOC in Toronto have a long history of creative, collective efforts towards self-determination that fail to correspond with the modes of inclusion authored by state institutions (see also chapter 2 by Catungal and chapter 3 by Dryden). As the following pages highlight, this history informed my informants' accounts in particular ways. In this chapter, I use the insights from my larger study to demonstrate how an analysis of the arts can yield productive insights into dynamics of tension, conflict, and hierarchy in QTPOC and other community-building efforts.

I experienced great trepidation in writing this chapter. As someone who lived, worked, and socialized among the people that I wrote about before I began this research, I worried that asking some critical questions about queer and trans of colour social dynamics would constitute a kind of betrayal. I also worried about the potentially negative repercussions of the representations that I have offered. Would discussing conflicts among QTPOC enable dominant outsiders to blame us for our challenges and/ or detract attention from the mechanisms of racism, sexism, transphobia, homophobia, and class oppression that viscerally characterize our daily realities? The editors of this book suggested that I frame this chapter as a love letter to Toronto-based QTPOC community organizers, and while I am untrained in the act of writing about love, a profound sense of care does, in fact, motivate this work. I offer this chapter in the spirit of contributing to an already robust dialogue about how QTPOC can more effectively engage in sustainable community development.

"Gaymousness" and "Calling Out": The Double-Sidedness of Political Regulation

In sitting down to do a Skype interview with Catherine Hernandez, I came to understand that I was not the only one who recognized the importance of adhering to a particular kind of political practice. While I had met Catherine several years ago, I had not really had the chance to get to know her until I participated in the Asian Arts Freedom School

(AAFS) workshop cycle that she facilitated in the fall of 2013. AAFS was established in 2005 as an art-based radical history and activism program for Asian youth in Toronto, and it has since changed its focus from pan-Asian youth to youth of colour more generally. Given her busy schedule as a single mother who operates an independent day care business and works on her artistic practice in her scant spare time, Catherine suggested that we speak over Skype after several thwarted attempts to meet in person.

In this interview, I hoped to get a sense of Catherine's thoughts about Toronto's QTPOC community, and she spent some time talking about her experience of being "called out." I include an extended quote from Catherine as it illustrates well how calling out regulates other people's politics.

I started performing at ReadGood,[1] and performers had a choice of being given an honorarium or being given rental space there. … At that time, Kim Crosby and I were planning a fundraiser for the Brave New Girls retreat, which is designed for queer femmes of colour. We were looking for a space that was affordable, and, of course, I thought about ReadGood because I had already earned eight to ten hours of space there, and we would basically get it for free. But I knew that there were some conflicts in that some QPOC [queer people of colour] did not feel welcome there as people of colour or Black people or Indigenous people. … We tried to fig-ure out different ways so that people who felt the space was not QPOC-friendly would understand our decision – including me approaching one of the co-owners about these concerns as a QPOC myself and Black ally – but I got numerous angry letters telling me, for instance, that I was anti-Black for wanting to book there. It was the first time that I was called out, and to be quite honest with you, it was abusive and brutal. It was not progressive. Boycotting is not progressive. It's easy. Allyship looks like difficult discussions and care. Not shaming a woman of colour and

---

1 This is a fictitious name for a community bookstore in Toronto. I originally de-signed this study to keep the individuals and organizations that I was working with anonymous and confidential. During the course of the project, however, I learned that several people and organizations wanted to be identified given the lack of documen-tation of queer and trans of colour organizing in the city. The project thus became one in which individuals and organizations could decide whether and how they were to be identified.

bullying her on a regular basis for years without a willingness to talk things out. It was the first time that people started to call me "activist," and I didn't, and still don't, feel comfortable with the word. ... I learned that as soon as you become public about your political views, some people will publicly shame you. I was being publicly shamed on Facebook and in community spaces.

The specific criticism of anti-Black racism is a significant one in Toronto QTPOC communities. Multimedia artist Nadijah Robinson (2014), whom I also interviewed (see below), clearly articulated the important stakes of anti-Black racism, and the complicity of non-Black people of colour, in her widely circulated article "Black Art Is Not a Free for All." Yet the situation that Catherine described is common in QTPOC community-organizing circles in Toronto, not only because it touches on issues of anti-Black racism but also because it points to a broader interactional dynamic. Catherine's story raises two important points for consideration that I would like to explore: first, the ways in which a particular orientation towards political practice becomes the basis for moral evaluation, and second, the ways in which these forms of evaluation are circulated in public venues and the consequences of this circulation.

On what basis was Catherine called out for her actions? Through my work with QTPOC community arts organizers, I came to learn that one could be called out for any number of reasons: for making a comment considered to be trans-misogynist, for behaving in ways interpreted to be racist, for organizing an event whose admission fees are deemed to exclude people with limited incomes, etc. The term *anti-oppression* was ubiquitous in these discussions, and its pervasiveness in conversations about queer and trans of colour organizing was such that abbreviations like "anti-o" or "AO" were frequently bandied about in the expectation that parties to the dialogue would not only automatically grasp the longer term that these shortened forms referenced but also understand the complex theoretical arguments that these forms indexed.

Anti-oppression is strongly associated with the field of social work (especially in the United Kingdom). As a political orientation, anti-oppression developed out of radical and critical social work movements in 1960s and 1970s and were deeply informed by social justice efforts led by various groups such as feminists, ethno-racial minorities, and people with disabilities (Dominelli 2002). In this regard, anti-oppressive orientations to social work moved to augment a strong class analysis by acknowledging the need to address other forms of social exclusion such as race and gender (Day 1992). Dalrymple and Burke (2006) maintain that anti-oppressive frameworks "recognize that macro social structures have an impact on social relations at all levels of society and provide a way of analyzing the causes of oppression and transforming the structures that sustain inequality" (11). If anti-oppressive approaches provide the framework through which social action is evaluated, we can see that Catherine was called out because her actions supported an institution whose operation was considered to enact social exclusion on the basis of race and sexuality.[2]

In her book *Terrorist Assemblages*, Jasbir Puar (2007) demonstrates how the pressure to adhere to a radical form of politics like anti-oppression can have regulatory effects. While she points to the way in which queer of colour analyses mobilize intersectional models that challenge, for example, how race and class norms are complicit with heteronorms, this adherence to a regulatory queerness "holds queer of colour organizing and theorizing to impossible standards and expectations, always beholden to spaces and actions of resistance, transgression and subversion" (23). Ultimately, she argues that the notion of queerness as automatically and inherently transgressive enacts specific forms of discipline. Within Puar's framework, anti-oppression becomes the regulatory ideal that produces specific forms of control among Toronto-based queer and trans of colour community organizers.

One realm of QTPOC socializing where anti-oppression-fuelled practices of calling out are especially pervasive is the fast-paced world of social media. A growing discourse critiquing "call-out culture" in online QTPOC communities, reflected in several online articles, blog entries, and Facebook posts, attests to the insidious nature of the harm inflicted in this way. For instance, trans Latina scholar Katherine Cross (2014) describes her fear of "falling into the abyss of 'call-out culture'

---

2 This chapter is concerned with a particular kind of political evaluation directed at "offending" individuals in (semi-)public settings. Yet QTPOC artists and organizers also discuss how similar types of criticism may be aired in the absence of these individuals. These kinds of criticism often circulate in social circles through gossip and influence the way in which particular individuals are perceived and treated. These individuals are often not aware of (and thus have no conscious control over) their social reputation and the kinds of information being shared "behind their back." QTPOC shared with me that they were frequently preoccupied with the kinds of information circulating about them without their knowledge. In this sense, as much as they feared being called out, they were also worried about what was *not* being called out. These more private preoccupations are beyond the scope of this chapter.

to be discredited with every slur and slander in the book ... [as] so much online social justice activism has become hyper-vigilant against sin, great or small, past or present" (n.p.). In his more recent online article, Toronto-based Asam Ahmad (2015) also elaborates on the potential toxic nature of calling out. He writes, "It isn't an exaggeration to say that there is a mild totalitarian undercurrent not just in call-out culture but also in how progressive communities police and define the bounds of who's *in* and who's *out*. ... We don't have a word to describe this kind of perverse exercise of power, [but] perhaps we could call it *anti-oppressivism*" (n.p.). Queer immigrant writer Verónica Bayetti Flores (2014) adds that calling out not only functions to exclude improperly political subjects but also to elevate those who engage in this practice. She writes, "I am so ready to let go of the America's Next Top Radical model of social justice. ... It seems as though some of us – us being folks invested in the advancement of social justice in some way or another – are calling folks out sometimes not to educate a person who's wrong, but to position themselves a rung above on the radical ladder" (n.p.).

The discourse of anti-oppression produces not only a social category of people who fail to be sufficiently radical (and who are subsequently called out) but also a special class of people who are eminently successful in enacting a transgressive political practice. Catherine alluded to this earlier in sharing that her increasing social prominence was tied to the perception that she was an "activist." As queer and trans of colour organizers and artists have shared with me, because celebrities are seen to have particularly praiseworthy politics, not only is it more difficult to call out a celebrity, but being called out by one also carries a particularly heavy weight.

This topic of celebritism and politics was raised at a meeting following the first "Unapologetic Burlesque" event. This "queer – antiracist – consensual – not your usual burlesque" night was held in response to the oppressive dynamics often found in more mainstream burlesque settings, and organizers kumari giles and Shaunga Tagore invited volunteers and performers to collectively envision what the second event would look like. One of the performers, Pandora Rockstar, said that she was uncomfortable with the fact that some people in the queer and trans of colour community arts scene had the opportunity to showcase their work more frequently than others. When I asked her to elaborate on this comment in our interview several weeks later, Pandora said,

I feel like we live in a "celebrity" culture where one person becomes the spokesperson for entire communities. ... They get chosen to perform/

represent a huge number of folks, which comes with certain advantages and privileges, and I find that to be a little unfair at times. ... Those "other" folks who maybe aren't that visible or don't take up too much space get completely ignored or pushed to the sidelines. We should strive to show-case, uphold, and mentor everyone who wants/needs/deserves to present their work.

This quote highlights how both calling out and elevation to the status of celebrity activist are tied to a mode of evaluation whose enactment produces social pressure among queer and trans of colour community artists, who then feel the need to take on a particular type of politics. This was echoed in my interview with emerging multimedia artist Melisse Watson. They explained, "Sometimes now I'm worried in this commu-nity that I'm not being radical enough, or not digging deep enough, or I'm way off base or I'm being politically incorrect. ... In this community, it can be terrifying to say something about something I'm experiencing and say it properly." This pressure to be a certain kind of political per-son is felt not only among less famous queer and trans of colour com-munity artists but also among so-called celebrities themselves. In fact, the challenges for popular, or "gaymous" (a clever combination of *gay* and *famous*), community organizers and artists were first made appar-ent to me in my conversation with Leah Lakshmi Piepzna-Samarasinha.

People are like, "You're a celebrity!" And I know people mean it as a com-pliment, but I think we have to be really careful with that because I think it can lead to a lot of unhealthy shit for everybody. ... I think a lot about the struggles with mental health and suicide among people who get to a certain point and who are seen as community leaders, and they have to be perfect, and if they do one thing wrong, it's, "Fuck you!," when they are actually just people, and a lot of times they do this work because they are just nerds and they want to be of service.[3]

In many ways, QTPOC community organizers and artists (whether they are celebrities or not) are justified in their fear of being called out. The stakes can be quite high when their ability to make a living depends on their reputation as a particular kind of political person in relatively

---

3 For more on Leah's ideas on the challenges of being "gaymous," see her widely circu-lated blog article (Piepzna-Samarasinha 2012).

small and insular social circles. In my interview with him, Vivek Shraya, a Toronto-based artist, said, "I've had years of experience [in commercial arts settings] where people don't like my stuff. But when someone calls your work ... discriminatory, that's a whole other level because these are people I work with. If you don't like my CD, and I see you the next day, it doesn't matter what you think. But if you think I'm discriminatory, and this is my job. ... I'm supposed to be a community organizer. It has such a broader impact, right?" In this statement, Vivek points out how being called out for failing to live up to the ideal of radical politics can have material consequences for those whose ability to work is tied to their capacity to translate these politics into practice.

In the process of carrying out the research on which this chapter is based, I learned that queer and trans of colour organizers create initiatives that are meant to serve as "safe spaces" or sites of refuge for QTPOC, who face racism, sexism, homophobia, and transphobia in their everyday lives. Yet I came to understand that these settings were not immune to mechanisms of differentiation and that they were enacted in sometimes extremely harsh ways. As a result, while QTPOC might turn to these safe spaces to catch their breath from the oppression they experience in more mainstream environments, they discover that they are then confronted with a different set of hierarchy-making practices oriented around the valorization of "radical politics."

(Un)making Humanity: On Shame and Lateral Violence

NADIJAH: I think that's probably something that we could work on more. Becoming more of a community. ... I think there's a lot of fear of being called out in this community that makes us only able to connect on certain levels.

MATTHEW: What do you mean?

NADIJAH: There's a lot of things, in order to create a safer space for everyone, there are a lot of things that we can't do, words that we can't say, things that support oppression, basically. Which is fine and great, but I think the danger is when someone slips up and does something like that, everyone jumps on them, and it's just like, "Oh you did this bad thing! We have to call you out. We have to make you accountable for your crime of saying this word." There's so much fear of that happening to you and you being known as the person who fucked up or the fucked-up person that it's just like, nobody can say anything. ... It feels very violent sometimes.

The role of radical politics in the interactive dynamic between safe spaces and calling out was explained to me by Nadijah Robinson, whose interview I excerpted above. Her description of the (anticipatory) fear and violence that call-out culture produces among community artists, as well as Catherine's description of the shame that she experienced when she was publicly criticized for her involvement with ReadGood, stand in stark contrast to QTPOC organizers' attempts to create safe space. While safe spaces invoke settings of tenderness and allowing, the enactment of anti-oppression politics produces settings characterized by fear and shame. Indeed, as I explore in this section, these affective settings are often experienced as spaces of violence, which call into question what it means to be human.

The significance of shame as a frequent object of analysis in the field of North American queer studies is often framed in terms of the relationship between queer minoritarian and phobic majoritarian contexts. For instance, Eve Sedgwick (2003) formulates a psychoanalytic approach to performativity that disrupts the conflation of shame with negativity per se. She argues that the stigma associated with being queer in mainstream straight environments is so powerful that its energy can, in fact, be made available to transform shame into pride. Experiences of rejection and humiliation need not be completely repudiated but rather can form the basis on which identities are constructed. Unlike Sedgwick, however, I am not primarily concerned with the consequences of shame as an interactional dynamic in spaces marked by racism, transphobia, and homophobia. Rather, I seek to understand how an affect like shame operates in queer and trans of colour social circles themselves, where they serve to hierarchize individuals according to the regulatory ideals of anti-oppression and radical politics.

Furthermore, I am interested in considering the ways in which QTPOC call each other out or accuse each other of failing to live up to the regulatory ideal of radical anti-oppressive politics as a kind of "lateral violence." Like Nadijah, many of the QTPOC organizers and program participants whom I spoke to understood the enforcement of the ideal of anti-oppression politics within the framework of violence. Echoing Melisse Watson's reservations about not being "radical" enough in their artistic practice, performance artist Masti Khor shared the following:

It's also really terrifying in our community to make a political statement, especially solo, because we're not nice to each other. ... There was a lot of

room for people to be, like, "That's fucked up! Your politics are fucked!" ...
I think we're really supportive around art pieces. It's like, you don't have
to be a good artist to be, like, to get on stage. But politically? If you do
something wrong politically, you can get torn down.

QTPOC organizers understand these and other practices of moral
judgment according to anti-oppression principles in terms of even
broader questions of what it means to be human. In my interview with
Jeff, one of the facilitators of AAFS, he spoke at length about the challenges of call-out culture in relationship to the notion of humanity.

> If I go to a space, and someone is doing fucked-up shit ... I might talk shit
> to the people I'm with to process and vent and whatever, but I think that
> it's really important to realize that it's super easy to critique people when-
> ever we want, but it's like, in what ways do we do that? And how often
> does that critique serve as a means to dehumanize other people? And once
> a critique is used as a means of dehumanization, then isn't it often feeding
> into and supporting a pre-existing cycle of violence?

In the interviews I conducted over the course of this project, the idea
of humanity came to the fore not just in discussions of being called
out but also in discussions of celebritism. Describing her struggles with
being seen as a community leader, Leah stated, "In a lot of ways, we all
just hustle, and we all want everybody to be able to do the work and
the idea of elevating up certain people ... when it's like, 'Oh my God,
I love you, you're perfect [and then suddenly, oh my God], I hate you.'
It's really weird, and it doesn't allow the person's full humanity, and it
stops people from supporting each other."

For both Jeff and Leah, the regulatory ideal of a radical political
practice is a problematic evaluative framework since it compromises
the humanity of those who are seen to fall short of political transgressiveness. By upholding this ideal , QTPOC community organizers
derive an understanding of humanity from discourses that produce its
opposite. This approach aligns with Feldman and Ticktin's contention
that "the human, the humane, the humanitarian, and the inhumane
are clearly all at play in the elaboration of humanity, and they just
as clearly lend sometimes contradictory meanings to this category ...
the inhumane is not only a threat to humanity, however. Sometimes
it is a threat that defines humanity" (2010, 4). More specifically,
queer of colour theorists have often pointed out how processes of

dehumanization occur by relegating racialized, gendered, and sexualized difference to a place outside the circle of humanity (Agathangelou 2013; Eng 2010; Reddy 2011).

I qualify this scholarship by describing how these processes of dehumanization are not only externally imposed because Toronto-based queer and trans of colour organizers mobilize anti-oppression practices in ways that dehumanize other QTPOC: minoritarian subjects, too, can participate in their own (de)humanization.

Looking for a Way Forward: Exploring Transformative Justice

How might we begin to address the negative consequences that stem from the enactment of a regulatory ideal of radical politics in the form of anti-oppression? The key word in this question is *enactment*. QTPOC organizers note that it is not the principles of anti-oppression politics in and of themselves that bring about harm in community arts settings. Sara Ahmed's (2010a) insistence on the importance of feminist killjoys (those who get in the way of other people's happiness by pointing to politically problematic conditions) is instructive in this regard. Rather than the problem lying in the principles themselves, it lies in how these principles manifest themselves in social relations. Thus, QTPOC in this study would never say that they oppose the dismantling of racism or the destruction of heteropatriarchy. They do, however, take issue with the way in which challenges to racism or heteropatriarchy operate to hierarchize social relationships and inflict harm on other QTPOC.

The key question in the previous paragraph used the word *we* because I am not the first to point out the ways in which the struggle against oppression can perpetuate harm in QTPOC social circles. And not only are QTPOC organizers, activists, artists, and scholars well aware of the kinds of social dynamics that I describe, but many have also begun to develop a wide range of analytics that seek to address the violence that these dynamics produce within marginalized communities. In the final section of this chapter, I propose one of these analytics, transformative justice, often used in tandem with community accountability, as a response to gaymousness and calling out as regulatory ideals of transgressiveness among QTPOC organizers.

In her preface to *The Revolution Starts at Home*, Andrea Smith (2011) elaborates the emergence of transformative justice as a counterpoint to both the formal criminal legal system and newer models of restorative justice. Drawing on her own experiences organizing anti-violence events in the United States, she points out how earlier iterations of these efforts were problematic in that they relied on the criminal legal system as an approach to ending violence against women of colour. "[Why were we] supporting a system that was increasingly incarcerating poor communities and communities of colour" (xiv)? In contrast to the criminal legal system, which operates within a punitive framework, models of restorative justice emphasize restoration and reconciliation. While the criminal legal system focuses on punishing perpetrators and removing them from society through incarceration, restorative justice approaches attempt to involve all parties in determining the appropriate response to a crime in a bid for community restoration. Yet in their introduction to the same collection, Chen, Dulani, and Piepzna-Samarasinha (2011) question the extent to which "community restoration" is necessarily positive. "There are serious limits to restoring the situation to what it was before the harm – what if the situation was shitty in the first place" (xxvi)?

For Smith, problematic social dynamics within collectives jeopardize their ability to hold perpetrators of violence accountable for their actions. In contrast to both a punitive criminal legal system and a model of restorative justice that leaves problematic community dynamics intact, approaches to transformative justice seek to create communities of accountability. Sara Kershnar et al. (2007) state, "Transformative Justice seeks to provide people who experience violence with immediate safety and long term healing and reparations while holding people who commit violence accountable within and by their communities" (5). Ultimately, transformative justice seeks to address the way in which social justice movements tend to replicate the patterns of oppression they claim to oppose. It stipulates that successful movements must prefigure the kinds of societies they seek to build.

Like many QTPOC, I look to transformative justice, or community accountability, as a way to address the harmful social dynamics that I have described in this chapter. As discussed earlier, the ways in which the ideal of anti-oppression politics are enacted among QTPOC community organizers bring about a kind of dehumanizing lateral violence that produces affective atmospheres of (anticipatory) fear and shame. This ideal negatively affects both those who are elevated to the status of celebrity for their political radicalness and those who are viciously called out for their improper politics because both must be constantly vigilant about maintaining a particular kind of political personhood. In many ways, the practice of calling out replicates the criminal legal system because of its harsh, punitive nature. In both cases, the perpetrators of violence can be isolated from their communities: in the first, the perpetrator is incarcerated by the criminal legal system, while in the second, the called-out perpetrator is pushed out of their social circles, either actively or by being shamed for their political "crime."[4]

As a transformative justice alternative to calling out, Ngọc Loan Trần (2013) proposes the practice of "calling in." Trần writes that

> the first part of calling each other in is allowing mistakes to happen. ... When confronted with another person's mistake, I often think about what makes my relationship with this person important. I start "call in" conversations by identifying the behavior and defining why I am choosing to engage with them. I prioritize my values and invite them to think about theirs and where we share them. And then we talk about it. We talk about it together, like people who genuinely care about each other. ... Because when I see problematic behavior from someone who is connected to me, who is committed to some of the things I am, I want to believe that it's possible for us to move through and beyond whatever mistake was committed.

Note that in Trần's formulation of calling in, the solution is not to do away with the ideal of anti-oppressive politics but rather to change the way in which this ideal is enacted. Calling in continues to invest in an anti-oppressive political practice by helping its participants live up to this ideal in a way does not lead to shame-inducing, harsh public criticism or to an environment in which QTPOC are fearful of political failure.[5]

Yet while QTPOC community artists and organizers recognize the toxic effects of radical norms on their social relations, and often identify

---

4 As an important caveat, a friend pointed out to me that it is crucial to qualify the comparison of call-out culture to the workings of the criminal legal system because (1) QTPOC and the state occupy vastly disparate positions of structural power and (2) the (social) consequences of being publicly chastised are not comparable to the actual experience of incarceration.

5 It is important to note that principles, concepts, and practices of transformative justice are by no means only a recent phenomenon. For instance, Audre Lorde's (1981) open letter to Mary Daly serves as an example of the criticisms that women of colour came to level against white feminists in what would later be referred to as second-wave feminism in North America. Yet, in her critique, Lorde refrains from "writing off" Daly and instead emphasizes the importance of working through differences.

transformative justice as a way to address this issue, they acknowledge that changing the ways in which they interact with each other is often difficult. Farrah, a Toronto-based queer of colour community organizer, shared the challenges that she had experienced in trying to resolve a conflict along the lines described by Trần. "It's heartbreaking because you're like, 'Can we sit down and talk about it?' But the scary thing is that people can't actually do that. They can vilify you online, write a blog post about you, they can talk about you at parties, but to actually have a conversation with you is a challenge." Many QTPOC identi-fied similar difficulties in practising transformative justice to resolve conflicts based on political (and personal) differences. The high stakes and painful nature of the circumstances that necessitate these kinds of conversations may serve to block these conversations from happening at all. What to do when the other person does not want (or finds them-selves unable) to engage in such difficult discussions?

The issue of consent becomes particularly challenging in situations where conflict involves individuals who are positioned in different ways. I became acutely aware of this difficulty while speaking to a for-mer employee of a QTPOC community arts program who described the grossly unjust treatment that she had received in her position. For her, this was not an isolated incident but a pattern. "This one thing keeps happening in arts organizations in my life and not just to me but dif-ferent people. I mean, like, people's work gets exploited, and people get burned out, and a lot of the time, it's the people who're doing this work and being exploited, it's gendered. It's not a coincidence that I'm a queer femme of colour that got fired from a job without any fair rea-son." She went on to explain to me that she felt as though she could not share her experience with others, not only because of the celebrity status of the director whom she identified as the source of her troubles but also because she did not want to damage the reputation of a much-needed community program. She pointed out the inherent asymmetry in the relationship between an employer and an employee and ques-tioned the extent to which someone in such an advantaged position would be motivated to change their behaviour. As earlier discussions of celebritism have shown, social relations among QTPOC in community arts organizing circles can be far from horizontal. This poses significant challenges to applying transformative justice principles in practice.

Ultimately, while QTPOC community artists and organizers turn to transformative justice to address the harm that comes about as a con-sequence of how the regulatory ideal of anti-oppression is manifest in

QTPOC social relations, they recognize both the challenges of implementing this ideal and the importance of doing so in less harmful ways. Having dedicated this chapter to identifying what we are up against, I am left feeling disappointed by my own desire to impart solutions for making these kinds of struggles easier. While Sara Ahmed (2010b) reminds us not to push for a happy ending, as a social worker I nevertheless feel remiss at my inability to fully address the harmful dynamics that I have described. As consolation, I hope to have offered a clearer understanding of how we might begin to think about the problem. In this spirit, I conclude with the evocative words of writer, community educator, and organizer Mia Mingus, who captures the urgency and difficulty of working through the kinds of challenges that QTPOC in Toronto are currently grappling with.

> We cannot, on the one hand have sharp analysis about how pervasive systems of oppression and violence are and then on the other hand, expect people to act like that's not the world we exist in. Of course there are times we are going to do and say oppressive things, of course we are going to hurt each other, of course we are going to be violent, collude in violence or accept violence as normal.
>
> We must roll up our sleeves and start doing the hard work of learning how to work through conflict, pain and hurt as if our lives depended on it – because they do. We have to learn how to have hard conversations and get skilled at talking about and dealing with shame, guilt, trauma, hurt, and anger. ...
>
> We must work to transform our selves, each other and the systems we're up against. ...
>
> Because the truth is, we need each other. (Mingus 2012, n.p.)

References

Agathangelou, Anna M. 2013. "Neoliberal Geopolitical Order and Value: Queerness as a Speculative Economy and Anti-Blackness as Terror." *International Feminist Journal of Politics* 15 (4): 453–76. https://doi.org/10.1080/14616742.2013.841560.

Ahmad, Asam. 2015. "A Note on Call-Out Culture." *Briarpatch Magazine*, 2 March. Accessed 8 May 2015. http://briarpatchmagazine.com/articles/view/a-note-on-call-out-culture.

Ahmed, Sara. 2010a. "Killing Joy: Feminism and the History of Happiness." *Signs* 35 (3): 571–94. https://doi.org/10.1086/648513.

– 2010b. *The Promise of Happiness*. Durham, NC: Duke University Press. https://doi.org/10.1215/9780822392781.

Bayetti Flores, Verónica. 2014. "On Cynicism, Calling Out, and Creating Movements That Don't Leave Our People Behind." *Feministing*. Accessed 8 May 2015. http://feministing.com/2013/12/20/on-cynicism-calling-out -and-creating-movements-that-dont-leave-our-people-behind/.

Chen, Ching-In, Jai Dulani, and Leah Lakshmi Piepzna-Samarasinha. 2011. Introduction to *The Revolution Starts at Home: Confronting Intimate Violence within Activist Communities*, edited by Ching-In Chen, Jai Dulani, and Leah Lakshmi Piepzna-Samarasinha. Brooklyn, NY: South End Press.

Chin, M. 2016. "Enacting Politics through Art: Encounters between Queer and Trans of Color Organizers and the Canadian City." Unpublished doctoral dissertation, University of Michigan, Ann Arbor.

Cross, Katherine. 2014. "Words, Words, Words: On Toxicity and Abuse in Online Activism." *Nuclear Unicorn* (blog), 3 January. Accessed 8 May 2015. http://quinnae.com/2014/01/03/words-words-words-on-toxicity-and -abuse-in-online-activism/.

Dalrymple, Jane, and Beverley Burke. 2006. *Anti-Oppressive Practice: Social Care and the Law*. London: McGraw-Hill International.

Day, Lesley. 1992. "Women and Oppression: Race, Class and Gender." In *Women, Oppression and Social Work: Issues in Anti-discriminatory Practice*, edited by Mary Langan and Lesley Day. London: Routledge.

Dominelli, Lena. 2002. *Anti-Oppressive Social Work Theory and Practice*. London: Macmillan. https://doi.org/10.1007/978-1-4039-1400-2.

Eng, David L. 2010. *The Feeling of Kinship: Queer Liberalism and the Racialization of Intimacy*. Durham, NC: Duke University Press. https://doi.org/10.1215/ 9780822392828.

Fajardo, Samantha. 2016. "Why Toronto Is the Most Multicultural City in the World." *Narcity*, 23 November. Accessed 20 May 2017. https://www.narcity .com/ca/on/toronto/lifestyle/why-toronto-is-the-most-multicultural-city -in-the-world.

Feldman, Ilana, and Miriam Ticktin. 2010. "Government and Humanity." In *In the Name of Humanity: The Government of Threat and Care*, edited by Ilana Feldman and Miriam Ticktin, 1–26. Durham, NC: Duke University Press.

Henry, Frances, and Carol Tator. 1994. "The Ideology of Racism: 'Democratic Racism.'" Special issue, *Canadian Ethnic Studies* 26 (2): 1–14.

Kershnar, Sara, Staci Haines, Gillian Harkins, Alan Greig, Cindy Wiesner, Mich Levy, Palak Shah, Mimi Kim, and Jesse Carr. 2007. *Toward Transformative Justice: A Liberatory Approach to Child Sexual Abuse and Other Forms of Intimate and Community Violence*. San Francisco: Generation FIVE.

Lorde, Audre. 1981. "An Open Letter to Mary Daly." In *This Bridge Called My Back: Writings by Radical Women of Colour*, edited by Cherrie Moraga and Gloria Anzaldúa. Watertown, NY: Persephone Press.

Mingus, Mia. 2012. "On Collaboration: Starting with Each Other." *Leaving Evidence* (blog), 3 August. Accessed 11 February 2015. https:// leavingevidence.wordpress.com/2012/08/03/on-collaboration-starting -with-each-other/.

Piepzna-Samarasinha, Leah Lakshmi. 2012. "Suicidal Ideation 2.0, Queer Community Leadership, and Staying Alive Anyway: Part One of a Work in Progress." *Brown Star Girl* (blog), 16 December. Accessed 8 May 2015. http://www.brownstargirl.org/blog/suicidal-ideation-20-queer -community-leadership-and-staying-alive-anyway.

Puar, Jasbir K. 2007. *Terrorist Assemblages: Homonationalism in Queer Times*. Durham, NC: Duke University Press. https://doi.org/10.1215/9780822390442.

Reddy, Chandan. 2011. *Freedom with Violence: Race, Sexuality, and the US State*. Durham, NC: Duke University Press. https://doi.org/10.1215/9780822394648.

Robinson, Nadijah. 2014. "Black Art Is Not a Free for All." *Black Girl Dangerous* (blog). 9 September. Accessed 31 October 2015. http://www .blackgirldangerous.org/2014/09/black-art-free/.

Sedgwick, Eve. 2003. *Touching Feeling: Affect, Pedagogy and Performativity*. Durham, NC: Duke University Press.

Senger, Emily. 2013. "Michael and Michael Celebrate 10 Years of Legalized Same-Sex Marriage in Canada." *Maclean's*, 10 June. Accessed 20 May 2017. http://www.macleans.ca/general/michael-and-michael-celebrate-10-years -of-legalized-same-sex-marriage-in-canada/.

Smith, Andrea. 2011. Preface to *The Revolution Starts at Home: Confronting Intimate Violence within Activist Communities*, edited by Ching-In Chen, Jai Dulani, and Leah Lakshmi Piepzna-Samarasinha. Brooklyn, NY: South End Press.

Trần, Ngọc Loan. 2013. "Calling IN: A Less Disposable Way of Holding Each Other Accountable." *Black Girl Dangerous* (blog), 18 December. Accessed 11 February 2015. http://www.blackgirldangerous.org/2013/12/calling -less-disposable-way-holding-accountable/.

PART TWO

Cartographies of Resistance

6 Calling a Shrimp a Shrimp: A Black Queer Intervention in Disability Studies

NWADIOGO EJIOGU AND
SYRUS MARCUS WARE

As queer, trans, and allied black people in disability studies, we have witnessed a profound disavowal of an intersectional analysis that could theorize disability, race, gender, class, and sexuality together in ways that are essential for disabled, Deaf, mad, and crip people on the margins (Crenshaw 1989). Such theorizing could foster lasting change both within these areas of study and within the social movements upon which many of them are built. The white supremacist and anti-black narratives in both queer studies and disability studies that we will discuss in this paper are symptomatic of a larger problem: specifically, the need for in-depth consideration of interlocking systems of oppression.

This chapter began as a classroom essay and has since been circulated widely, first as a paper at the Society for Disability Studies 21st Annual Conference at the City University of New York in 2008, then as a text assigned on several academic syllabi. We wrote it while negotiating the same academic space – specifically, a disability studies classroom. This allowed us to not only formulate an early critique of the whiteness of a discipline that, several years later, has only just begun to grapple with the question of race but to also offer alternative ways of knowing that are grounded in storytelling – a method that, as this book collection illustrates, has a long history in queer and trans black, Indigenous, and people of colour (QTBIPOC) communities. In the place of a disembodied canon that often stays white, then, we practise an activist scholarship (Pulido 2008; Oparah and Okazawa-Rey 2007) that valorizes shared and collectively theorized elements of experience and engages in forms of knowledge production that are collaborative and in the service of social movements.

The early disability studies canon often predicated its main argument on a constructed dichotomy between disability and other experiences of oppression that was seen as being mutually exclusive. Such a theory advocated the replication/appropriation of black and racialized or queer and trans liberatory movements by disabled activists to achieve what was mistakenly assumed to have been already achieved by other marginalized groups – namely, self-determination.[1] Similarly, the late Chris Bell (2006) stated,

> It is disingenuous to keep up the pretense that the field is an inclusive one when it is not. On that score, I would like to concede the failure of Disability Studies to engage issues of race and ethnicity in a substantive capacity, thereby entrenching whiteness as its constitutive underpinning. In short, I want to call a shrimp a shrimp and acknowledge Disability Studies for what it is, White Disability Studies. (275)

Grounded in disability movements, disability studies is an emerging interdisciplinary field of enquiry that provides scholars, activists, and community members with an exciting opportunity to critically examine notions of embodiment, difference, and normalcy. From multiple angles, scholars have offered analytics and frameworks from which we can think about how disability manifests itself and is produced through the everyday realities of disabled and non-disabled people. It is disappointing, however, that much of the scholarship in this promising field has proceeded to erase how disability has been mutually constituted by, with, and from racial, sexual, class-based, and gendered categories that reflect colonial legacies through history.

We both began studying disability studies as graduate students in a course in disability theory offered at a school that we will call "a Canadian university." We had separately incorporated a disability justice perspective from doing course work outside the discipline. We were both excited about the possibilities of this emerging discipline and about the work we were about to undertake in the course. As racialized people who had experienced various forms of marginalization based on gender, gender identity, sexuality, and racialization, we welcomed a chance to bring these experiences into our analysis. However, we found that many of the course readings and class discussions

---

1 This is consistent with the logic described by Allan Bérubé (2001).

were not grounded in an intersectional analysis. We found that the course framework attempted to set up such an exchange, but that the readings and classroom discussions with other students instead recreated a limited understanding of disability and the discipline. By analysing our shared classroom, we reflect on our experiences in this field as a means of understanding and tracking how power works in disability studies.

Our chapter begins by considering what we mean when we refer to *disability studies*. One of the primary concerns of disability studies is to disrupt the medicalization of disability, thus challenging the notion that disability is an individual problem, located in disabled peoples' bodies and minds, that needs to be cured, fixed, or managed (Oliver 1996; Linton 1998; Begum 1992, 71). As noted by Jennifer James and Cynthia Wu (2006), disability studies calls attention to "how built and social environments disenable those with physical, sensory, or cognitive impairments and privilege those who are normatively constituted" (1). By uncovering disability as a social construction, disability theorizing creates rich possibilities for addressing the ways that categories of social difference are codependent on each other and on disability.

Writing this text together has been important to us because it reflects collective and shared elements of experience and knowledge production. We want the chapter to speak to how we have experienced and theorized the classroom similarly in spite, or because, of our different social locations. The chapter is also a testament to finding ways of bringing into our pedagogy the collectivity present in the community organizing and activism we partake in outside the academy.

We analyse the interdependencies of disability, race, gender, gender identity, class, and sexuality by examining our own stories and how we came to be involved in the disability studies project. Both of us have complicated relationships with notions of disability and the space created when we begin to explore disability in relation to other experiences of marginalization. One of the meaningful concepts we took from this disability studies classroom was the need to bring narrative into scholarship and research. In one of the few readings on the course syllabus that discussed non-white experiences, Parin Dossa (1999) states, "Narratives of minority persons with disabilities reveal different ways in which they negotiate socially constructed labels of Othering and claims to subjectivity" (306). We took this scant mention as an invitation to develop our own narratives of how we negotiate our marginalized and normative identities.

This chapter is dedicated to this task. We begin by positioning ourselves: telling our own stories of how disability, racialization, homophobia, class, and gender intersect in our own lives. We meditate on some of the ways that the dominance and presumption of whiteness has been produced and reproduced in our classroom. Specifically, we are interested in offering up an analysis of specific vignettes from our shared classroom experience to interpret the implications of conceptualizing disability and race as mutually exclusive categories and (mis)using colonialism as a trope for disability. In doing so, we hope to highlight some of the openings that an integration of critical race and anti-colonial studies can bring to critical disability praxis and vice versa. These narratives demonstrate a need for intersectionality in disability studies and ask just what it is that we need disability studies to "be" to make sense of the world and create the change we want to witness in it.

Our Stories (or: How and When We Enter Disability Studies)

Syrus's Story

I, Syrus, have been in and out of the psychiatric system since I was a child – being treated short-term for depression or for related mood disorders. In each encounter with a psychiatric professional, I was given a different explanation of my condition; being mixed-race/black, being gay, being transsexual. In my early twenties, I became an outpatient at the Centre for Addiction and Mental Health [in Toronto], where I developed a physical disorder called akathisia, a rare neurological complication associated with high doses of antipsychotic medications. Akathisia creates the simultaneous conditions of muscles spasms, sedation, and the constant urge to move all of one's limbs at once. After being diagnosed, I talked to my psychiatrist about reducing the number of medications I was taking. I had been given a cocktail of medications – some of which were causing the "side effect"[2] of akathisia, some of which had been prescribed to treat the condition, and some that

---

2 I would like to trouble the seemingly dichotomous notion of effect and side effect in medication dosing. A patient experiences all effects of medication as primary effects, I would argue, and creating a secondary "side effect" terminology can take away possibilities and agency from folks who wish to talk about the way that they experienced side effects.

came with their own side effects, which were *also* being treated with yet another layer of medication. At one point, I was taking antidepressants and antipsychotic medication, but also Parkinson's medication to treat the akathisia caused by the antipsychotic medications and then orally administered eye drops to treat the extreme salivary dryness caused by the Parkinson's medication. The doctor did not want to listen to any of my concerns about his treatment methods and about being overly medicated. He didn't want to discuss anything about my past except the stories centring on me being gay. He repeatedly told me that if I wasn't depressed about being gay, then I should be.

I was in the psychiatric system for years before I found a physician who could see me as a person and who saw my psychiatric disability as its own experience, rather than as a product of my mixed-race heritage, of being queer, or of being black. I've been involved in the psychiatric industry for the past eleven years. I have taken on the identity of a psychiatric survivor as I very nearly did not survive my encounters with the industry. I am still involved. My current doctor has repeatedly tried to connect my trans identity with the psychological trauma I experienced as a child, rather than simply recognizing transsexuality as a chosen or celebrated identity.

In my story, race, sexuality, gender, and class were interwoven to create a makeshift explanation of my "problem" – that is, the experience of depression. Depending on the context, doctors used my experience of racialization, being transsexual, and being from a working-class neighbourhood and upbringing to discount my own expert understanding of my lived experience. Rather than exploring what I thought were contributing factors in my own pain, these feelings were explained away through stereotypes around sexuality, class, gender, and race in relation to disability and mental health. Medical research is historically implicated in working to create connections among race, class, sexuality, gender, and disability. Sandy Stone (2006), for example, traced the historical connections between transsexuality and medicalization in her manifesto "The 'Empire' Strikes Back." She critically examined the research of Leslie Lothstein and quoted from her 1970 book as follows:

> In a study of 56 transsexuals the results on the schizophrenia and depression scales were outside the upper limit of the normal range. The authors see these profiles as reflecting the confused and bizarre life styles of the subjects. (Stone 2006, 223)

How troubling is this conflation of disability and the experience of gender fluidity? These "confused and bizarre" conditions were subsequently used as explanations for other medical or psychiatric symptoms like depression and schizophrenia.[3] I knew that there was something inherently wrong with this pathologization, and I turned to disability studies for some kind of alternative analysis. I was eager to explore how this field would connect issues facing psychiatric survivors with additional experiences of marginalization. I wanted to explore how (and why) my mental health status had been explained through the tropes of systemic racism, homophobia, and transphobia. I wanted to understand the experience of being institutionalized through a disability studies perspective. Last, I wanted to understand how my experiences of racialization, gender, and class influenced my experience of the psychiatric industry.

Nwadiogo's Story

Disability is one of many interacting social categories that have shaped how I have come to know myself and understand the world of which I am a part. For instance, like many black students, at an early age, my preschool teacher applied the label "slow learner" to describe me. Unfortunately, my teacher did not think to explore the barriers to education that I was experiencing in the classroom. These barriers included negotiating two languages in a school system that privileged English and experiencing bullying and gendered racism as a dark-skinned, middle-class black girl with an Indigenous African name in a predominantly white school. Categorizing particular individual mind-bodies as having a "problem" makes discussions about the barriers that prohibit access to learning environments disappear.

Before I suggest what I think this personal and collective narrative offers disability studies, I would first like to speak to the non-disabled privilege that I have, as these labels that my preschool teacher

---

3 Although medical programs designed to "treat" trans people began much earlier, transsexualism was not "accorded the status of an 'official disorder' until 1980, when it was first listed in the American Psychiatric Diagnostic and Statistical Manual" (Stone 2006, 223). Indeed, the medicalization of transsexuality precluded the creation of documents like this manual; transsexuality and what is now called gender dysphoria were seen as abnormal conditions.

assigned to my body are not ones that stuck throughout and beyond my educational experience. My intention in sharing this concluding piece of my story is not to distance myself from those who are continuously labelled as having or being a problem (distancing oneself being a strategy enacted by many marginalized groups to fight inequities and thereby reinforcing ableism) but rather to acknowledge my albeit transient, non-disabled privilege, which interacts with the many other ways in which I experience privilege and marginalization (Baynton 2001; Clare 1999, 67; Erevelles, Kanga, and Middleton 2006, 79). For instance, while the number of black women in academic spaces, especially those who have and continue to experience poverty, is small, I still have the privilege of accessing and moving through these spaces with relative ease. I have the privilege of never having been institutionalized, confined, and/or segregated based on historically informed categories of normalcy and deviance.

While I hesitate to say that academia was built with me and my identity composite in mind, especially when considering how academic institutions have been and continue to be created by and for white-dominant bodies, I am nonetheless able to find and create spaces. I have non-disabled privilege to say that this was the first and last time a person in an authoritative role of expertise such as an educator ever labelled me as having a disability. Nonetheless, this practice of categorizing particular bodies and minds in a marginal position is one that has implications for myself and for the larger communities of which I am a part. It is one of my many entry points into the field of critical disability studies and larger disabled peoples' movements. This narrative also helps us recognize that disability is codependent on racial, sexual, gender, class, and more categories of socially constructed cultural difference (James and Wu 2006, 1; Stubblefield 2007).

Although it is impossible and extremely problematic to attempt to trace the origins of how and why my preschool teacher came to understand me as having a problem, I do think that culturally specific conceptions of "normal" child behaviour and development affected her interpretations. For instance, some of the questions that have continuously arisen from reflecting on this experience are, How are experiences of and reactions to gendered racism translated into "symptoms" of a disability? What are the ways in which cultural difference compounds notions of Otherness and abnormality? To draw on the main thematic of disability studies, when disability appears, how is it inextricably linked to cultural, racial, class, gender, and sexual differences?

One Classroom, Multiple Experiences

Having given context to what brought us to disability studies using examples taken from our history, we explore in this section the specific experiences in the classroom setting that demonstrated how its pedagogies, teaching materials, and teaching methods (specifically, group discussions) contributed to the re-traumatization of marginalized, disabled people. This exploration points to a need for intersectionality in the disability studies project that, a decade later, remains valid. In revisiting the classroom, we employ a reflexive sociological method that centres lived experience as valuable data, as detailed by Viviane Namaste (2000) in *Invisible Lives*. We turned to our lived experiences in the classroom as data for our analysis.

Discussions of race, colonialism, and disability in our classroom elicited multiple sites of provocation and violence, but also openings for change. In this section, we explore how whiteness was reproduced in our classroom. We examine what critical race and anti-colonial studies can bring to critical disability praxis and vice versa. We do so by collectively revisiting vignettes that shed light on how disability, race, and coloniality are mutually constituted, in ways that cannot be reduced to a metaphor. Several scholars have pointed to how race and disability have been constructed as separate, distinct phenomena and have discussed the limitations of such posturing. As Jennifer James and Cynthia Wu note, these frameworks implicitly assume that disabled people are white and racialized people are able-bodied, thereby "erasing those who are disabled and non-white" (2006, 2; see also Mollow 2006, 284; Vernon 1999, 387; Dossa 2006, 352). We would like to use this theorizing to interrogate particular instances in the classroom in hopes of tracing how power is being enacted and to think about whose interests are being served and who continues to be marginalized.

Along with another student of colour in the class, we conducted a presentation in which we wanted to create linkages between disability studies and the multiple perspectives that we access when making sense of our lives, histories, and the world. Our presentation focused specifically on queerness and (post)colonialism, the main thematics for the course week. During the allotted discussion period following our presentation, a student noted that we had only three hours in the class each week and therefore it was impossible to "discuss everything." They went on to state that an exclusive focus on disability was crucial. They urged us to consider the number of courses at the university that had *race* in the title versus the number of courses with *disability* in the course name or description. This student suggested that it was possible to separate disability from experiences of marginality on multiple fronts, and they relied on the age-old trope that race and experiences of racialization had been well integrated into the university context, something that (white) disability studies should attempt to replicate.

While we agree that it is important to recognize the ways that disability and disabled people have been and continue to be marginalized in academic spaces, we disagree that this marginalization warrants framing discussions of disability as being disconnected from experiences of race, gender, and class. We also challenge the post-race perception and claim that the task of anti-racist scholarship is now complete and that white supremacy has been dismantled in the university and in society at large.

The comment above goes beyond the individual student who made it; it reflects a wider sentiment in the course and in disability studies that says that when we are talking about race, we are not talking about disability, and when we speak about disability, we are not talking about race. Here we are not trying to allude to discussions that posit race as a disability or disability as race since some have problematized those discussions as causing the realities of disabled racialized people to disappear (Lukin 2006, 2). What we are referencing are theories of intersectionality and interlocking oppressions, which explain how systems of categorization normalize dominant identities (Vernon 1997, 3; Mohanty 2003; Dyer 1997; Serano 2007; Driedger 1993). For instance, when people think of a Canadian, they/we usually assume them to be straight, non-disabled, non-trans/male, Anglo-Saxon, Christian, English-speaking, middle-class, not confined, and a Canadian citizen. If we take seriously the need to decentre the dominance of particular identity categories, a disability studies that does not critically engage with processes of racialization becomes perceptible as one that continues to reproduce the presumption of whiteness.

As Ben-Moshe (2016) demonstrates, disability studies normalizes whiteness by reducing colonialism to a metaphor for theorizing ableism and the marginal position that disabled people (read: white, disabled people) inhabit in dominant spaces. What we are specifically speaking to are the ways in which white, disabled people are understood as "colonized" by normate culture and pedagogies. While it is necessary to pay close attention to the many types of violence done to particular bodies to maintain notions of able-bodiedness, intelligence, sanity, and productivity in a capitalist market, the appropriation of the term *colonialism* erases violent histories and contemporary realities. As people who carry with us transgenerational injuries as a result of legacies of colonialism and slavery, but who also benefit from ongoing gendered, colonial violence enacted on First Nations peoples in Canada, this (mis) use erases this violence, while ignoring the messy ways in which power, privilege, and domination work (Smith 2005; Lawrence 2002). In the article "(Post)colonising Disability," Mark Sherry (2007) importantly states that "disability should not be treated as a metaphor for post-colonialism, and ... post-colonialism should not be treated as a metaphor for disability. Each experience may share some similarities, but they are also quite distinct" (19). In addition, if we are not careful to notice both the distinctness of and interconnections between disability and colonialism, how can we begin to truly disrupt the dominance of whiteness in the field by centralizing the experiences of disabled racialized and Indigenous peoples?

We wish to draw on another experience that we had in the same classroom to explore how disability studies as a disciplinary formation is not only resistant to discussing issues facing disabled people who are racialized but also directly implicated in creating and recreating experiences of trauma for those who experience intersecting marginalization. One student stated that he had decided long ago to disregard any other form of oppression and just focus on disability. He provided a context for this decision in the form of a narrative from his childhood. In his story, two friends had been the objects of racial and homophobic slurs in the same week by other students in their school. Although our classmate prefaced his narrative by stating that he would not repeat the slurs, he did so anyway, in graphic detail. He explained that the students who had used the slurs had been punished by being suspended from school. In that same week, he continued, a friend who used an electric wheelchair had had the Off switch pushed as a prank, leaving them stranded in an elevator, unassisted. He explained that no one had been suspended in response to that instance of violence, partly because the school did not know exactly who had flicked the power switch and thus did not know whom to suspend. In this narrative, our classmate connected these three acts of violence and drew specific conclusions – namely, that racism and homophobia were taken more seriously than ableism.

What are we to make of this story? The student's retelling oversimplified the interconnectedness of racism, homophobia, and ableism.

We are not told the sexual orientation or race of the student experiencing ableism. We do not know whether the students who were the object of the racial and homophobic slurs were disabled or whether the slurs were read in such ways because of the students' race or sexuality. This narrative re-inscribes the notion that disability, queerness, and race are mutually exclusive groups vying for recognition. Retold in our classroom, the story acted as a justification for why the student felt it appropriate to focus exclusively on disability, without recognizing that for disabled people who experience multiple modes of systemic and interpersonal discrimination, it is impossible to just focus on disability. There was a pervasive myth in our classroom that critical race studies, queer studies, and trans studies were well supported and were fully integrated into academic institutions. Likewise, there was a belief that experiences of racism, sexuality, and gender were taken seriously in the academic environment. These notions disconnect the ways in which systemic ableism and the medicalization of marginalized people have intertwined across systems of ability and raciology.

If we do not take seriously questions of racialization and colonialism in disability studies – by theorizing disability with, through, and from race and vice versa – we run the risk of (re)producing whiteness and further reinforcing white supremacy. We also run the risk of assuming disabled people to be white and racialized people to be non-disabled, thus continuing everyday and structural practices of compulsory able-bodiedness (Kafer 2003). In addition, the analogical and anti-intersectional framing of race in disability theory hyper-marginalizes disabled people of colour and Indigenous people and constructs them as a "different kind of disabled" that is other and separate from (white) disabled people. It contributes to their marginalization in programs, community-building, and services because they are all built on the same single-identity theory of disability. Essentially, the risks are too high for us *not* to be part of creating a disability studies that takes into consideration multiple axes of difference and, as accurately as possible, reflects all our realities.

Conclusion: Creating Epistemic Spaces beyond Camps

One of the problems with an analysis that is not grounded in intersectionality is that it prevents those of us who are affected by multiple experiences of marginalization from bringing our full selves to our work. Audre Lorde (1984) explains.

My fullest concentration of energy is available to me only when I integrate all the parts of who I am, openly, allowing power from particular sources of my living to flow back and forth freely through all my different selves, without the restrictions of externally imposed definition. Only then can I bring myself and my energies as a whole to the service of those struggles which I embrace as part of my living. (121)

Lorde further stresses that this ability to bring our whole selves to our organizing and our work is not only helpful; it is also essential to bring about lasting change. She states,

The future of our earth may depend upon the ability of all women to identify and develop new definitions of power and new patterns of relating across difference. (123)

To us, Lorde's prophetic statement resonates with Paul Gilroy's (2000) more recent call to assess the impact that is created when we flatten our experiences into one dimension. He links this impact to the creation of "camps" within academia, meaning discipline-based separations that flatten our understanding of what is happening at any given time in society.

As academics in an emerging discipline, there are important steps we must take in creating scholarship that has a broader impact for those marginalized in the academy. We need disability studies and other disciplines to help us understand our society, dynamics of power in and outside academia, and our lives. We need scholarship to work across disciplines and take inspiration from what is happening beyond the walls of the institution. Disability studies is a discipline that has roots in community activism and organizing outside the academy. Considering this history, what is lost as a result of institutionalizing disability activism in academe? Addressing these questions might involve replacing "camp-based thinking" (Gilroy 2000) with "relating across difference" (Lorde 1984, 123) and beginning rather than ending our discussions in academia on the intersection. By creating a space for difference in our classrooms, our scholarship, and the academy, we create a liminal space in which to understand and analyse how power and its resulting systems of violence and oppression work within society and how organized resistance to systemic power and oppression works across communities and locations. A disability studies that brings into its scholarship a layered understanding of marginalization across multiple systems of power would move closer to truly creating change, both in the academy and in larger society. In addition, it would reflect some of the work that is already happening in various communities, such as by Black Lives Matter Toronto, Blockorama, and the Asian Arts Freedom School as well as several other forerunning examples that are the subject of this book (see the Introduction in this book).

Such an activist scholarship would be grounded in, supportive of, and accountable to the various ways in which people resist ableism and organize for social change. This would mean centralizing the struggles and perspectives of people whose multiple marginal subject positions shape the ableism they encounter differently. Specifically, we need to begin asking questions such as the following. How can we take seriously the importance of both accessible spaces and ongoing colonial legacies in this space that is now called Canada? If we agree that people of colour and First Nations people are over-represented in disabled communities, how do we stay accountable and work to pay close attention to their/our heterogeneous experiences and barriers (O'Toole 2004, 294)? With the awareness that people with cognitive disabilities fill marginal spaces both in the academy and beyond, how do we begin, or continue to address and make atonement for, this erasure (Johnson and Traustadottir 2000, 13)? How does the incarceration and confinement of disabled people, both in psychiatric institutions and in prisons, perpetuate racialized, gendered, sexualized, and classed ableism and dichotomous notions of normalcy and deviance? How do we hold in tension both the injurious ways in which the biomedical discourse continues to strongly invest in various interlocking forms of domination and the ways in which marginalized people are not able to access suitable health care as a result of systemic inequities? What role does disability studies play in the struggle to stop all forms of violence against black, Indigenous, and people of colour; trans and queer folks; and women and femmes transnationally? Last, how is disability studies accountable to people who bear the brunt of violent projects such as economic globalization, imperialism, militarization, and war, which Rachel Gorman (2013) has named as some of the most important processes or projects of "disablement"?

A disability studies that passionately engages us is one that grapples with these questions and is committed to teaching about and learning from the limitations, successes, and possibilities present in current and past disabled peoples' theorizing and strategies for building community. Examples of what this might look like abound. As Matthew Chin (chapter 5) and Janaya Khan and LeRoi Newbold (chapter 7) argue in this book, black and QTBIPOC organizers in Toronto have long, prefigured movements whose methods and analytics are grounded in the needs and experiences of disabled people of colour. Scholars such as Ayesha Vernon (1997, 1999) and Diane Driedger (1993) attest to the marginalization of black communities and women in disability rights movements in the United Kingdom and Canada, respectively. Leroy Moore, "a black disabled poet, organizer, advocate and lecturer," writes a column called "Illin n' Chillin" in *Poor Magazine* that is particularly interested in reporting on instances where race, disability, and sometimes gender intersect. In addition, he has "formed a Bay Area organization for and by people of color with disabilities called Disability Advocates of Minorities Organization, DAMO" (Moore 2007). Authors like Dean Spade (2003) are developing thoughts on how the medicalization of transsexuality has affected trans people, particularly racialized trans women. Loree Erickson (2007), a Toronto-based artist, activist, and scholar, uses disability theory, queer theory, and sex-positivity in both her research and her creative practice. Eli Clare, author of *Exile and Pride* (1999), also uses creative practice to understand his experiences of class, whiteness, disability, and gender and the ways in which they relate to his life experiences.

Further examples of this important work include Chris Bell (2006), with whose article, "Introducing White Disability Studies," we began this chapter. Anna Mollow's (2006) article, "When Black Women Start Going On Prozac ...," provides a valuable template for making meaningful connections among the experiences of medicalization of disabled and non-disabled racialized and marginalized people. Tanya Titchkosky's (2007) "Pausing at the Intersections of Difference" complicates our understandings of the events surrounding racism, classism, and ableism in post-Katrina New Orleans. Parin Dossa's (1999) "Towards a Methodology for Dis-Ability" examines how racialization affects nonwhite, disabled people.

To affirm consistency with all the people mentioned above, we fully acknowledge the need for intersectionality across disciplines. Disciplines like queer and black queer studies, trans studies, and critical race and ethnic studies, as well as the social sciences and humanities as a whole, need to respond to the disabled movement and the development of disability studies in the academy and beyond.

In conclusion, in offering accounts of how and when disability has appeared in our lives and how it interacts with the rest of our identity composites, we hope that we have both troubled the presumption of whiteness that currently exists in disability studies and highlighted the necessity of an intersectional analysis. What we need is a critical disability studies that challenges the dominance of specific modes of being and knowing, and that is invested in, and part of, resistance movements that are already attempting to make intelligible, interlocking systems of oppression to create meaningful, sustainable change.

References

Baynton, Douglas C. 2001. "Disability and the Justification of Inequality in American History." In *The New Disability History: American Perspectives*, edited by Paul K. Longmore and Lauri Umansky, 33–57. New York: New York University Press.

Begum, Nasa. 1992. "Disabled Women and the Feminist Agenda." *Feminist Review* 40 (Spring): 70–84.

Bell, Chris. 2006. "Introducing White Disability Studies: A Modest Proposal." In *The Disability Studies Reader*, 2nd ed., edited by Lennard J. Davis, 275–82. New York: Routledge.

Ben-Moshe, Liat. 2016. "Movements at War? Disability and Anti-occupation Activism in Israel." In *Occupying Disability: Critical Approaches to Community, Justice, and Decolonizing Disability*, edited by Pamela Block, Devva Kasnitz, Akemi Nishida, and Nick Pollard, 47–61. New York: Springer.

Bérubé, Allan. 2001. "How Gay Stays White and What Kind of White It Stays." In *The Making and Unmaking of Whiteness*, edited by Birgit Brander Rasmussen, Irene J. Nexica, Matt Wray, and Eric Klinenberg, 234–65. Durham, NC: Duke University Press.

Clare, Eli. 1999. *Exile and Pride: Disability, Queerness, and Liberation*. Cambridge, MA: South End Press.

Crenshaw, Kimberle. 1989. "Demarginalizing the Intersection of Race and Sex: A Black Feminist Critique of Antidiscrimination Doctrine, Feminist Theory and Antiracist Politics." *University of Chicago Legal Forum* 140: 139–67.

Dossa, Parin. 1999. "Towards a Methodology for Dis-Ability: Research among Ethno-cultural Minorities." In *Disability in Different Cultures: Reflections on Local Concepts*, edited by Brigitte Holzer, Arthur Vreede, and Gabriele Weigt, 303–13. Bielefeld: Transcript.

– 2006. "Disability, Marginality and the Nation-State: Negotiating Social Markers of Difference – Fahimeh's Story." *Disability & Society* 21 (4): 345–58.

Driedger, Diane. 1993. "Discovering Disabled Women's History." *And Still We Rise: Feminist Political Mobilizing in Contemporary Canada*. Toronto: Women's Press.

Dyer, Richard. 1997. *White*. New York: Routledge.

Erevelles, Nirmala, Anne Kanga, and Renee Middleton. 2006. "How Does It Feel to Be a Problem? Race, Disability, and Exclusion in Educational Policy." In *Who Benefits from Special Education? Remediating Other People's Children*, edited by Ellen Brantlinger, 77–99. Mahwah, NJ: Lawrence Erlbaum Associates.

Erickson, Loree, 2007. "Revealing Femmegimp: A Sex-Positive Reflection on Sites of Shame as Sites of Resistance for People with Disabilities." *Atlantis: Critical Studies in Gender, Culture & Social Justice* 31 (2): 42–52.

Gilroy, Paul. 2000. *Between Camps: Nations, Cultures and the Allure of Race*. London: Allen Lane.

Gorman, Rachel. 2013. "Mad Nation? Thinking through Race, Class and Mad Identity Politics." In *Mad Matters: A Critical Reader in Canadian Mad Studies*, edited by Brenda LeFrançois, Robert Menzies, and Geoffrey Reaume, 269–80. Toronto: Canadian Scholars' Press.

James, Jennifer C., and Cynthia Wu. 2006. "Editors' Introduction: Race, Ethnicity, Disability, and Literature: Intersections and Interventions." *Melus* 31 (3): 3–13.

Johnson, Kelley, and Rannveig Traustadottir. 2000. *Women with Intellectual Disabilities: Finding a Place in the World*. London: Jessica Kingsley.

Kafer, Alison. 2003. "Compulsory Bodies: Reflections on Heterosexuality and Able-Bodiedness." *Journal of Women's History* 15 (3): 77–89.

Lawrence, Bonita. 2002. "Rewriting Histories of the Land: Colonization and Indigenous Resistance in Eastern Canada." In *Race, Space and the Law: Unmapping a White Settler Society*, edited by Sherene Razack, 21–46. Toronto: Between the Lines.

Linton, Simi. 1998. *Claiming Disability, Knowledge, and Identity*. New York: New York University Press.

Lorde, Audre. 1984. "Age, Race, Class and Sex: Women Redefining Difference." In *Sister Outsider: Essays and Speeches by Audre Lorde*, 114–23. Freedom, CA: Crossing Press.

Lukin, Joshua. 2006. "Black Disability Studies." *Temple University Faculty Herald* 36 (4): 6–10. Accessed 1 December 2016. http://www.temple.edu/instituteondisabilities/programs/ds/facultyherald2.htm.

Mohanty, Chandra Talpade. 2003. "Under Western Eyes Revisited: Feminist Solidarity through Anti-capitalist Struggles." *Signs* 28 (2): 499–535.

Mollow, Anna. 2006. "'When Black Women Start Going On Prozac …': The Politics of Race, Gender, and Emotional Distress in Meri Nana-Ama Danquah's *Willow Weep for Me*." In *The Disability Studies Reader*, 2nd ed., edited by Lennard J. Davis, 283–99. New York: Routledge.

Moore, Leroy. 2007. "Illin n' Chillin." *Poor Magazine* (online news service), n.d. Accessed 1 December 2016. http://www.poormagazine.org.

Namaste, Viviane K. 2000. *Invisible Lives: The Erasure of Transsexual and Transgendered People*. Chicago: University of Chicago Press.

Oliver, Michael. 1996. *Understanding Disability: From Theory to Practice*. New York: St. Martin's Press.

Oparah, Chinyere (formerly Julia Sudbury), and Margo Okazawa-Rey. 2007. "Introduction: Activist Scholarship and the Neoliberal University after 9/11." In *Activist Scholarship: Antiracism, Feminism, and Social Change*, edited by Julia Sudbury and Margo Okazawa-Rey, 1–16. Boulder, CO: Paradigm.

O'Toole, Corbett Joan. 2004. "The Sexist Inheritance of the Disability Movement." In *Gendering Disability*, edited by Bonnie G. Smith and Beth Hutchison, 294–300. New Brunswick, NJ: Rutgers University Press.

Pulido, Laura. 2008. "FAQs: Frequently (Un)Asked Questions about Being a Scholar Activist." In *Engaging Contradictions: Theory, Politics, and Methods of Activist Scholarship*, edited by Charles R. Hale, 341–66. Berkeley: University of California Press.

Serano, Julia. 2007. *Whipping Girl: A Transsexual Woman on Sexism and the Scapegoating of Femininity*. Emeryville, CA: Seal Press.

Sherry, Mark. 2007. "(Post)colonizing Disability." *Wagadu* 4 (Summer): 10–22.

Smith, Andrea. 2005. *Conquest: Sexual Violence and American Indian Genocide*. Cambridge, MA: South End Press.

Spade, Dean. 2003. "Resisting Medicine, Re/modeling Gender." *Berkeley Women's Law Journal* 18: 15–37.

Stone, Sandy. 2006. "The 'Empire' Strikes Back: A Posttranssexual Manifesto." *The Transgender Studies Reader*, edited by Susan Stryker and Stephen Whittle, 221–35. New York: Routledge.

Stubblefield, Anna. 2007. "'Beyond the Pale': Tainted Whiteness, Cognitive Disability, and Eugenic Sterilization." *Hypatia* 22 (2): 162–81.

Titchkosky, Tanya. 2007. "Pausing at the Intersections of Difference." In *Exploring Gender in Canada: A Multi-Dimensional Approach*, edited by Bev Matthews and Lori Beaman, 135–7. Toronto: Pearson.

Vernon, Ayesha. 1997. "Fighting Two Different Battles: Unity Is Preferable to Enmity." In *Disability Studies: Past, Present, and Future*, edited by Len Barton and Mike Oliver, 255–62. Leeds, UK: Disability Press.

– 1999. "The Dialectics of Multiple Identities and the Disabled People's Movement." *Disability & Society* 14 (3): 385–98.

7 Black Lives Matter Toronto Teach-In

JANAYA KHAN AND LEROI NEWBOLD[1]

On 26 August 2015, the Toronto chapter of the Black Lives Matter movement (Black Lives Matter Toronto) held a teach-in for the public at A Different Booklist.[2] At the time, Black Lives Matter Toronto (BLM-TO) had organized together for almost a year, creating important interventions into the everyday imaginary of white, cis, able-bodied queer and trans communities and into the bureaucratic mechanisms of the city.

The teach-in was facilitated by BLM-TO members Janaya Khan and LeRoi Newbold and was designed to reflect on the ways that anti-blackness plays out within the city, to explore the work of BLM-TO up until that point, and to discuss plans for future organizing. Since then, BLM-TO has ramped up its organizing, creating several highly mediated interventions into public space and life in the city. These include the takeover of Toronto Police Headquarters in the spring of 2016, which lasted over three hundred hours, a sit-in in the middle of the Toronto Pride Parade in the summer of 2016, and the occupation of Ontario's Special Investigations Unit (SIU) office in Mississauga in response to the killing of Abdirahman Abdi at the hands of Ottawa police in the fall of 2016 (see a full discussion of police actions in chapter 8 by Tara Atluri). The Pride sit-in explicitly intervened in LGBTQ organizations and communities

---

1 We thank Gloria Swain for transcribing this interview.
2 A Different Booklist is an independent, multicultural bookstore specializing in books from the African and Caribbean diaspora, located close to Bathurst and Bloor. This area of Toronto has held a particular significance within black communities and has been a home to many queer social events.

to address their anti-black racism and the increasing convergence with the carceral and neo-liberal city.

The following early public conversation prefigures the ways in which BLM-TO has risen to become one of the most important mass movements in the city's recent history, in direct genealogy with an emergent black queer resistance that builds on decades of earlier organizing by black queer and trans people in Toronto since the early 1970s (see chapter 3 by OmiSoore H. Dryden). Leadership by and from black queer, trans, and disabled organizers is celebrated in this teach-in, which points to a long history of organizing by black queers, who have undeniably made their mark on the city (Walcott 2006).[3] Black queer organizing thereby emerges as central to the development of black community spaces in Toronto and to shaping political responses to police violence in the city.

LEROI NEWBOLD: We are Black Lives Matter Toronto, a movement responding to deaths, state and police violence, and cultures of anti-Black racism in Toronto and beyond. We're in a state of emergency, which is why this place is so packed and all of us are here. But we're not just responding to emergency; we are also investing in the type of world that we can create, through our own community-building practice. I want to talk about Black Lives Matter and some of these projects. We believe that Black communities have power right now, so we don't need to just be lobbying the government, and we don't need to simply encourage our young people to reach those places of power before they can have a voice or can make change. That's why our projects focus on the power that young people already have.

For example, we have been involved in organizing demonstrations in response to police violence, but we're also working on building the Black Lives Matter Freedom School. It will be a space where Black youth can access Blackness and liberation and an education that's not Eurocentric. It will be a three-week-long summer program to give young people an entry point into the Black Lives [Matter] movement. The program will encourage them to build

---

3 Rinaldo Walcott, "Black Men in Frocks: Sexing Race in a Gay Ghetto (Toronto)," in *Claiming Space: Racialization in Canadian Cities*, ed. Cheryl Teelucksingh (Waterloo, ON: Wilfrid Laurier University Press, 2006), 121–33.

skills around technology and art that can be used for resistance, to create chant squads, and learn in a radicalized environment that supports our kids and that loves them.

JANAYA KHAN: One might ask, why these particular actions? The answer is that we are resisting but also building alternatives because Black bodies are being criminalized and are at risk of violence everywhere we are. Black youth are being pathologized, they're being told that they have mental health challenges, they're being told that they can't obey orders or authority, and then they are being streamlined into [the] care of the Children's Aid Society and pushed out of schools. In Toronto, we have a 40 per cent push-out rate in our schools. We have teachers who are afraid of them, and we have police in our schools. The police in our schools create a militarized experience for black students and students on the margins.

There is an 80 per cent increase [in] African Canadian and Black people streamlined into Canadian federal prisons. On the street, we are four times more likely to be carded than anyone else.

That is why we started Black Lives Matter Toronto. We were angry, we were hurting, and we recognized that something had to happen. When Mike Brown was shot in Ferguson in 2014, we had our first protest in solidarity at the US consulate, and we spoke about the racism that exists in our backyard. That demonstration pulled in about three thousand people. How many of y'all were there for that? Thank you. It was beautiful; it was freezing cold. I remember I was on the news, and they were asking me all these questions, and I was like, "Girl, it is so cold, don't talk to me right now." After that, we began hosting protests about local police violence. When the SIU announced that no charges would be pressed in the case of Jermaine Carby's murder by Peel Regional Police, and when Andrew Loku was killed by Toronto police in July 2015 – both Black men shot to death by police – we had a day of action, and we shut down the Allen Road highway. Remember that? [Clapping.]

From the beginning, Black Lives Matter Toronto has been a community-owned endeavour. We're not an organization; we're a group of grassroots Black intellectuals. We are smart as shit. [Clapping.] Black Lives Matter Toronto has been a collaborative effort. We have worked with Justice for Jermaine, we've worked with A Different Booklist, and we are presently working with the Toronto Rape Crisis Centre to host "Take Back the Night." It has been collaborative because our membership is global. I was born in Canada, but I'm Trini. Where's the rest of us from? Jamaicans? [Clapping.] We have folks from Haiti, Bermuda, we have lots of folks in our membership who were not born here, but they recognize that our work is global work and our liberation will be globalized liberation, and so we are deeply invested in organizing that builds connections and relationships.

LEROI: One of the other new community-engagement pieces that we're working on now is a collaboration with the Toronto Rape Crisis Centre to host "Take Back the Night," a night march against sexual violence that has happened every year for many, many years in this city. This is the first year that it will focus on Black communities specifically. Black Lives Matter has hosted a lot of rallies and marches, but we wanted to do something nourishing for our communities and give back to ourselves. We live and breathe in conditions of anti-Black racism, so "Take Back the Night" will have a community-healing space, where healers will offer things like body work and spiritual healing, while focusing that healing towards Black trans people, Black cis women, and Black LGBT people. Black organizations in the city will also be giving [out] resources on mental health, housing, and employment. The night will also include a radical kids' space, where kids will be creating chants that they can do throughout the march and can be engaged in our movement.

JANAYA: And so with that in mind, because I'm about to get my Malcolm X on [clapping], I'm about to get my Ella Barker on. We'd like to hear questions from you, but we would like to ask that in the mic-sharing, if you have a burning question, hold off for a second and see who else is going to be at the mic. The experiences of Black people and Black femme or female-identified people are especially important right now; can we agree to that?

We believe in art as much as we believe in shutting shit down. We believe in the need for stats and research that focus on the lives and experiences of Black people and African people and Caribbean people here.

COMMUNITY MEMBER: Can you speak to what is unique about doing anti-Black racism organizing in Canada as opposed to other places?

JANAYA: We know deeply, as I'm sure some of you who do different social justice work here know, of the uphill battle trying to talk about social justice in Canada. They'll invalidate racism here and say we're not as bad as the US. When did our standards become so low that we can justify real violence by saying we're not as bad as the US? Because we don't have Black people dying every twenty-eight hours like they do? When did that become the standards of justice for Black people? We are legitimately in a state of emergency in Canada. We already were.

One major issue we've faced here in Ontario is our Special Investigations Unit [SIU], that's who we're supposed to look to in the event that police use force against persons in this province. They were supposed to be a group of civilians, but they're a group of ex-cops. According to their own report, from 2012 to 2013, there was a 22 per cent increase of incident reports of police officers using force against a person. There's been a 51 per cent caseload increase for this small group of people. That tells us that our police are actually getting more and more militarized and aggressive, and that our SIU is not changing in order to be accountable to its populace. It is changing to better support police officers in their masquerading. In their pretence of justice and pretence of law enforcement, which has just really manifested itself around anti-Black racism and the killing of Black people.

Here in Canada we recognize, particularly in Toronto, that it's not about critical masses as much as it is about critical connections. Everyone here in this space needs to be making critical connections. We need to be having conversations about anti-Black racism in Canada because for the first time, in a long time, people are talking about anti-Black racism here. In this era, Black Lives Matter Toronto is pushing that narrative. But revolution happens in cycles, and we're going to honour our elders, and look towards our Indigenous people and our Black people, as we read more and more about what's come before us. Histories of this work aren't accessible, they are not archived, but guess what – we already know they're there because we have been living and surviving in those conditions. This is why a space like A Different Booklist is so incredibly important. Because it is literally a part of Black Toronto; it's a part of Black Canada's history. That is why we need to support it.

Also, what we are dealing with here is fundamentally not about just the Harper government – get rid of it, get rid of it. What we're dealing with is not just one party, politician, or institution. If we were to get rid of the current government, anti-Black racism would continue to exist. What we are dealing with is a belief system. It is a belief system that Black people are [inherently] inferior, and that we actually don't feel pain, that we don't hurt, that we don't love. That is what anti-Black racism is. It manifests itself in locking us up. There's an article in the *Toronto Star* that said that Black youth spend the longest time in the Children's Aid Society's care. That's an extension of the prison industrial complex. I was one of those youth; I grew up in that. I can tell you it did not help. It made things increasingly difficult. It made me known to the police. Why? Because they treated me as an adult, and I was twelve years old. And then fourteen years old. These are the contexts our organizing is born out of.

COMMUNITY MEMBER: Sometimes I feel we speak too much about anti-Black racism all the time rather than speaking to white privilege operating within the justice system, shutting things down, obscuring justice. You often talk about anti-Black racism, and I am asking, how do you understand white privilege's role in all of this – in obstructing and denying justice for Black people?

JANAYA: I believe they work in tandem. I'm not sure what circles you're in, but I think it's wonderful that people are talking about anti-Black racism there. The reality is overwhelmingly that people are not talking about anti-Black racism and that people are also not talking about white privilege and white supremacy. Here's the thing: when we name anti-Black racism, we are automatically pushing against white supremacy; we are pushing against white privilege. We recognize how lost Black narratives get in social justice movements, and so we don't just say "white supremacy," we also say "anti-Black racism." Because a singular narrative of white supremacy suggests that all racialized people experience racism equally but differently. But we know that's not true. When we say anti-Black racism, we are looking particularly at the historical, economic, and political conditions that inform Black life and have informed Black life historically. When we name anti-Black racism, we automatically centralize the experience of Black people. When we name white supremacy, we can see it in a white, Canadian context; it's very visible. But I've experienced anti-Black racism in Asian communities. It is pervasive. It's everywhere. It is incredibly important to push back against white supremacy while also naming anti-Black racism. And so I will always name anti-Black racism.

COMMUNITY MEMBER: My second question is, what are your strategies for holding mayor John Tory accountable and our so-called Black police chief Mark Saunders?

JANAYA: How do we intend to hold Mark Saunders,[4] our kinfolk, and the mayor accountable? We have been in contact with the mayor. As some of you may know, he hit us up while we shut down Allen Road, and he agreed to meet. We found his response to us underwhelming. There was a lack of commitment to free Black people because we were clear in our demands. Our demands centred [on] Andrew Loku and Jermaine Carby, killed by Peel police last year in September, and also taking into consideration the fact there's two class-action lawsuits by the Black Action Defence Committee against Toronto and Peel police for racial profiling. Our demands included ending carding, police disarmament, and overhaul of the SIU.

If there's a class-action suit, it actually indicates that every other recourse and every other means of legal action has failed. You're correct that accountability needs to happen here. Like in the taking of Andrew Loku's life: a forty-five-year-old Sudanese man who was supporting his family here. He came here to escape a "war-torn country" – we all know the West's involvement in supporting war – and he was killed by Toronto police. His friend explained to Black Lives Matter Toronto that he was one of only four people who spoke his particular Sudanese dialect in Toronto. There are ramifications: his family is in South Sudan [and] didn't get to say goodbye. Who's going to support that family now? These are the implications that police don't think about. And that our communities often don't think about, either. To heal from that, we have to create accountability and build strategies for alternatives to the trauma of racist police violence. Also, if somebody knows where John Tory or Mark Saunders lives, feel free to holler.

COMMUNITY MEMBER: Can you explain about carding strategies?

---

4 Mark Saunders is the current chief of police in Toronto. He is a Black man and is one of the first Black police chiefs in Canada. He infamously ignored BLM-TO's calls for meeting and consultation in the wake of the SIU decision about Andrew Loku's death, prompting the occupation of police headquarters, #BLMTENTCITY, in spring of 2016.

JANAYA: Some of you may have seen there's been some recent consultation surrounding carding. This supposedly random stopping and questioning of people known as carding, or officially the Community Contacts Policy, which allowed police to "randomly" stop people and ask for their names and information. This rightfully caused outrage in Toronto. Carding practices are particularly prevalent against Black people. Black Lives Matter Toronto is not interested in reforming the policy; we want it abolished. In the meantime, we're working in collaboration with the African Canadian Legal Clinic and other organizations so we can push back against it while we work on its abolishment. Because the answer to racial profiling, and to keeping youth safe, isn't in dressing differently or pulling up our pants. We're absolutely pushing for abolition first and foremost and looking forward to working in collaboration with a few organizations and legal groups to ensure that it happens. We're also deeply invested in looking at transformative strategies – non–prison-and-police-based strategies for our communities.

COMMUNITY MEMBER: Can you give us some examples of transformative justice that we can participate in now? What do we do with one another instead of calling the cops? What do we do with one another instead of calling security, whatever that surveillance is? How do we work with one another so that we don't need to do that?

JANAYA: That's a phenomenal question. What does that look like? What is community accountability? What is transformative justice? Community accountability is a non–prison-and-police-based strategy [for] dealing with violence in our communities. First and foremost, we need to look at models that already exist. Where does it already exist? We need to look to our elders because everything that could possibly happen in our communities and is happening has happened before. We need councils of elders. They exist in a lot of communities, but in a lot of other communities, they don't because of anti-Black racism. But let's really go to the bottom here and see where community alternatives exist. Like Black trans sex workers. When a client is violent or dangerous, they can't call the cops. Sex work is not decriminalized here. In fact, it's heavily criminalized. And so, Black trans sex workers have invented and implemented safety strategies in order to keep each other safe because it's not an option to call the police. I've also lived in apartment complexes where we agreed we wouldn't call the police. And when there was a fight in the neighbourhood and it got real nasty, there was a group and a team of people who responded to that fight. And then there was an accountability process and continuity plan that looked like acknowledgment, apology, and amends to action. Acknowledgment: I know that I said or did this thing. Apology: I'm sorry that I said or did this thing. Amends: what do we need to do to restore balance to this situation and action? How am I going to self-direct and educate myself so that this particular thing never happens again? That's the type of investment that we have. That's a model of transformative justice.

So, we can agree that if something happens, we will not call the police. These agreements can be made in an apartment complex, in a neighbourhood, in a building, or among a group of friends. But then what? We also need to start empowering our communities to be able to deal with violence and injustice in our community, to create a system of values and practices that we adhere to. That's the proactive element. We need to do some political education because oftentimes, the mainstream too often looks at the individual responsible for their actions and says, Why did you do that? Why did you perpetrate this act of violence? But we don't look at the social, economic, and political conditions that inform these behaviours. We don't look at mental health. We don't look at poverty. There's not enough of us for us to keep punishing and exiling each other, if we keep cutting people out, because we will bleed out. Responsible transformative justice must involve the healing and self-determination of the community. No one knows how to heal itself better than those who have been harmed and impacted.

LEROI: One of the places that we can have these conversations around transformative justice, and we will have them, is at "Take Back the Night," a community space. There's going to be a transformative justice demonstration stage modelling different ways we can respond to different situations, intimate partner violence and community violence, without police.

COMMUNITY MEMBER: Can you talk a bit about the ways that Black Lives Matter takes up issues of homophobia and transphobia? And the way that cis-genderism tends to work to erase the lives of those of us who are queer and fiercely femme?

JANAYA: Black Lives Matter is important because we're challenging a police system with a belief system. We're bringing forth a set of ideas. A vision, an idea that says that Black people are the fulcrum of liberation, are the fulcrum of white supremacy, that if we centralize the experiences of Black people, that if we give the most marginalized what they need, then we all have what we need. Because there is no one more equipped to fight for freedom for all than those at the very bottom. [Clapping.] And how do we know, how do we know who's at the bottom? We need only look to our prisons. We need only look to who is dying at the hands of police. We need only look at the most disenfranchised. Because even within the narrative of Blackness, we know it is queer Black people. It is trans Black people. It is poor Black people. And disabled Black people. We are an organization that is deeply invested in a Black, trans, feminist politic. What does that mean? It means that we centralize the experiences of Black women. We centralize the experience of Black trans women who are queer, who are disabled, who are poor, who are deaf and hard of hearing. We recognize and build capacity around that type of leadership. So if you want to be a part of this movement, then we need to learn together. To love together. To create space for that beautiful plurality together. Because again, when the most marginalized have what they need, we all have what we need.

8 Black Picket Signs/White Picket Fences: Racism, Space, and Solidarity[1]

TARA ATLURI

Black Lives Matter. The matter of skin and bone, of material and emotive bodies exist in spatial and temporal worlds that determine their political vitality.

This piece of writing discusses the racialization of queerness as a set of spatial practices that bar Blackness from entry into nationalist queer zones of being/belonging, thus supporting white supremacy. It thereby intervenes in mainstream discussions regarding queer space and queer world-making, which often identify white queer subjects as being marginal to nationalist discourse and nationalist branding. Discussing processes of queer world-making that blur divisions between the public and the private, Lauren Berlant and Michael Warner (1998) argue,

> Making a queer world has required the development of kinds of intimacy that bear no necessary relation to domestic space, to kinship, to the couple form, to property, or to the nation. (548)

And yet, in making no reference to "race" and racism, the authors implicitly assume that white people are the subjects and agents of queer world-making. In contrast, this chapter assembles scenes and moments

---

1 It is important to celebrate the collaborative and creative ways that conversations challenging anti-Black racism globally are emerging. This chapter, and the book it appears in, are part of the Marvellous Grounds archiving and mapping project, which also does this. The first issue of the blog accompanying this book features tent city as a model site in which alternative futures are prefigured and become imaginable in ways that this chapter is in direct conversation with (see, especially, Rodríguez and Kaur Panag 2016; Swain 2016).

of chilling racism and remarkable Black activism that structure anti-racist queer world-making in the context of common sense white supremacy. I argue that Black queer world-making challenges white-settler
collusions with state power and colonial ideals of domesticity and
settlement, which author Jasbir Puar (2007) refers to as "homonationalism." In the context of white supremacy, white queers on Turtle Island
can disavow their nationalist and familial relations to whiteness, while
simultaneously benefiting from the privileges born out of biopolitical
lineages of economic and embodied white-supremacist inheritance.

In this piece of writing, I attempt to map the resilient and inspiring activism of Black Lives Matter Toronto (BLM-TO) as a necessary
divergence from the neo-liberal spatialization of homonationalism in
white-settler Canada. Whiteness is materialized in Toronto through
genealogies of white-settler nationalism that form recognized and
intelligible cartographies of queerness. BLM-TO unearths anti-colonial
genealogies and geographies, erecting new monuments of anti-colonial
sexual politics that reroute the mythologies of material spaces from
those rooted in racism.

This chapter explores this theme with regard to four scenes of public reckoning, all of which expose the insidious racism of white-settler
Canada and highlight the tenacity of Black queer world-making and
space-making: first, the BLM-TO tent city occupation outside Toronto
police headquarters following the racist murder of Andre Loku, a disabled refugee from Sudan, by Toronto police; second, the protest held
by BLM-TO in Premier Kathleen Wynne's front garden; third, efforts by
BLM-TO to politicize the Toronto Pride Parade, unsettling queer com-
forts of "home" grounded in white-settler celebrations of racist murder;
fourth, Andrew Loku's home, or private residence, as a site of state-led
infiltration and white-supremacist murder.

These four moments, politicized through a distinctly anti-racist,
anti-colonial, *and* queer lens, are in tension with the claim that gender
and sexuality are the most salient factors explaining exclusion from
the nation. They resonate with Rinaldo Walcott's (2016a) argument
that Canadian Blackness is constructed through a paradoxical posi-
tionality of both hyper-visibility and invisibility. Thus, Black bodies
are subject to racial profiling and hate crime but also a white gaze
that makes Black people invisible in the dominant national imaginary.
Simultaneously, the Black body becomes a site of intense securitization and spectacle. The notion that anti-Black racism renders Black
lives and places both hyper-visible and invisible is echoed in the

activism and organic intellectualism of BLM-TO, whose occupations of space are the subject of this chapter. On its Facebook page, BLM-TO describes its ethos, stating,

Rooted in the experiences of Black people in this country who actively resist our dehumanization, #BlackLivesMatter is a call to action and a response to the virulent anti-Black racism that permeates our society. We adopt this language because to us, the need to acknowledge black lives is global. State-sanctioned violence against black lives is a global phenomenon. Anti-blackness is a global phenomenon. Pervasive anti-black racism is a global phenomenon. (2016)

The BLM-TO occupation that I focus on in this chapter took place in March 2016. BLM-TO occupied the square in front of police headquarters at College and Yonge Streets, in the centre of downtown Toronto. Members stayed for fifteen days, despite the police's immediate attempts to brutalize and expel them, during chilling weather conditions. The murder of unarmed Black people such as Andrew Loku and Jermaine Carby by police had been at the centre of political agitation since the group's founding in 2014. After the Special Investigations Unit of the police stated that the officer who had murdered Loku would not face any penalties, BLM-TO again took to the streets to protest. Anti-Black racism in Toronto was further inflamed with the city's decision to cut back Afrofest, the annual music festival, from two days to one day. In a context of ubiquitous erasures of Black lives in white-settler Canada/ Turtle Island, these among other instances of anti-Black racism led to the occupation. On the BLM-TO blog, co-founder Janaya Khan documents the innovative ways in which Black geographies materialized outside police headquarters in the face of the state's efforts to violently erase the newly formed spaces of #tentcity #blackcity. Khan writes,

BLMTO held an action this Sunday March 20th, and began BLMTO tent city, an occupation of Nathan Phillips Square that began as a rally. The Toronto Police bullied and threatened arrest. The community, the fire keeping people warm, tents and art were all threatened by police. (2016, n.p.)

If, as Black feminist geographer Katherine McKittrick (2002) argues, Black geographies involve both the violent erasure of Black lives from material spaces and the transformation of landscapes by Black people, the tent city occupations are representative of how Black protest creates new monuments and landmarks. The space outside police headquarters in Toronto was transformed into landmarks of insurrectionary Black politics. According to Khan, the tents at Black city were named after several people who had been murdered by the Canadian state, including those killed in immigration detention. They further commemorated Black Canadian spaces that had been targeted for erasure.

[Tents] were named Africville and Afrofest, one a Black settlement that Canada made every effort to erase and another a Pan-Afrikan festival the City of Toronto attempted to demean, just as they did with massive budget cuts to Caribana. (Khan 2016, n.p.)

While BLM-TO and its allies were sleeping on the concrete in the brutal cold for three hundred hours, gaining global media attention and receiving support from people throughout the world, political leaders did little to seriously address the demands of activists. After being brutalized by police and ignored by politicians, BLM-TO staged a demonstration outside the home of Kathleen Wynne, the current premier of Ontario. Kathleen Wynne's lucrative self-branding as a white lesbian politician contrasts starkly with the state-led violence that Black queer and transgender people face in white-settler Canada. Many trans and queer Black people who occupy leadership positions in BLM-TO are represented in the mainstream media as a "terrorist" threat to ostensible Canadian values, civility, and civilization. This became amply clear in the public reactions to Black-activist transgression, which involved crossing the symbolic boundaries of a racist, white-settler society in which Blackness had been constructed as out of place in Wynne's sanctified zone of domesticity. In the white-supremacist media and mainstream public imaginary, the homonationalist space of Wynne's home could not have been further removed from the outlaw Black geography of tent city. Hence, Black bodies daring to set foot on white-settler, lesbian property were imagined as "terrorizing" the colonizing quietude of Canadian homonationalism.

The White Names You Recognize: Racist Queer World-Making

Familiar, mainstream queer spaces and places in Toronto are often constructed with implicit and explicit reference to the white family and white-settler genealogies. Mainstream queer life-worlds are structured by a familiar relation to whiteness as the embodied ideal that constitutes a recognizable image of who and what is queer. As Sara Ahmed (2000) argues, the figure of the stranger is one who is unfamiliar and unwelcome, foreign and exterior to the zones of civility occupied by recognized members of a community and/or nation. White queerness becomes recognizable and celebrated as queerness by constructing a boundary that excludes people and practices that appear foreign to homonationalist narratives. In the context of white-settler anglophone, francophone, Christian, and Catholic Canada, queerness gains entry into normative nationalist narratives by making racialized and religious "others" strange to the point of expulsion, invisibility, and murder.

Jasbir Puar (2007) uses the term "homonationalism" to describe the inclusion of "respectable" queer people in the national imaginary against Muslim and Brown bodies, whose queerness in relation to national ideals is unassimilable in a racist, Islamophobic "war on terror." Queer people, Puar argues, were once associated with the death of the nation state in mainstream homophobic culture due to the North American AIDS crisis. The rise of the so-called global war on terror has given rise to a valorization of affluent, white, gay men who are invited to support the vitality of the North American dream against vilified images of racialized terrorists.

Puar discusses "recognition and incorporation" as materializing spatially based on the assumed proximity of intelligible white sexualities in space. To be recognized, Puar argues (implicitly echoing Ahmed's reading of strangers), involves being familiar. What was once seen as deviant about (white) queer life becomes incorporated into institutional life, state power, and market capitalism, as something to be studied, surveilled, managed, and branded. Puar writes,

> The politics of recognition and incorporation entail that certain – but certainly not most – homosexual, gay, and queer bodies may be the temporary recipients of the "measures of benevolence" that are afforded by liberal discourses of multicultural tolerance and diversity. This benevolence toward sexual others is contingent upon ever-narrowing parameters of white racial privilege, consumption capabilities, gender and kinship normativity, and bodily integrity. (2007, xii)

Far from an image of benevolence, Puar sees homonationalism as a process of life and death. Certain queer bodies are invited to live only by virtue of the death of others. The author writes, "The cultivation of these homosexual subjects folded into life, enabled through 'market vitality' and 'regenerative reproductivity,' is racially demarcated and paralleled by a rise in the targeting of queerly raced bodies for dying" (ibid.).

This chapter similarly interrogates how, in white-settler Canada, white queer bodies are "folded into life" through a spatial, affective, and political alignment with state power; European, white-settler narratives of conquest; and market capitalism. As I discuss, affluent, white queer politicians such as Ontario Premier Kathleen Wynne rise to ascendancy against the systematic denigration of Black humanity by the state. The pervasive and murderous nature of anti-Black racism in Canada was clearly demonstrated by the state-led murder of Andrew Loku. The marking of Andrew Loku's body for death is symptomatic of how the vitality of affluent Western nations is produced through the denigration of racialized lives in and from the Global South. White supremacist discourse simultaneously justifies the state-led murder of Black people, while also constructing narratives of the white, Western "salvation" of racialized people in the Global South. The white-enlightenment narrative of the Western "rescue" of Black refugees masks the economic benefits that the state reaps from exploiting the labour of refugees, migrants, and racialized people, while institutionalized racism compromises their lives. Locating violence as something that happens in formerly colonized places in the Global South allows white-settler violence to remain unspoken and unspectacular.

The exclusion of Black, including queer Black, subjects from life-affirming spaces at various scales – from the "local" to the "global" – complicates the celebration of white LGBT cultures, scenes, and archives, which in North America often form dominant political narratives of queer time and space. This celebratory white queer rhetoric wilfully ignores a growing body of Black Canadian scholarship, which demonstrates that the question of space on Turtle Island has historically and continues to be deeply structured by anti-Black racism. For example, Katherine McKittrick (2002) argues that race and racism "structure and limit black lives and places," yet "black identities and places continually emerge despite spatial domination" (28). This spatial domination attempts to fix the meanings of Canadian identity as always already white and absent of Blackness.

> Geographies of domination and rupture reveal how the broader geographical imaginary of Canada, as rational, white, and cohesive is necessarily contested. (ibid, 33)

If anti-Black racism has a distinctly spatial character, so does the struggle for Black lives, which is one of the most important movements of our times. Drawing on the important lessons and leadership of BLM-TO, the remainder of this article highlights new geographies of city space that reimagine the city and its possibilities through uses of space by queer Black activists.

BLM-TO's impassioned activism has indeed modelled new ways of engaging with space in white-settler Canada. Through their occupation of the square in front of the police station, and of premier Wynne's front garden, the group challenged temporal and cartographical stasis by creating queer life-worlds whose present conjuncture is informed by anti-colonial politics. Through the timeless reverence of Black protest, one bears witness to an anti-colonial rupturing of sequential narratives of Eurocentric enlightenment progress and succinct national borders.

Fair Is Fair, Eh? The Currency of Whiteness

The protest outside Wynne's home during the BLM-TO tent city occupation was met with reactions that are symptomatic of the phobic hostilities of white settlers to Blackness. Sandy Hudson, an organizer and co-founder of BLM-TO, discusses the protest with a CBC reporter.

> Members were outside the home after 10 p.m. for about 20 minutes and left a card with an invitation to meet with them, a wreath, wine – actually an empty wine bottle filled with water … – and cheese. (CBC News 2016a, n.p.)

Hudson's explanation for placing these items outside Wynne's home is cited in the mainstream press as follows: "It was like, you know, here we are inviting you, this is like a warm welcome. … It was peaceful. It was not loud in any way. It was respectful" (ibid.). Hudson's implicit citation of Western traditions of civility as protest is reminiscent of the tactics used by Haitians demonstrating against French colonial rule. Haitian revolutionaries demonstrated the hypocrisy of Western "civility" when they demanded that its ethics and understandings of ontology be extended to Black people. Using a language of Western hospitality was tactical as it revealed the ruse of liberal traditions of meritocracy and sociality (James 2009, 51–70; Žižek 2008).

Simultaneously, the hospitality of protesters wishing to enter into a meaningful conversation about racism reflects their commitment to feasible change. As the media's and politicians' responses to BLM-TO reveal, these dreams of reciprocity exist in the context of white supremacy. They are enacted within the material spaces and histories of a Canada of affluent white people with cottages, canoes, and condominiums, implicitly supporting urban Aboriginal homelessness and the gentrification of Blackness. The contrast between spectres of Black and Aboriginal outcasts and affluent white settlers is also clearly demonstrated by Wynne's and her partner's response to the protest. The headlines of mainstream newspapers suggest that Wynne's partner was disturbed by the protestors. "Wynne was not home, but the items were discovered Friday morning and it 'unnerved' her partner, Jane Rounthwaite, the premier said" (CBC News 2016a, n.p.). While seeing Black people protest outside one's home is written in the mainstream press as supposedly "traumatic," Aboriginal women are murdered and go "missing" in alarming ways. As Kerry Clare writes, "The history of violence against Indigenous women can be traced to colonization, systemic racism, denial of culture, language and traditions, and laws designed to destroy identity, dislocate, and fragment families" (Clare 2015, n.p.). Clare further writes,

> It would be disingenuous to say that violence against Indigenous women has changed to a degree that things are getting better. The numbers of those missing and murdered have not slowed down, and there has been no uptick in charges against those responsible for violence against Indigenous women. (ibid.)

One is left with an image of a petrified, white middle-class settler peering through the curtains, scared of the Black and Indigenous people who remain on the other side of white picket fences. Interestingly, far from the domestic sphere, Wynne later appeared at a BLM-TO protest outside the Ontario legislature at Queen's Park and stated that she would like to meet with the organization. Wynne announced this publicly, at a rally held in the exterior spaces of city streets, far from her home. The politician made this declaration before the news media, staging a public spectacle in which she purported to offer solidarity to BLM-TO, while her domestic realm remained one in which Black bodies were unwelcome. Wynne stated, "I would like for the protest to happen other places than my home and you know, quite frankly, it's not just about my home, it's about the neighbours as well" (CBC News 2016a). This resonates with Stuart Hall's assertions regarding the importance of spatial metaphors in understanding racism. Hall suggests that when characteristics and positions of power often reserved for white people are occupied by Black people, anxieties erupt regarding colonial categorization (1997, 236). Hall cites the writing of Mary Douglas, stating that,

> Every culture has a kind of order of classification built into it and this seems to stabilize the culture. You know exactly where you are, you know who are the inferiors and who the superiors are and how each has a rank, etc. What disturbs you is what she calls "matter out of place." You don't worry about dirt in the garden because it belongs in the garden but the moment you see dirt in the bedroom you have to do something about it because it doesn't symbolically belong there. (ibid.)

In the juxtaposition of Black picket lines and white picket fences outside Wynne's home, Blackness is barred from entering zones of white-settler intimacy. This threat to the intimate spaces of homonationalism was magnified when BLM-TO once again took to the streets a few months later, in the summer of 2016.

The War against Blackness: Homonationalism and the Terrors of White Entitlement

Who is imagined to belong in the nation state is often expressed in familial metaphors. Mother countries belong to good mothers, and wise patriarchs govern fatherlands. It is interesting that Wynne and her partner are both women, perhaps offering evidence of how middle-class, liberal, white queerness finds a happy home in the nation state. Indeed, Wynne's sexual identity is often used in the mainstream press to brand Ontario and Canada as being hospitable to queers and feminists (Brennan 2015). Following the protest outside Wynne's home, an empty bottle filled with water became associated with "terrorism." This paranoid reaction to any traces of racialized presence in proximity to zones of white intimacy is an example of Puar's assertions regarding homonationalism as a scripting of white queer respectability that needs the figure of the racialized terrorist to proclaim white-settler innocence. The CBC states,

> The police's chemical, biological, radiological, nuclear and explosive unit was called in because it was not immediately known what substance was in the bottle. (CBC News 2016a, n.p.)

The rhetoric of the ostensible terrorism of radical Black politics continued to be discursively invoked at another widely mediated BLM-TO action half a year after tent city, in summer 2016. This time, BLM-TO infiltrated white queer territory to stage a sit-in at the 2016 Toronto Pride Parade to protest the racism of white queer spaces in Toronto and, in particular, the growing alignment of white queer politics with policing and other murderous functions of the state (Haritaworn, Kuntsman, and Posocco 2014). In a courageous display of activism, BLM-TO, which had ironically been invited as an honoured group in the 2016 Pride Parade, stopped the usual march and occupied the city streets to stage a sit-in at Yonge and College Streets, not far from the site where tent city had been staged a few months earlier. It asked the organizers of Pride Toronto to comply with a series of demands, which Rinaldo Walcott outlines as follows:

> They ask for solid financial support for the Blackness Yes group who stage Blockorama, and for a central and fully supported stage for Black Queer Youth. Additionally, the group wants Indigenous, Black and trans people and those living with disabilities to have better access to paid positions within the Pride organization. They also demand the return of the South Asian stage and the removal of police floats from the parade. This last demand has overshadowed all the others. (Walcott 2016b, n.p.)

Highlighting the action's re-politicization of Pride, Walcott further states,

> BLM-TO's Pride protest has steered the conversation back to deeper and more important, even philosophical, questions of queer life. We need to meditate on them. Those questions, when honestly confronted, demonstrate that BLM-TO's demands should be met posthaste. (ibid.)

While representatives of Pride Toronto signed BLM-TO's list of demands, they later recanted their support. Journalists John Rieti and Shanifa Nasser (2016) quote Janaya Khan, who theorizes this act of eroding queer Black spaces to appeal to conservative white queers as an example of pinkwashing. "Pinkwashing" refers to the depoliticization of queerness through an alignment of LGBTQ space with a neo-liberal, capitalist understanding of "success," an inclusion in biopolitical nationalist fantasies, and a valorization of legalistic discourses of equality and entitlement (see the Introduction; chap. 9; Puar 2007). Khan reportedly stated,

> This type of pink-washing that's happening, where it's like, "We're in alignment with gender and sexually diverse people, but not in alignment with racialized people," we can't stand for that. (Quoted in Rieti and Nasser 2016, n.p.)

Despite the underwhelming response by Pride Toronto, the BLM-TO sit-in successfully intervened in a gentrifying ethos of contemporary queer politics, which uses police power to protect affluent white bodies and corporate interests. While many people stood in solidarity with BLM-TO at the 2016 Toronto Pride Parade, others screamed at the group in contempt and even threw bottles at Black activists. This disturbing treatment is again reflective of Walcott's assertion that Blackness is both hyper-visible and invisible (Walcott 2016a). While mainstream white queer elites and politicians want to "see diversity" as a means of supporting nationalist and city-wide branding, Black politics and radical Black activists disappear. Organizations such as BLM-TO are asked to "diversify" queer space by publicly appearing as Black and queer to the extent that they do not politicize their oppression. This narrative of depoliticized diversity is challenged by a movement for Black lives that actively centres Black queer lives. In the article "Debriefing Black Lives Matter Toronto's 15 Day Occupation (Part 2)," David Gray-Donald cites an interview with BLM-TO organizer and co-founder LeRoi Newbold, who states,

> The Black Lives Matter movement itself is founded by queer Black women. And the leadership of queer and transgender people within Black Lives Matter is something that can be noted within every chapter, and BLMTO is no different. Our steering committee is composed exclusively of queer and trans people and women, Black women. This movement is a crossroads. This is who is meant to be in leadership of the movement at this time in history. (Quoted in Gray-Donald 2016, n.p.)

According to Newbold, Black queer people are at the forefront of Black Lives Matter precisely because anti-Black racism is so deeply imbricated in normatively gendered and sexual ideologies.

Similar insights into how sexual violence is fundamentally racialized and structures the lives and deaths of Black people were missing from the media commentary after Pride. There was a common refrain in the mainstream press and among online commentators that BLM-TO had "hijacked" the parade and taken Pride Toronto "hostage" (Aravosis 2016, n.p.). This language of anti-nationalist criminality supports Puar's assertion that homonationalism is the process of the mainstreaming of queerness, which recognizes and valorizes white gay patriots, while vilifying politicized, queer people of colour (Puar 2007). The language of hijacking also implies that queerness belongs to white settlers, constructing Black queer bodies as invisible and foreign to queer world-making in Toronto. As Desmond Cole writes,

> The idea that BLMTO "hijacked" the parade to advance its own agenda assumes that the black struggle is somehow separate from that of Pride. This assumption – that blackness is somehow divorced from queerness and queer politics – explains why blacks have been so unwelcome within one of the largest queer celebrations in the world from the beginning. (2016)

The Toronto Pride Parade is part of a genealogy of violence that is often traced back to the bathhouse raids by the Toronto police; these led to the formation of the Citizens Independent Review of Police Activities, in which Black, racialized queers played an active role (ibid.). The whitening of queer history constructs Black politics as being incidental to queerness in wilfully racist and ahistorical ways. Vitriolic hate speech emerged following the BLM-TO occupation of Pride, often by those who purport to be part of the queer community. Echoing the homonormative and homonationalist narratives that accompanied the action at Wynne's house earlier that year, BLM-TO was referred to by white queers as "guests in someone else's home" (#PrideTO 2016). The language of "Black guest" and white homeowner reflect the exile of Black people from queer communities vested in ideologies of white-colonial entitlement (see also the Introduction to this book).

This exiling of Black queer bodies is a chilling image, one that stands in stark contrast with the welcome extended to police officers at Pride 2016 and those who defended them. One of the demands made by BLM-TO at its Pride sit-in was the removal of police floats from the event. Following this, a letter written by a gay police officer appeared in the mainstream media, justifying police presence in the Toronto Pride Parade as a necessary validation of gay police officers, who grapple with their sexuality (CBC News 2016b, n.p.). Besides being a police officer, the author highlighted that he was a former soldier who had fought in Afghanistan as part of the global "war on terror." The letter thus invoked a disturbing rhetoric of "inclusion" and empathy whose proper objects are warring white men. Within a racist schema, white men who participate in and profit from murderous Islamophobic wars should be celebrated as queer heroes. Simultaneously, those who threaten the common sense violence of white nationalism are imagined as vigilantes, troubling a sense of "peace" that is made possible only through routine, racist murder, war, and shocking denial.

While this chapter focuses on BLM-TO's tent city occupation and the group's politicization of queer Pride in 2016, the effects of this courageous Black activism are important to note. Due to the impassioned activism of BLM-TO at queer Pride 2016, the Toronto police were barred from appearing in uniform during the 2017 queer Pride Parade. Again, this decision generated a great deal of debate in the city of Toronto. Like the 2016 queer Pride events, BLM-TO's successful campaigns to demilitarize Pride and remove visible symbols of racist state power from queer spaces led to many deeply racist comments online and publicly. The occupation of white queer space and white queer archives by Black transgender and queer activists is met with constant hostility, revealing the un-homely racism that shapes a white-supremacist society.

"Love Thy Neighbour?" Hatred, Hostility, and Impossible Hospitalities

The microcosm for the nation and city is the neighbourhood, a place where certain bodies are invited to play house. Following the BLM-TO protest outside her home, Premier Kathleen Wynne stated, "I would like for the protest to happen other places than my home and you know, quite frankly, it's not just about my home, it's about the neighbours as well" (CBC News 2016a, n.p.). The neighbours and the citizens who are imagined in this narrative are white, middle class, and lacking in any commitment to radical politics.

The reference to "neighbours" resonates in chilling ways with the ravages of racism and war that threaten the precarious lives of racialized people in a white-settler colony. For example, Andrew Loku was a child soldier who had immigrated to Canada, only to be murdered by the police. Omar Khadr, a Canadian citizen detained in Guantanamo Bay at the age of fifteen, is also referred to as a child soldier. Khadr was subject to abhorrent abuse. He states that military interrogators told him that if he did not comply with their demands, he would be "raped to death by a big black man," a threat of torture, which repeats racist tropes that garner their currency from slavery (Atluri 2011). Racialized people who are deemed to be radicals and terrorists are not home in Canada and can be forcibly removed from the nation state, stripped of all citizenship rights, and murdered by supposedly "peacekeeping" Canadians.

For Loku, home was the site of his brutal and sickening execution. Khan discusses how Loku's death happened after a series of conflicts with a neighbour.

> If there are any of you reading this who has ever felt driven to the edge by a loud neighbour, one who constantly bangs on your ceiling, who ignores every effort you've made to bargain and plead, who doesn't care for the days and months of accumulated sleep loss, imagine being in that place again. *Now imagine being executed for it.* Andrew Loku, like many of us before, went upstairs to rebut his neighbor for the umpteenth time on their constant noise. He used a hammer to bang on their door, and banged the hallway and stairway railing as he made his way back down to his floor. That was just before midnight, by just after midnight he was dead. (Khan 2016, n.p.)

Within seconds of seeing Loku, the police officer who was called to the scene shot and killed him. Judith Butler discusses how a racist visual schema, structured by white paranoia, informs visual perception. She comments on the case of Rodney King, a Black man who was brutally beaten by police officers in Los Angeles. Despite video evidence showing King being viciously beaten by police officers, Butler states that an existing visual schema of white supremacy shaped by paranoid anti-Black racism causes Black male bodies to appear as "threatening." This perceived "threat" is structured by visual perceptions that have been shaped by long genealogies of anti-Black racism. The Black male body appears as a figure of imagined deviance within the popular imaginary due to endless discursive renderings of Black male bodies as sites of danger to tactical mirages of white innocence that appear again and again in mainstream political and popular culture. Similarly, Andrew Loku was threatened by his neighbour, and yet, within a white supremacist schema that structures perception, it was he who was imagined to be a threatening presence in ways that justified his murder (Butler 1993).

This contrasts with an affluent, white-colonial notion of domesticity and neighbourliness that is strictly reserved for white citizens. Kathleen

Wynne and her partner recast themselves as damsels in distress in the presence of Blackness. In a deeply racist imaginary, Blackness is somehow always imagined to threaten whiteness and, particularly, the bodies of white women, who are seen to be forever innocent. This irrational fear of Blackness as threatening must wilfully ignore the obvious privileges afforded to white people in white-settler Canada and particularly those who occupy powerful political positions, such as Premier Kathleen Wynne. The intimate proximity of the Black body is guarded against to the point of murder. The Judeo-Christian ethic of "Love thy neighbour," which is seamlessly woven into the mythologies of supposed Western secularism, is tempered by white supremacy (Žižek 1997, 45). Black people are a threat to neighbourhoods of imagined white people, who are spatially and ideologically at home, entitled to occupy Indigenous lands and turn the brutality of genocide into quaint domestic scripts. Jacqui Alexander discusses imperialism as a palimpsest, using the metaphor of a parchment that is written over again and again (Alexander 2005). The originary violence of Canadian colonialism, the white European slave trade, and the colonization of African and Caribbean nations haunt Turtle Island. Similarly, the un-belonging and partial citizenship rights of Black people are part of an ongoing imperialist palimpsest. As Janaya Khan writes,

> #TentCity is bringing together this country's legacy of colonial violence, its anti-Black racism and three centuries of enslavement, its mass incarceration of Black and Indigenous people, Indigenous genocide, its racist and deadly migrant and immigration practices, its transphobia and misogyny, its deeply embedded Islamophobia apparent in terrorism with our actions. The lie, one that has caused uphill battles for so many of us who live in Canada, is being exposed. (2016)

Before one sheds tears for the racist anxieties of white lesbians in lily-white homes, one can and should perhaps think of Andrew Loku and the many other murdered Black people who will never be at home in white-settler Canada, or in the world.

Marvelling: Spaces of Imagi/nation

The anthology of writings by queer and trans Black, Indigenous, and people of colour that this chapter is part of involves a mapping and archiving project called Marvellous Grounds. The name *Marvellous*

Grounds gestures to the importance of art in imagining worlds beyond the "murderous inclusions" (Haritaworn, Kuntsman, and Posocco 2014) that currently govern the LGBT-friendly nation states of the Global North. Like the Introduction to this book, this piece of writing draws on Suzanne Césaire's concept of the marvellous, which Robin Kelley (2003) discusses in regard to the close relationship between surrealism and revolutionary Black politics. According to Kelley, Césaire's surrealism "was not an ideology but a state of mind, a 'permanent readiness' for 'the marvellous'" (170). This orientation towards a different future involved seriously acknowledging the violence of the past and present to construct radical futures. Kelley further writes about Césaire, "When she speaks of the domain of the marvellous, she also has her sights on the chains of colonial domination, never forgetting the crushing reality of everyday life in Martinique and the rest of the world" (ibid.). Césaire's "domain of the marvellous" resonates with the writings of queer of colour theorist José Muñoz. In *Disidentifications: Queers of Colour and the Politics of Resistance*, Muñoz (1999) marvels at how racialized, queer people who must navigate a hostile public sphere find ways to not only survive but also create spaces of resistance and inspiring texts that rewrite history.

One such inspiring archive of imagi/nation can be found in the creativity of Syrus Marcus Ware, co-editor of this book and BLM-TO organizer. Ware is an acclaimed Black transgender artist whose artistic praxis comments fiercely and beautifully on violence and political resistance. Interviewed by the *Real News* at a BLM-TO demonstration, Ware stated,

> Here we are again, talking about Jermaine Carby, talking about Andrew Loku, talking about all these people. We keep coming back to this cop shop to say enough is enough, enough of anti-black racism, enough of targeting of our communities, enough of the prison industrial complex. We want justice. We said that in 1992. We said that in 1999. We said that in 2016. (Real News 2016, n.p.)

Ware's comments gesture to the long history of movements against anti-Black racism in Toronto. The material monuments often found in cities such as Toronto celebrate white-colonial genocide and ever-emerging spaces of market capitalism. The vulgar racism of Turtle Island is managed spatially. Enduring histories of radical Black and Indigenous politics are buried under a haze of skyscrapers, affluent housing developments, and statues of victorious white colonizers. Far from cop shops, white picket fences, ivory towers, and other hostile spaces of everyday racism, Ware constructs marvellous artistic spaces of political integrity and historical memory.

In *Activist Love Letters*, Ware remaps normative ideas of love and history. This installation project, which has existed since 2012, draws on ongoing interdisciplinary methods to create political histories and archives of inspiring, emotive survival.[2] Ware discusses this deeply meaningful and moving installation, which has been staged several times in Toronto.

> I screened two films that spoke of activism, hope, rage, and social change. Following the films, I read aloud from activist-penned letters – specifically, (a) a letter that author James Baldwin (1970) sent to Angela Davis while she was in prison, (b) a letter that Leonard Peltier wrote from within prison to Mumia Abu Jamal, also in prison, encouraging him to stay strong, to keep fighting, and (c) a letter that Toronto activist Tooker Gomberg (2002) wrote to all community mobilizers, encouraging each of us to take care of each other and ourselves. I then invited the audience to write their own letters to someone active in our communities, as kind of an "Activist Love Letter."[3]

In Ware's installation, home is found in the inspirational narratives and histories of queer people of colour. As Ware states,

> I choose to create bios about mostly activists of colour – BIPOC, queer, and trans people – folks working on sex worker activism, trans rights, disability activism, HIV/AIDS, Indigenous sovereignty. In this way, I ended up

---

2 Interestingly, given our argument about the erasure of Black queer activism in this book, recent controversies have arisen over the plagiarism of Ware's work by the US-based Museum of Impact. A petition against this act of plagiarism and a letter of support for Ware states, "In 2015, the Museum of Impact began using Ware's project concept, even copying the exact title of the work, 'Activist Love Letters,' and the hashtag #activistloveletters, while presenting it in art galleries and museums in the US as their own creative content. The Museum of Impact does not credit or cite Syrus' work, he is not paid royalties or artist fees, and have refused to communicate with the artist despite his repeated attempts [6] to establish a connection and begin a discussion" (Change.org 2016, n.p.).

3 Syrus Marcus Ware, interview by the author, September 2014.

shaping some of the "who" – who people wrote to – but also the "what" – some of the things that people wrote about. Some of the beauty of the performance is that people have also written to people close to them – strangers, often, to me – and I end up developing a relationship through the process with new communities and other activists.[4]

Ware also offers insight into how opening up art worlds to activists may alter the affective dimensions of the artistic space.

The project has been wonderfully received – I have adapted it for each community that I do it in – having short bios about local organizers from that location for people to write to. Before mailing the letters, I include a little blurb about the project in the envelope and invite people to reply. The replies have inspired me to keep the project going. The majority of people who reply are stunned to have received a letter reaching out, sharing a story, or thanking them for their work.[5]

The installation asks people to write letters of tribute to activists, even if they may never receive the object. Rather than functioning as property held in place, the letter represents boundless emotion and transnational artistic and activist energies. In the striking work of Syrus Marcus Ware, a creative cartography points one in new directions not contained by the borders of nation states.

Edward Said (2000) argues that exile is interesting to consider but deeply painful to experience. Yet Said also triumphs the artistic energies of exiles, those whose acute alienation allows them to stand at a distance from the mainstream and to emerge as creative visionaries. While affluent white-settler politicians are invited to play house, BLM-TO erects tents in the bitter cold and stages sit-ins despite violent attacks and vilification from a racist public. Beyond spaces of "polite" white denial, there are defiant new cartographies unravelling in tent cities, artistic exhibitions, occupations of city streets, and the precious space of texts such as this one.

Between these words and their reader, whole worlds of possibility emerge.

Black Lives Matter.

---

4 Ibid.
5 Ibid.

References

#PrideTO. 2016. Twitter account. Accessed 19 July 2016. https://twitter.com/ pridetoronto.

Ahmed, Sara. 2000. *Strange Encounters: Embodied Others in Post-coloniality.* New York: Routledge.

Alexander, Jacqui. 2005. *Pedagogies of Crossing: Meditations on Feminism, Sexual Politics, Memory, and the Sacred.* Durham, NC: Duke University Press. https://doi.org/10.1215/9780822386988.

Aravosis, John. 2016. "Black Lives Matter Shuts Down Toronto LGBT Pride: Demands Cops Be Kicked Out of Parade, Wins." *America Blog*, 4 July. Accessed 30 December 2016. http://americablog.com/2016/07/black-lives -matter-shuts-toronto-lgbt-pride-demands-cops-kicked-parade-wins.html.

Berlant, Lauren, and Michael Warner. 1998. "Sex in Public." *Critical Inquiry* 24 (2): 547–66. https://doi.org/10.1086/448884.

BLM-TO (Black Lives Matter Toronto). 2016. Facebook page. Accessed 19 July 2016. https://www.facebook.com/blacklivesmatterTO/.

Brennan, Richard. 2015. "Kathleen Wynne Feels 'Responsibility' as First Lesbian Premier." *Toronto Star*, 8 April. Accessed 25 July 2016. https:// www.thestar.com/news/queenspark/2015/04/08/kathleen-wynne-feels -responsibility-as-first-lesbian-premier.html.

Butler, Judith. 1993. "Endangered/Endangering: Schematic White Paranoia." In *Reading Urban Uprising*, edited by Robert Gooding-Williams, 140–3. New York: Routledge.

CBC News. 2016a. "Black Lives Matter Protest Goes to Kathleen Wynne's Home." 1 April. Accessed 19 July 2016. http://www.cbc.ca/news/canada/ toronto/black-lives-matter-kathleen-wynne-1.3516893.

– 2016b. "This Gay Toronto Cop Sent an Open Letter to Pride Toronto about the Black Lives Matter Protest." 4 July. Accessed 20 July 2016. http://www.cbc.ca/news/canada/toronto/gay-cop-black-lives-matter -letter-1.3663323.

Change.org. 2016. "Support for Syrus Marcus Ware's Activist Love Letters (2012–Ongoing)." Accessed 28 December 2016. https://www.change .org/p/monica-o-montgomery-founding-director-the-museum-of-impact -support-for-syrus-marcus-ware-s-activist-love-letters-2012-ongoing.

Clare, Kerry. 2015. "Angela Sterritt: The Legacy of Violence against Indigenous Women in Canada." *49th Shelf* (website), 6 March. Accessed 25 July 2016. http://49thshelf.com/Blog/2015/03/06/Angela-Sterritt-The-Legacy-of -Violence-Against-Indigenous-Women-in-Canada.

Cole, Desmond. 2016. "Pride Has Divorced Blackness from Queerness: Cole." *Toronto Star*, 7 July. Accessed 25 July 2016. https://www.thestar.com/

opinion/commentary/2016/07/07/pride-has-divorced-blackness-from -queerness-cole.html.

Gray-Donald, David. 2016. "Debriefing Black Lives Matter Toronto's 15-Day Occupation (Part 2)." *Briarpatch Magazine,* 13 April. Accessed 25 July 2016. https://briarpatchmagazine.com/blog/view/debriefing-black-lives-matter -torontos-15-day-occupation-part-2.

Hall, Stuart. 1997. *Representation: Cultural Representations and Signifying Practices.* London: Sage.

Haritaworn, Jin, Adi Kuntsman, and Silvia Posocco, eds. 2014. *Queer Necropolitics.* London: Routledge.

James, C.L.R. 2009. *You Don't Play with Revolution: The Montreal Lectures of C.L.R. James.* Oakland, CA: AK Press.

Kelley, Robin. 2003. *Freedom Dreams: The Black Radical Imagination.* Boston: Beacon Press.

Khan, Janaya. 2016. "The Great White Nope: What BLMTO Is Exposing about Canada through #TentCity." *JanayaKhan.com,* 23 March. Accessed 30 December 2016. http://janayakhan.com/home/.

McKittrick, Katherine. 2002. "'Their Blood Is There, and They Can't Throw It Out': Honouring Black Canadian Geographies." *Topia* 7: 27–37.

Muñoz, José Esteban. 2009. *Disidentifications: Queers of Colour and the Politics of Resistance.* Minneapolis: University of Minnesota Press.

Puar, Jasbir. 2007. *Terrorist Assemblages: Homonationalism in Queer Times.* Durham, NC: Duke University.

Real News. 2016. "Toronto City Council Asks Province for Police Review as Black Lives Matter Occupation Intensifies." 3 April. Accessed 20 July 2016. http://therealnews.com/t2/index.php?option=com_content&task=view&id= 31&Itemid=74&jumival=16036.

Rieti, John, and Shanifa Nasser. 2016. "Pride Says It 'Never Agreed' to Exclude Police, as Black Lives Matter Slams Police for 'Pink-Washing.'" *CBC News,* 4 July. Accessed 19 July 2016. http://www.cbc.ca/news/canada/toronto/ black-lives-matter-pride-protest-1.3663250.

Rodríguez, Río, and Amandeep Kaur Panag, eds. 2016. "QTBIPOC Space: Remapping Belonging in Toronto." *Marvellous Grounds* (website), no. 1. Accessed 1 December 2016. http://marvellousgrounds.com/blog/ special-issue-1-qtbipoc-space/.

Said, Edward. 2000. *Reflections on Exile and Other Essays.* Boston, MA: Harvard University Press.

Swain, Gloria. 2016. "300 Hours: What I Learned about Black Queer and Trans Liberation at BLMTO Tent City." *Marvellous Grounds* (website), no. 1. Accessed 1 December 2016. http://www.cbc.ca/news/canada/toronto/ gay-cop-black-lives-matter-letter-1.3663323.

Walcott, Rinaldo. 2016a. "Invisible and Hypervisible: Black Canadian Life and Institutional Disregard." YouTube video, 52:34, from a lecture presented in the Race Literacies Series, 26 January. Accessed 1 December 2016. https://www.youtube.com/watch?v=CDSe5mjX2H0.

– 2016b. "Black Lives Matter and Misconceptions." *NOW Toronto*, 13 July. Accessed 16 July 2016. https://nowtoronto.com/news/black-lives-matter-and-misconceptions/.

Žižek, Slavoj. 1997. *The Plague of Fantasies*. London: Verso.

– 2008. *Violence: Six Sideways Reflections*. London: Picador.

9 Becoming through Others: Western Queer Self-Fashioning and Solidarity with Queer Palestine

NAYROUZ ABU HATOUM AND GHAIDA MOUSSA

Much attention has been given to queer people and organizations in Palestine in the last decade, and particularly so by Western queers who align themselves with radical[1] politics. This has been most notable since 2009, and it can, in part, be attributed to the internationalization of human rights values and the popularization of solidarity with Palestine through calls to action like the Boycott, Divestment and Sanctions (BDS) campaign. In addition, this phenomenon has been informed by the increasingly global use of gay rights as criteria for determining the "progressiveness" of nations. In particular, the Israeli state has mobilized the currency of "being gay-friendly" in its public relations campaign to "pinkwash" its violence against Palestinian people. In this article, we interrogate this new-found Western queer interest in "the Palestinian queer." We offer an anti-colonial critique that is grounded in affect theory to interrogate what makes Palestinian queers an accessible political cause for radical queer communities in liberal democracies. We speak from our settler-colonial and diasporic context as dwellers of the city of Toronto, where, in 2008, we witnessed a strong mobilization of politicized queers against the Israeli pinkwashing campaign and the formation of Queers Against Israeli Apartheid (QuAIA).

This chapter is not a historical screening of the origins of queer solidarity with Palestine. Nor is it meant to delineate the history of Palestinian queer activism in Palestine. Instead, it is a theoretical exploration

---

1 While the term *radical* has many connotations, we use it in this chapter to refer to an orientation towards – without assuming, or excluding, a true investment in – social justice and anti-oppression.

of the narratives of solidarity, written from the perspective of its recipients. We will begin by providing some context of the Israeli pinkwashing campaign and the general environment that gave rise to Western queer solidarity with queer Palestine. Presenting this story then allows us to explore the shift that we have noticed from earlier criticisms of queer solidarity. We seek to identify the potential work that the Palestinian queer does *for* queer North American imaginations. Using QuAIA and the work of Sarah Schulman (2012) as cases in point, we claim that Western performances and allegiance towards a queer Palestine mobilize Palestinian queer subjects at the service of a nostalgic brand of radical Western queer subjectivity that fashions itself as radical.

What drives this self-fashioning, we argue, is a desire to remedy an aching "queer nostalgia" (Haritaworn 2015) for political activism within queer communities, understood in Haritaworn's terms as "an active investment in murderous times and places that the nostalgic subject ostensibly seeks to overcome" (142). We borrow this term from Haritaworn to make sense of the fabricated proximity between the nostalgic Western queer subject and Palestinian queers. We turn to Dina Georgis's (2013) work in *The Better Story*, and particularly her suggestion that resistance is the better story of postcolonial subjects, to propose that *Western queers have in some ways appropriated Palestinian struggles.* We consider how the return of the slogan "The first Pride was a riot" in relation to QuAIA's fight to march in the Toronto Pride Parade points to the ways that solidarity with Palestinian queers through the appropriation of their struggle has helped remedy the nostalgia for Stonewall, an idealized era of Western queer politicization. This reading ultimately suggests that the arrival at radical political subjecthood in the West happens through allyship with queer Palestine.

Israel's Pinkwashing and the Rise of Solidarity with Queer Palestine: A Brief Contour of the Context

The spark of Western queer solidarity with Palestine emerged roughly in 2009 as a response to Israel's educational and visual rebranding campaigns such as the Blue Star Campaign, which began in 2005. This public relations campaign is a massive effort to market Israel as a modern and progressive state and society. It capitalizes on what, at the time, had emerged as criteria of modernity and progressivity, which were being newly recognized in the international human rights arena: the acceptance of gays and lesbians. In sum, in this campaign, Israel is portrayed as a gay haven, standing in contrast to its Middle Eastern neighbours, claimed to be integrally homophobic and regressive. This campaign is directed towards the West and aspires to secure Israel's status as a modern nation – or, quite plainly, as the West within the heart of the East. At the same time, it serves to mask and justify Israel's continued violence towards Palestinians living within its sovereign borders and within its military reach in the West Bank and the Gaza Strip. The strength of this campaign came largely from its portrayal of Arab, and particularly Palestinian, homophobia as a "timeless pathology" (Ritchie 2010, 559), thus framing Israeli occupation, apartheid, and state violence as needed forms of discipline that are "natural (if not unavoidable) and irresolvable" (Hochberg 2010, 502).

This state-sanctioned propaganda was emphatically resisted by local queer organizations, such as Aswat and alQaws,[2] as early as 2004. Both groups have a solid understanding of how Israel is using its gay citizens and gay liberal-rights framework to distract the world from its violation of human rights against the Palestinian people, from its actual treatment of its own gay and lesbian citizens, and from the existence and resistance of Palestinian queers. This state practice has come to be known as *pinkwashing*. Amal Amireh's (2010) work has been particularly influential to our understanding of pinkwashing as a violent strategy meant to uphold state power. Amireh argues that one of the results of Israel's pinkwashing campaign is the silencing of Palestinian queer subjects, who are given right to speech only if they serve the interest of the state by reproducing its homonationalist discourse. Further, Amireh reminds us that the gloated-about freedoms afforded to gay Israeli citizens come at the expense of Palestinians – a fact that is further confirmed by Stein's (2010) observation that gay rights and anti-Palestinian policies were introduced simultaneously by the Israeli government in the 1990s.

Palestinian queer resistance to Israel's pinkwashing campaign led to the queer Palestinian call for BDS against Israel in 2010 – for example,

---

2 alQaws (www.alqaws.org) is a non-governmental organization promoting sexual and gender diversity in Palestinian society. It is a group of lesbian, gay, bisexual, transgender, questioning, and queer Palestinian activists, who work collaboratively to break down gendered and heteronormative barriers. Aswat (www.aswatgroup.org) is a group of lesbian, bisexual, transgender, intersex, questioning, and queer Palestinian women.

the Palestinian Queers for Boycott, Divestment, Sanctions (PQBDS) and Pinkwatching Israel campaigns. Its reach was wide and gave rise to multiple groups in North America advocating for LGBTQ boycotts of Israeli gay tourism, criticism of Israel's overall "gay" rebranding campaign, and offers of support to Palestinian queer groups in Palestine, such as the "General Assembly Declaration – Queer Visions at the World Social Forum: Free Palestine" (Pinkwatching Israel 2016). Over social media, in one-on-one conversations, and through interactions with some of these groups, we have witnessed how many white, North American queers proclaim solidarity with Palestine, the intimate resonances of which we investigate in this chapter.

The most visible of these groups in our local Toronto context is QuAIA, which was formed in 2008. As a group that describes its work as being in solidarity with queers in Palestine, QuAIA is one of the most well known of its kind in North America. Its celebrity is in large part due to the media coverage it received in 2009 and 2010, when various local Zionist groups so strongly and loudly opposed its use of the word *apartheid* to describe the Israeli state that its participation in the Toronto Pride Parade was thrown into question. Despite the massive lobbying against it, QuAIA rallied a huge number of supporters and successfully fought the city's censorship and original decision to ban QuAIA from participating in the parade (Abunimah and Activism and BDS Beat 2015; Dale 2013; Foreman 2014; Watson 2014).

Queer solidarity with Palestine was also crystallizing in other North American cities, including New York[3] and Seattle.[4] Notably, in January 2012, an LGBTQ solidarity delegation consisting of academics, writers, artists, and activists from the United States visited Palestine and met with Palestinian queer organizations and a small number of Israeli queer anti-occupation activists. The delegation generated multiple statements, writings, and documentations (Guy-Sheftall et al. 2012; Puar 2012), some of which were later presented at the "Homonationalism and Pinkwashing Conference," held in 2013 at the City University of New York.

The political discourse at the conference demonstrated some of the problems with North American queer solidarity with Palestine

---

3 See New York City Queers Against Israeli Apartheid: http://queersagainstisraeliapartheid. blogspot.ca/.

4 See QuAIA Seattle: http://quaiaseattle.org/.

movements. Participants were mainly white North American and a few brown and Black academics. A central focus, as reflected in the papers that were presented, was the issue of Israeli pinkwashing and queer solidarity with Palestine. In addition, there were a few sessions that debated other queer issues in the Middle East. Only a handful of conference papers were critical of the concept of solidarity or suggested a reflexive interaction among the ways in which colonialism, nationalism, and liberal queer desires in North America were cultivated and orchestrated together (Kouri-Towe 2013; Morgensen 2013a; Upadhyay and Jackman 2013).

Very few Palestinians presented at or participated in the conference; one exception was Haneen Maikey, the director of alQaws. In her keynote address, Maikey (2013) problematized North American queer solidarity with Palestine by interrogating the practice of "pinkwatching," the term increasingly used to refer to queer activism aiming to denounce and resist Israeli pinkwashing. In particular, she questioned whether this practice simply enhanced the politicization of the LGBTQ movements in the West or actually helped Palestinian queers resist the occupation. This is precisely the question we explore in our chapter.

To do so, we first review some of the critical literature on solidarity to understand how colonial dynamics have been reiterated in relation to solidarity with Palestine. We then ask what function is served for Western queers by what we have come to know as *solidarity*. We wish to break out of essentialist discourses about what constitutes good solidarity activists or solidarity receivers and to trouble the binary thinking that mythologizes oppression as happening "elsewhere" rather than in politicized spaces themselves. As such, we are *not* implying that white subjects cannot be in solidarity with racialized groups, but argue that this solidarity does not stand outside of power dynamics. Having articulated this, our aim is not to shut down political alliances. For instance, we acknowledge how Toronto's QuAIA has confronted Israeli international pinkwashing efforts and supported Palestinians' call for BDS. We also realize that there is a thin line separating QuAIA's positive intentions from the effects of their praxis on the political work of solidarity with Palestine. What we ask, therefore, is for a more nuanced, reflexive engagement among privileged subjects, which aims primarily to dismantle the material, discursive, and abstract tools that allow a reproduction of hierarchal structures and oppressive dynamics.

Western Epistemologies on Queer Solidarity

In the North American context, queer solidarity with Palestine was largely built through local conversations and organizing among queer politicized groups. A large portion of this organizing was based on uncritical premises of solidarity, which strongly relied on the reproduction of colonial power dynamics and on a denial of the historical and current racialization of Palestinians. As a concept, solidarity relies on a thread of commonality, which often engages an identification that assumes a shared struggle; in our case, sexual identity is mobilized by Western queers to establish the imagined Palestinian queer Other as familiar and as worthy of solidarity. Such an imaginative construction is made possible after twenty years of "internationalization" – or rather "hegemonization" – of Western LGBTQ, gay, and/or queer cultures and discourses worldwide (Massad 2002). In Massad's account, sexuality played a central role in the colonization of the Arab world through the representation and disciplining of the Arab body as sexually deviant, while later, and still today, imperialism and warfare are justified as means of disciplining Arab societies for their alleged *repression* of sexual freedoms.

Our notion of Western queer solidarity as an extension of colonialism, or as employing colonial dynamics, is largely indebted to a British-based study of queer transnational movements by Haritaworn, Tauqir, and Erdem (2008). The authors position the new-found interest of queer transnational movements in the well-being of Arab and Muslim queers as part of the post–9/11 global political context, which is shaped by the Islamophobic and racist civilizing mission that accompanied the war on terror (manifested in the occupation of Afghanistan and Iraq). According to Haritaworn, Tauqir, and Erdem, solidarity movements are able to intervene because they conceive of Arab and Muslim queers as powerless and voiceless victims in need of saving from their integrally homophobic and oppressive cultures. This project is made possible by Western queer subjects' own identification as sexually liberated beings in whose footsteps others must follow to emancipate themselves. The authors describe this narrative of progress, which relies on the self-determined superiority of Western queer subjects, as a saviour narrative, one that justifies a neocolonial "solidarity" project based on Western needs, ideals, processes, and epistemologies.

In so doing, Haritaworn, Tauqir, and Erdem draw attention to the metonymy between Western transnational feminism and queer transnational movements, which construct the figure of the "Third World queer" in close repetition with that of the "Third World Woman" (Mohanty 1997). Reflecting on another such metonymy – the recent attention Palestine has received from international groups – Jasbir Puar (2013), specifically referencing Sarah Schulman's (2012) work and writing about queer solidarity with Palestine, asks in what ways Joseph Massad's (2002) identification of the "gay international" has been replaced by a "queer international" (Puar 2013, 37). One further figure, whose emergence as a comfortable object of solidarity is the subject of this chapter, is that of the Palestinian queer. This figure is created as ahistorical, unchanging, always oppressed and without agency, and thus continuously awaiting the benevolence of a West that will set it free. If we may "queer" Gayatri Spivak's 1988 statement (in "Can the Subaltern Speak?"), "white men save brown women from brown men" (quoted in Kapoor 2004, 627), "white queers save 'brown' queers from 'brown heterosexuals'" (Moussa 2011, 23).

Furthermore, one could expand Spivak's statement to queer such solidarity with Palestine by arguing that this process is enabled through the premise of North American white queers saving Palestinian queers from Israeli pinkwashing and homonationalism. For Haritaworn, Tauqir, and Erdem (2008), it is against this oppressed figure that the "representational power of white queers" is produced (87). Western queer subjects' voices and writings, all based on Western experiences and epistemologies, hereby rise as one-size-fits-all blueprints for sexual oppression and sexual liberation, rendering alternative voices and ways of being silent or non-existent. What is more, this monopoly on a one-dimensional queerness harms racialized subjects as it sustains internal conceptions of queerness as a Western and imperial foreign product of colonization (Kuntsman 2008).

The discourses and practices that emerge from this type of neocolonial solidarity between the West and Palestine are multiple and productive of various political subjectivities, thus making it difficult to ignore the entanglements of the homonationalist and the anti-apartheid gay, who, in some circumstances, might be one and the same. In this chapter, we argue that radical political queers have adopted Palestine as a comfortable political niche on the radical side of both queer politics and North American politics. Such political investments serve the continuous self-fashioning of political subjects, a process that, we argue, is not based on contextual knowledge about Palestine and its political complexities. Instead, these investments are informed by premises of solidarity, which are derived from a calculation of the sociocultural proximity and distance of the object of solidarity. Namely, does the Other – the object of solidarity – have a familiar proposition on queerness and politics? Does the Other speak the radical queer language spoken in the Global North?

The international queer solidarity movement with Palestinian queers consists solely of the support of a limited selection of communities or even specific persons in Palestine. Today, the light of queer North American political solidarity is shed on two queer groups, which are the only two visibly active organizations: alQaws and Aswat (with alQaws getting far more international solidarity attention than Aswat). Here we might question how much the comfort with which Western queer solidarity groups approach Palestinian queers derives from their assumption that being sexually and socially queer is enough to imagine commonality with other queers living under drastically different political circumstances, such as apartheid or military occupation. On the other end of solidarity, some queers in Palestine complain about these types of alliances, built with international solidarity groups, and the direction, discourses, and rhetorics that these groups coerce locals into adopting.

One critique of this quest for international allyship was raised by Palestinian feminist blogger Nisreen Mazzawi (2014) in an article she wrote in Arabic in *Assafir*, a Lebanese newspaper. Mazzawi claims that Palestinian queers need to revisit their priorities. While many have focused on combatting Israeli pinkwashing campaigns or critiquing the singling out of queers in international solidarity efforts, not enough efforts, in Mazzawi's view, have gone into strengthening queer groups in Palestine to empower themselves. Her critique stems from a response to a letter written by the forty-three Israeli intelligence officers who revealed that the threat of outing is a method used against Palestinian queers in military interrogations (Weiss 2014). Mazzawi (2014) criticizes Palestinians' rushed call for international condemnation, specifically the one by alQaws, whose issuing in English she argued could potentially alienate many Arabic-speaking queers. Hence, she asks her readers to use the Israeli state's oppressive discourse and practice as an opportunity to build stronger local work aimed not only at condemning the state's bullying and policing of queer Palestinian bodies but also at interrogating the conditions that make such threats useful tools for Israeli intelligence services. Mazzawi also notes that the urgency to battle Israeli pinkwashing should not be directed at looking outwards for international support but at looking inwards for internal support from local Palestinian organizations, communities, and political parties.

Mazzawi's concern is justified when we consider that Arabic academic and artistic productions do not receive any international attention due to the lack of international efforts to translate this material. In the meantime, any communication written in English on social media is picked up by Western solidarity groups outside Palestine, singled out, and reduced to "the queer voice" of Palestine. The epistemological value embedded in the English language, as well as in the status of Western academics who are often only loosely connected to Palestine, if at all, is rarely problematized, despite unsettling queer Palestinian movements and burdening all Palestinian queers with one selected narrative to be adopted internationally. Needless to say, Palestinian queers do not always share the same political vision of liberation with internationals, such as one-state or two-state solutions, the political nature of the future state, or strategies of liberation like negotiation, BDS, popular civilian struggle, and armed struggle. They may also not adhere to the same political discourse on identity, such as the identity politics framework that is prevalent among queer communities elsewhere. These differing visions may form a barrier for queers in Palestine to building relationships with an international language of solidarity.

Language, too, can form a barrier. Palestinian queers who are capable of speaking English, or who adopt North American radical political terminologies to publicly present themselves as queer and claim a voice in international discussions, are the ones who are heard and selected as worthy collaborators and recipients of solidarity. Connections with Palestinians, in other words, are informed by a specific conceptualization of solidarity that is sustained by the familiarity of the Other as well as the flexibility of the other. This familiarity and flexibility must be performed by Palestinians using a balancing act involving the adoption of familiar discourse and an identification that positions them as authentic signifiers of radical politics. This observation does not serve to dismiss the hard work of local queer activists, who might speak the language valued in the West or have access to travel and heightened mobility. Rather, it serves to challenge the Western grid of intelligibility, which limits the West to relating only to what has the potential to be visible. These processes produce exclusion and a simplification of the complex realities in Palestine. The imagined Palestine that is produced and reproduced this way is often divorced from the ordinary life experiences of local or diasporic Palestinians.

Western Queer Self-Fashioning

Andrea Smith's (2013) article, "The Problem with 'Privilege,'" a reflection on the way privilege has been used among political-left communities, sheds light on our concerns about some of the premises fuelling queer activist discourses in the West. Smith argues that the apparently reflexive practice of confessing privilege, "while claiming to be anti-racist and anti-colonial, is actually a strategy that helps constitute the settler/white subject" (ibid). This is possible, she continues, through the use of racialized and/or Indigenous bodies that become the point of entry for self-discovery and, we add, recovery of self-politicization post-Stonewall.

In the remainder of this chapter, we will build on the theorizations of Western solidarity by postcolonial feminist theorists and their reworkings by queer of colour theorists, discussed above. We argue that we are witnessing a potential shift, or perhaps a reversal, which should be duly noted. While suggesting that Western queers are attempting to save Palestinian queers, could we not claim that *Palestinian queers save Western queers from their political identity crisis*? After all, as the above-cited theorists note, colonial processes and progress narratives have always depended on the construction of "self" through the other. As we will argue next, this process of subject formation involves the maturation of this latter subject – the self – more than has been claimed so far. In other words, this rite of passage assures Western queers' arrival at radical political subjecthood.

Sarah Schulman's (2012) book, *Israel/Palestine and the Queer International*, is one of the most recent examples of how, for many Western queers, radical identity can take shape through their self-identified allyship with queer Palestine. Schulman managed to move from her activism in HIV/AIDS–related issues to leading and mobilizing anti-pinkwashing campaigns in the United States as well as organizing talks and conferences on queer activism and solidarity with Palestine, such as the "Homonationalism and Pinkwashing Conference"[5] in New York, which we mentioned earlier. While it is essential for us, in true feminist and queer spirit, to celebrate others' successes, it is also important to critically reflect on the politics and economies of such celebrations. Schulman's book describes her personal journey to Palestine as a logical

---

5 See http://homonationalismconference.eventsbot.com/, accessed 9 October 2013.

chapter in her family history because she is a Jewish American whose family fell victim to Nazi Germany during the Holocaust. This narrative is reflexive and self-critical: Schulman discusses her own past complicities with Zionism and her shifts to new forms of political affiliations with Palestine through the queer gate. The narrative culminates in her confrontation with Zionists and liberal gays in the United States and Israel.

For us, the significance of this book is in its honest discussion of the processes, procedures, networking, and correspondence between Schulman and, predominantly, other Jews in Israel and the United States. Throughout the first half of the book, Schulman writes at length about the birth of her solidarity visit to Palestine and the organizing that led to her discovery of a world of politics that was new to her and enabled her to make new connections around the world. At the height of this organizing, Schulman brings three Palestinian queer activists – Ghadir from Aswat as well as Haneen Maikey and Sami from alQaws and PQBDS – for an awareness-raising tour through the United States. The book is a good manifestation of how solidarity with Palestine, during the years 2009 to 2013, became an overtly international issue, engineered and constructed by a few actors in some US cities, who happened to be mainly white and Jewish. The network of queer solidarity for Palestine that was knitted together involved other, predominantly Jewish, people – highlighting, paradoxically, the centrality of the non-Palestinian context and the marginalization of Palestinian queers' agency in the making of queer solidarity for Palestine.

In this way, and in the specific narrative of Schulman's book, affiliation between queer solidarity and "radical" politics on the one hand and Palestine on the other functions not only as an identifier but also as a process of self-fashioning: a journey to the self and a reconciliation with a family history. Alternatively, Palestine is another available academic front to be occupied, with old and new conceptual linkages – namely, "queering" solidarity with Palestine. The point drawn here is that solidarity and identification with Palestinian queers is, to a large extent, a product of internal Western epistemologies rather than the result of an intimate relationship with Palestine or Palestinians.

This point is also reflected in the Toronto context that we are part of. We noticed that through the first year of QuAIA's existence, a few Arab, Palestinian, and non-Palestinian participants took an active part in organizing it. However, by the end of the second year, most Arabs, one of the authors of this article included, stepped away from active organizing with QuAIA as its work was focusing more on the politicization of the Pride Parade in Toronto and less on building ties with queer groups in Palestine, and this change in focus alienated diasporic Arabs who wished for a solidification of relationships with queers in Palestinian and other Middle Eastern countries. Those who gradually stepped away, however, remained supporters of QuAIA and continued to attend its events.

Local Toronto-based scholar Dina Georgis has been influential in our reading of the logic that allows the premise and gesture of Western queer solidarity to take the path identified thus far. Her book, *The Better Story* (2013), invites us to consider emotion and narratives when attempting to understand political conflicts and identities. Georgis defines "the better story" as "the affective dimensions of how postcolonial people are constructing their lives and writing their histories" (19). In particular, resistance frequently figures as the better story of postcolonial survival that holds together postcolonial communities. Our analysis of QuAIA and Sarah Schulman's book has led us to question the ways in which Palestinian resistance – the better story of Palestinian (queer) subjects – has been appropriated by Western queers longing for the political era of Stonewall. After reading this sentence, one might immediately hear the echo, or the continuous return, of the slogan "The first Pride march was a riot," which re-emerges any time Western queer groups urge for the re-politicization of Pride marches in the West, such as during the debate about QuAIA's participation in the Toronto Pride Parade. Queers in solidarity with Palestine not only identify with the subjects of their solidarity – that is, Palestinian queers – but also trace their struggle for (Western) queer liberation in the story of Palestinian queer survival. This appropriation is melancholic and violent as it places Palestinian queer struggles into the story of Western politicization and effaces how these struggles have their own histories, emerging from a long line of anti-colonial resistance, Palestinian feminist organizing, and national and labour movements.

The violence of this narrative also lies in how it erases a story here, in North America, that Indigenous, non-white, and Palestinian activists and scholars have shed a light on recently, thereby opening a gate to deeper discussions about queer Western nationalism, homonationalism, imperialism, and settler-colonialism in North America. Needless to say, these discussions should have been explored and pushed forward decades ago. An important outcome that we have witnessed is that the discourse on North American queer solidarity with Palestine has enabled a reflexive conversation at "home," in North America, about how queer North Americans are complicit in settler-colonialism in the lands they are living on and the state they are implicated in. Among the authors engaging in such a critical reflection are Jasbir Puar and Maya Mikdashi (2012), who propose an internal critique of North American queer solidarity work with Palestine in their opinion article in *Jadaliyya* entitled "Pinkwatching and Pinkwashing: Interpenetration and its Discontents." In particular, they interrogate the links between pinkwatching and homonationalism.

> Pinkwatching has become the primary, myopic lens through which queer youth (but not only youth) are asked to (and allowed to) be politicized around the issue of Palestine – a cycle which reinforces the myriad ways in which solidarity for Palestine/Israel in the United States is often articulated through the presence of different identity groups staking "their claim" in the debate (Jewish-American, Arab-American, Gay-American). One is tempted to call the production of such a narrow and reductive framework, through which American queers are to become politically engaged in foreign policy, an exercise in homonationalism. (Puar and Mikdashi 2012, n.p.)

Puar and Mikdashi go so far as to suggest that (North American) pinkwatchers have to recognize that they are living on colonized lands and in a state that also practises pinkwashing, while maintaining military rule and occupations overseas. In their words, "Pinkwatching activism in the United States by and large ignores the ways that the use of gay rights discourses and bodies have been used to legitimize *American* colonial and military ambitions" (n.p.).

This critique was also advanced by Scott L. Morgensen (2013b) in his opinion article in *Jadaliyya* entitled "Settler Colonialism and Alliance: Comparative Challenges to Pinkwashing and Homonationalism." Morgensen forces the critique of queers' complicity in settler-colonialism further and argues for a queer settler solidarity with (queer) Indigenous peoples. Of note for our current discussion, he asks how allyship with Palestine without an acknowledgment of Israel as a settler-colonial state can "reflect our desire to naturalize settler colonialism 'at home'" (n.p.).

Along the lines of the aforementioned critiques, we call for a greater regard for how the United States' and Canada's "war on terror" – which has led to increased border control, deportation, and criminalization of Indigenous and racialized people, coupled with these countries' undying support for Israel as a settler-colonial nation – always ties in with the double and joint movement of consolidating empire both within and without their colonial borders (Smith 2005). As Sunera Thobani (2014) reminds us in the prologue to *Queer Necropolitics*, the collection by Haritaworn, Kuntsman, and Posocco, "It should not be forgotten that the chief architects of this 'war on terror' are the settler-colonial societies established by Euro-America" (xvii). When Israel serves as a model for North America's war technology, and, conversely, when war exercises for missions abroad are tested on Indigenous communities (Smith 2005), we cannot envision an analysis of solidarity movements that does not centre the interlinked forces, dynamics, and systems at work to uphold settler colonialism, racial thinking, capitalism, patriarchy, homonationalism, and, lately, Islamophobia. In addition, we might ask how the "radical self-fashioning" we are discussing might apply to solidarity with Indigenous populations at home. After all, Morgensen himself has gained traction as an expert in "settler-colonial studies," which has become a site of professionalization in which white academics take space to air out how much space they take, while Indigenous scholars are consistently pushed out of the academy and silenced.

Conclusion

In this chapter, we have argued that the examined Western solidarity communities treat Palestinian queers' *better stories* of survival as sources of identification and self-politicization; in other words, they reduce them to a plot for *their own better story* as queers. We have further argued that this conversation is a melancholic one, acting as a balm for the loss of the queer political époque of Stonewall. Thus, our chapter does more than simply offer another critique of the politics of representation by suggesting that Western politicized queers simplify, decontextualize, or de-historicize, Palestinian queer politics. It also reveals that Western queer mourning for an idealized lost past of queer politicization since Stonewall has involved a reclamation of the political nature of queer, one that has displaced a Western queer story of survival and liberation to a Palestinian story of resistance and liberation.

As diasporic Arab activists and scholars in the West who have deep-rooted ties to Palestine and the Arab world, we hope to incite a vigorous mobilization among queer communities that is attentive to the ways in which power is not external to our communities. The brand of solidarity that we have critically analysed in this chapter has indeed felt violent. It has forced us to always look outward when we are trying to look within, to navigate – in collaboration with other Arab queers in the Arab world, in Toronto, and across the globe – how to articulate ourselves or live our lives outside the grid of intelligibility of the same West that we have long attempted to contest as a colonizing and imperialist power. When our identities come to be at the service of Western power – whether queer or not – we witness a familiar reconfiguration of archetypal colonial dynamics. We still find ourselves unable to speak of/ for/among ourselves, speak among others, or articulate the raw conditions of our lives and realities. We find ourselves speaking in poetry and through metaphors because our existence is at best only tangible in moments of rage, pain, mourning, or celebration. We are noticing that our stories are often recuperated by those whom we intended to call into reflexive accountability. In other words, power dynamics can be hidden under a coat of solidarity, and queer solidarity activists can uncritically employ well-articulated anti-oppression politics to deflect responsibility. Yet Palestine, to us, is a home that is beyond the grasp of the current instrumental role it occupies in the Western imagination.

References

Abunimah, Ali, and Activism and BDS Beat. 2015. "Toronto Queer Group That Won Right to Say 'Israeli Apartheid' Wraps Up." *Electronic Intifada*, 27 February. Accessed 1 December 2016. https://electronicintifada.net/blogs/ali-abunimah/toronto-queer-group-won-right-say-israeli-apartheid-wraps.

Amireh, Amal. 2010. "Afterword." *GLQ: A Journal of Lesbian and Gay Studies* 16 (4): 635–47. https://doi.org/10.1215/10642684-2010-009.

Dale, Daniel. 2013. "Queers against Israeli Apartheid: No Grounds to Ban Activist Group, City Legal Chief Says." *Toronto Star*, 27 May. Accessed 1 December 2016. https://www.thestar.com/news/city_hall/2013/05/27/rob_ford_mayors_drug_scandal_affecting_city_hall_allies_say.html.

Foreman, Rob. 2014. "Pride Parade Funding Takes Centre Stage in LGBTQ Debate." *Eyeopener*, 23 September. Accessed 1 December 2016. https://theeyeopener.com/2014/09/pride-parade-funding-takes-centre-stage-in-lgbtq-debate.

Georgis, Dina. 2013. *The Better Story: Queer Affects from the Middle East*. Albany: State University of New York Press.

Guy-Sheftall, Beverly, Katherine Franke, Roya Natarajan, Lisa Weiner-Mahfuz, and Darnell L. Moore. 2012. "TFW Forum on Palestine." *Feminist Wire*,

26 January. Accessed 30 December 2016. http://www.thefeministwire
.com/2012/01/tfw-forum-on-palestine/.

Haritaworn, Jin. 2015. *Queer Lovers and Hateful Others: Regenerating Violent
Times and Places*. London: Pluto Press. https://doi.org/10.2307/j.ctt183p5vv.

Haritaworn, Jin, Tamsila Tauqir, and Esra Erdem. 2008. "Gay Imperialism:
Gender and Sexuality Discourse in the 'War on Terror.'" In *Out of Place:
Interrogating Silences in Queerness/Raciality*, edited by Adi Kuntsman and
Esperanza Miyake, 71–95. York, UK: Raw Nerve Books.

Hochberg, Gil Z. 2010. "Introduction: Israelis, Palestinians, Queers: Points
of Departure." *GLQ: A Journal of Lesbian and Gay Studies* 16 (4): 493–516.
https://doi.org/10.1215/10642684-2010-001.

Kapoor, Ilan. 2004. "Hyper-Self-Reflexive Development? Spivak on
Representing the Third World 'Other.'" *Third World Quarterly* 25 (4): 627–47.
https://doi.org/10.1080/01436590410001678898.

Kouri-Towe, Natalie. 2013. "Homonationalism and the Politics of Transnational
Queer Activism in Toronto's Pride Parade." Paper presented at the
"Homonationalism and Pinkwashing Conference," City University of New
York, New York City, 10–11 April.

Kuntsman, Adi. 2008. "The Soldier and the Terrorist: Sexy Nationalism,
Queer Violence." *Sexualities* 11 (1–2): 142–70. https://doi.org/10.1177/
1363460707085468.

Maikey, Haneen. 2013. Keynote address presented at the "Homonationalism
and Pinkwashing Conference," City University of New York, New York
City, 10–11 April.

Massad, Joseph A. 2002. "Re-orienting Desire: The Gay International and
the Arab World." *Public Culture* 14 (2): 361–86. https://doi.org/10.1215/
08992363-14-2-361.

Mazzawi, Nisreen. 2014. "Al-Khetab Al-Queeri Al-Falastini: Dhed Al-Ehtilal,
Baa'eedan A'an Waqea'ahe [The Palestinian queer discourse: Against the
occupation, but far from reality]." *Assafir*, 23 July. Accessed 30 December
2016. http://palestine.assafir.com/Article.aspx?ArticleID=3063.

Mohanty, Chandra T. 1997. "Under Western Eyes: Feminist Scholarship and
Colonial Discourses." In *Dangerous Liaisons: Gender, Nation and Postcolonial
Perspective*, edited by Anne McClintock, Aamir Mufti, and Ella Shohat,
255–77. Minneapolis: University of Minnesota Press.

Morgensen, Scott. 2013a. "Challenging Settler Colonialism in Israel, the
United States and Canada." Paper presented at the "Homonationalism and
Pinkwashing Conference," City University of New York, New York City,
10–11 April.

– 2013b. "Settler Colonialism and Alliance: Comparative Challenges to Pinkwashing and Homonationalism." *Jadaliyya*, 3 April. Accessed 30 December 2016. http://humweb.ucsc.edu/feministstudies/news/morgensen-settler-colonialism.pdf.

Moussa, Ghaida. 2011. *Narrative (Sub)Versions: How Queer Palestinian Womyn "Queer" Palestinian Identity*. Ottawa: University of Ottawa.

Pinkwatching Israel. 2016. "General Assembly Declaration – Queer Visions at the World Social Forum: Free Palestine." Accessed 30 December 2016. http://www.pinkwatchingisrael.com/2012/12/10/wsf-declaration/.

Puar, Jasbir. 2012. "The Golden Handcuffs of Gay Rights: How Pinkwashing Distorts Both LGBTIQ and Anti-Occupation Activism." *Feminist Wire*, 30 January. Accessed 30 December 2016. http://www.thefeministwire.com/2012/01/the-golden-handcuffs-of-gay-rights-how-pinkwashing-distorts-both-lgbtiq-and-anti-occupation-activism/.

– 2013. "Homonationalism as Assemblage: Viral Travels, Affective Sexualities." *Jindal Global Law Review* 4: 23–43.

Puar, Jasbir, and Maya Mikdashi. 2012. "Pinkwatching and Pinkwashing: Interpenetration and Its Discontents." *Jadaliyya*, 9 August. Accessed 30 December 2016. http://www.jadaliyya.com/pages/index/6774/pinkwatching-and-pinkwashing_interpenetration-and-.

Ritchie, Jason. 2010. "How Do You Say 'Come Out of the Closet' in Arabic? Queer Activism and the Politics of Visibility in Israel-Palestine." *GLQ: A Journal of Lesbian and Gay Studies* 16 (4): 557–75. https://doi.org/10.1215/10642684-2010-004.

Schulman, Sarah. 2012. *Israel/Palestine and the Queer International*. Durham, NC: Duke University Press. https://doi.org/10.1215/9780822396536.

Smith, Andrea. 2005. *Conquest: Sexual Violence and American Indian Genocide*. Cambridge, MA: South End Press.

– 2013. "The Problem with 'Privilege.'" *Andrea366* (blog), 14 August. Accessed 30 December 2016. https://andrea366.wordpress.com/2013/08/14/the-problem-with-privilege-by-andrea-smith/.

Stein, Rebecca L. 2010. "Explosive: Scenes from Israel's Gay Occupation." *GLQ: A Journal of Lesbian and Gay Studies* 16 (4): 517–36. https://doi.org/10.1215/10642684-2010-002.

Thobani, Sunera. 2014. Prologue to *Queer Necropolitics*, edited by Jin Haritaworn, Adi Kuntsman, and Silvia Posocco, xv–xviii. London: Routledge.

Upadhyay, Nishant, and Michael Connors Jackman. 2013. "Whose Occupation Does Pinkwashing Obscure? Queer Politics and Indigenous Colonization in Canada." Paper presented at the "Homonationalism and Pinkwashing Conference," City University of New York, New York City, 10–11 April.

Watson, H.G. 2014. "John Tory Says QuAIA Has No Place in Pride Parade." *Daily Xtra*, 20 September. Accessed 30 December 2016. http://www .dailyxtra.com/toronto/news-and-ideas/news/john-tory-says-quaia-place -in-pride-parade-93258.

Weiss, Philip. 2014. "Israel Surveils and Blackmails Gay Palestinians to Make Them Informants." *Mondoweiss*, 12 September. Accessed 30 December 2016. http://mondoweiss.net/2014/09/blackmails-palestinian-informants/.

10 Compulsory Coming Out and Agentic Negotiations: Toronto QTPOC Narratives

AZAR MASOUMI

We, as queer and trans Black and people of colour, have a troubled and troubling relation to space. My trouble with space was impossible to ignore even in the process of this research, research that critiqued the stronghold of coming out over queer and trans people from an anti-racist perspective. I was repeatedly asked to come out publicly before my call for participants could be forwarded or posted by the groups and organizations I had approached. To some extent, these requests were understandable; coming out publicly, it seemed, was the only way I could make myself understood and understandable. Yet it was ironic that my critique of coming out had to travel through the pre-given routes of coming out. Carving out a space for a "queer of colour" critique, it seemed, was both troubled and troubling work; it was an unsettlingly incomprehensible task that always necessitated negotiated comprehensibility.

As queer and trans Black and people of colour, we have a multiply troubled relation to space as the spaces we "take," no doubt, are not intended for us (see chapter 2 by Catungal), both as racialized people in the white-centred Canadian nation and as queer and trans people in a deeply transphobic, heteropatriarchal landscape. Our space-taking is also troubled by our inevitable implication in the settler-colonial occupation of Indigenous lands in Canada (see chapter 9 by Abu Hatoum and Moussa). Our space-taking is further troubled in a neo-liberal homonationalist (Puar 2007) regime in which at least some non-heterosexual people are asked – in fact, invited – to come out and be part of the proud nation. Our space-taking is troubled by the fact that we are told, repeatedly, that non-white peoples and communities are "still" struggling with coming out, living visible lives, and demanding rights.

Taking space, as I experienced first-hand during this research, involves costs, negotiations, and compromises.

While celebrating our space-taking is what makes our pleasures and survivals possible, this paper considers the troubles and troublings of space-taking and space-making by racialized queer and trans people in Toronto. Toronto is often celebrated for its remarkably diverse composition because close to half its residents are first-generation immigrants (Anisef and Lanphier 2003). Yet Toronto's highly praised diversity and "multiculturalism" follows a long history of racism and racial marginalization that continues to this date (see chapter 7 by Khan and Newbold). As Eve Haque (2012) has shown, far from demolishing racial hierarchies, Canadian multicultural policy has consolidated the primacy of whiteness as the unquestioned state of Canadian nationhood by situating non-white people in an eternally unequal position in relation to whites.

Toronto is also highly celebrated for its "progressive" sexual politics: a so-called progressive city in a supposedly already progressive nation, where gay men and lesbians enjoy almost all the rights associated with full citizenship. Toronto's vibrant Gay Village and its world-known Pride are often noted with awe as a sign and evidence of Toronto's tolerance and open-mindedness. What these accounts, of course, fail to acknowledge is the growing commercialization, depoliticization, elitism, gentrification, and policing in the Gay Village (Kinsman 1996; Nash 2006; Rosser, West, and Weinmeyer 2008; Sears 2005), which unevenly serve those in positions of socio-economic privilege that overlap with gender conformity, whiteness, and cis-maleness.[1]

The complex racial politics of Toronto and its Gay Village mean that urban, including queer urban, spaces remain marginalizing to queer and trans Black and people of colour (see chapter 2 by Catungal). This, of course, does not mean that queer and trans Black and people of colour live on the margins of the city or are unable to leave any marks of their presence (see chapter 3 by Dryden). Quite the contrary. As Jin Haritaworn, Ghaida Moussa, Río Rodríguez, and Syrus Marcus Ware note in the Introduction, queer of colour communities have had a long-standing and unmistakable influence in shaping the landscape of queer art and organizing within and outside the confounds of the Gay Village

---

1 *Cis-male/female/gender* refers to a person whose gender identity matches the gender they were assigned at birth.

and politics in Toronto. Yet, as these authors aptly note, these interventions and contributions somehow never quite cut into the official or recorded maps and archives of Toronto. This lack of recognition and conversation makes memories of these interventions easily discarded, creating the illusion that they were never made. The result is a constant sense of absence, of the need to remake the same interventions time and time again. As the editors put it, we remain eternal newcomers to a scene we have long inhabited and often shaped. For those of us who came of age in the aftermath of the most visibly politicized era of gay and lesbian organizing in Toronto, I and most of the participants in my study included, entering the queer space in Toronto as a non-white subject feels at times like the daunting task of walking a path never traversed before. But, of course, the path has been walked by many of us, many times.

Despite these difficulties with "queer" spaces in Toronto, taking and making space have been integral to sexual politics and struggles in that city and North America more generally. But taking and making space necessarily rely on some form of coming out; and in the landscape we inhabit, coming out has become a compulsory step in the production of "proper" queer and trans subjecthood. Compulsory coming out tells us, as Foucault (1990) noted, again and again that professing our "true" selves to ourselves and the world is integral to our emotional health, self-actualization, personal fulfilment, and freedom. Our space-making and space-taking occur in a context in which coming out has become *the* marker of queer and trans subjecthood.

But as queer and trans Black and people of colour, we have a troubled relationship with coming out and its compulsory forces as coming out is deeply racialized. In liberal, rights-based frames of politics, coming out is entangled with discourses of progress. Like many other things that modernist thinking takes as inherent aspects of civility and progress, coming out, too, is conceived as having been initiated in the Global North and then only gradually spreading among non-white peoples. It is only a matter of time, we are told by sexuality study scholars such as Ken Plummer (1995), before more and different people come out and join the march towards liberation. The fact that queer and trans people of colour "lag behind" their white counterparts in this procession towards freedom is only a question of pace. Some are simply quicker at being liberated than others. But everyone will, eventually, come out and be free. Compulsory coming out relies on and naturalizes Euro-American vanguardism.

Of course, many queer of colour scholars have brought these narratives of coming out under great scrutiny for their racial undertones and criticized the overblown emancipatory role attributed to living open and visible sexual lives. Centring discussions of race, racism, and geopolitical inequalities, these scholars have demonstrated that coming out is not equally liberating to all subjects. My analysis in this paper is informed by this scholarship – in particular, the works of Gayatri Gopinath (2005b, 2005a, 1998, 1997, 1996) and Carlos Decena (2011) but also Jasbir Puar (2007, 1998, 1994), Martin Manalansan (2003), David Eng (2010, 1997), and Rinaldo Walcott (2012, 2007). Together, these authors convincingly argue for the importance of reading gender and sexuality through race and vice versa. Their empirical research and theoretical explorations destabilize the assumed mutual exclusivity of racial Otherness and gender and sexual non-conformity; they "colour" the queer and "queer" the colour. These scholars' works demonstrate that by exclusively emphasizing the importance of sexual visibility, compulsory coming out prioritizes gender and sexual non-conformity over racialization and overlooks the ways in which sexuality and racialization constitute one another.

Moreover, queer of colour scholarship helps us understand the ways in which the rhetoric of coming out fails to acknowledge the unequal access of people of colour to spaces of visibility materialized through the nation. Being "Canadian," for example, is not equally available to all legal citizens. As Himani Bannerji (2000) has noted, Canadian multiculturalism recreates racial hierarchies that maintain the nation white and white-centred: multiculturalism receives, centres, and situates certain bodies under the banner of "culture" and turns others into "multi-cultures." At a transnational level, queer of colour scholars show that compulsory coming out takes "modernity" as a prerequisite for sexual liberation, in ways that establish non-Westerners as the underdeveloped pasts of Western people, and they draw a developmental path from the pre-modern, homoerotic subject to the modern, liberated gay (Gopinath 1998; chap. 9).

This paper engages with the narrative of compulsory coming out from the perspective of twelve first- and second-generation, immigrant queer women and trans Black and people of colour in Toronto. Moving away from the common academic practice of using respondents' narratives as simply empirical "evidence" for theoretical explorations, in this paper I foreground my respondents' stories and present them as detailed, lived, and felt life stories. The participants in this study were recruited through my personal and academic networks, and the interviews took place between February 2013 and April 2014 in Toronto, at university campuses, participants' homes and workplaces, and coffee shops. All respondents, except for three, were born outside Canada. The Canadian-born respondents were children of first-generation immigrant parents. Eleven of the twelve respondents had at least one post-secondary degree. My respondents were primarily of working-class or lower-middle-class backgrounds, and the majority of them had strong cultural, and sometimes religious, affiliations.

Not/Selective Coming-Outs

Initially, my aim in interviewing people was to learn about the ways that racialization affects sexual subjectivity and politics. Thus, in the first few interviews, I placed very little emphasis on questions around coming out. Yet repeatedly and organically, the conversations turned to the meanings, possibilities, and un/desirability of living an open life as a gender and sexually non-conforming subject, indicating the centrality of coming out to the ways in which respondents experienced their gendered, sexual, and racial embodiment. To accommodate this unexpected flow of input, I reframed my questions in the following interviews to more directly enquire about my respondents' thoughts about and experiences with coming out. The stories that interviewees told – of their lives, their families, and their intimate relationships – provided a counter-narrative to the mainstream formulations of coming out. My informants repeatedly criticized the "developmentalist" assumptions that equated visibility with liberation (Gosine and Wekker 2009). Their complicated relationships with compulsory coming out demonstrated the ways that racial positioning and their lack of or precarious access to citizenship, national belonging, and whiteness fractured being out as a purportedly seamless state of freedom and fulfilment. This section expands on my respondents' critical engagement with coming out.

Sexual Racism and the Limits of an Encompassing Trans and Queer Subjecthood

Coming out as gay or lesbian has, without doubt, had a tremendous political significance in the sexual liberation movements in Europe and North America (Plummer 1995). Nonetheless, compulsory coming out presumes that living openly as gays and lesbians is the only or the most important concern for gender and sexually non-conforming subjects. This assumption – which can hardly be upheld given individuals' daily struggles with racism, displacement, and precarious legal status, to just name a few – shapes the lives of many queer and trans Black and people of colour (Decena 2011; Manalansan 2003). Ironically, and significantly, conventional formulations of visibility render trans subjectivities completely invisible (Edelman 2009; Stryker 2006; Zimman 2009). Living openly as subjects that are primarily or exclusively defined through their non-conforming genders and sexualities is not always an option for those whose everyday experiences are shaped by racialization, migration, and non-citizenship.

The queer women and trans Black and people of colour whom I interviewed made it abundantly clear that race and racialization are integral to their positioning in the social world. My respondents repeatedly highlighted the ways in which their non-conforming genders and sexualities affected and were affected by their racialization. For them, gender and sexual non-conformity was inseparable from their ongoing experiences of racialization, and their coming out was complicated by factors that were seemingly unrelated to gender and sexuality.

In numerous instances, participants spoke about the ways in which their own perceptions of their gender and sexuality came into conflict with racial stereotypes of what Asian, Brown, Black, Muslim, and Arab "women" and "men" are or ought to be. The deeply transphobic nature of dominant racist imaginations meant that trans respondents had also been placed in and subjected to gendered racial formulations based on what their genders appeared to be to onlookers.

A number of cis-gender respondents, too, spoke about the imposition of heterosexuality on their female bodies by racial stereotypes. Ella's entire self-presentation was formed in response to the hyper-heterosexualization of Asian women in mainstream Canadian culture. A "one-point-five" generation, Chinese Canadian, queer, cis-gender woman, she was fed up with being desired by men for "the shape of my eyes." She consciously chose androgynous clothing and hairstyles, sometimes against a deeper appreciation for her own femininity. For her, defying the submissive femininity that was forced on her supposedly heterosexually desirable body required continual and conscious effort and sacrifice, and strategic self-presentations that resisted men's preying eyes.

Elham, a Middle Eastern Arab queer woman, also shared stories of sexual racialization. Being Arab meant that she was not only often presumed to be heterosexual but also assumed to be married or married against her will. Disclosing her non-heterosexuality, moreover, exposed her to racial assumptions about her "struggles" against the supposed inability of her culture to accept her sexuality. Of course, Elham found these assumptions deeply demeaning. Not only did these assumptions degrade the culture she cherished, they also undermined the sense of agency, autonomy, and independence she exercised daily.

Lily, a Black Caribbean queer woman, also had to negotiate social contexts in which she was not, and could not, be merely a queer subject. In at least one painful incident, Lily's Blackness had overshadowed her queerness: she had been in a same-sex relationship, and when the ex-partner's family discovered this, they had reacted more negatively to her Blackness than to the queer nature of the relationship. A lifetime of experience with anti-Black racism had shaped Lily's decisions about whether and when she was to come out. Growing up with racist assumptions about her purported aggression and "hard-headedness" had made Lily wary of having to continually educate people about herself, including about her sexuality. Her Black femininity, and lack of interest in dressing "like a dandy," made her queerness unimaginable. She expressed her sense of exhaustion with coming out, which made her come out only "on an as-needed basis." In her own words, sometimes she "just want[ed] to be a person, and not ... a voice for anything."

Trans respondents also shared painful stories of gendered racism. Sparrow regularly experienced certain types of targeted harm on public transit due to their racialized and gender non-conforming embodiment. Amir also experienced hostility and aggression every day from white male strangers due to his Brown masculinity. His lived experiences before and after transitioning had made him an apt observer of the operations of male privilege, even if only partially accessible to him as a trans man, as well as gendered racism.

Sexual racism and racial stereotyping, however, were not exclusive to heterosexual circles or the general public. Nishka elaborated on the exotification of her Brown femininity by white lesbians, which in turn affected how she was read, approached, and treated in mainstream queer spaces. She was often positioned as an exotic Other whose exceptional sensuality made her a desired partner in "naughty" acts of threesome. Reliving Frantz Fanon's (1967) anguish over being read exclusively in terms of his skin colour in the encounter with a little girl in Paris, almost half a century later Nishka spoke about the painful experience of being entirely reduced to her race.

It's almost suffocating when you know that you're only ... you're only tangible to them in a particular way. That's how they perceive you.

Fundamentally, at the end of the day you're perceived by your [race], and you become desirable or undesirable to them based on ... your racialization.

Thus, being read purely in terms of their gender and sexual subjectivities was not a given for my informants. No encompassing gender or sexual subjectivity was accessible to them that would transcend their racialized positionings. As a result, race was an important factor in my participants' lives, and it sometimes determined whom they befriended, dated, or interacted with as well as their activism and community engagements. All participants spoke about the integral role of queer of colour spaces, friends, and communities in their lives. Some, like Pandi, a Brown, Indian, queer, cis-gender woman, felt completely relaxed, safe, and at ease only around other people of colour.

Being children of immigrant parents who had sacrificed much to make a better life possible for their children in Canada further complicated the situation for some of my respondents. Honouring these sacrifices and complying with familial cultures that refrained from direct discussions of sex, whether straight or queer, mediated decisions about coming out. AC had indefinitely delayed coming out in order to perform her role as the perfect daughter for her immigrant parents. Similarly, when Tino, the trans child of a Latino, single immigrant mother, came out, they were initially confronted with their mother's despair over what, in their mother's mind, amounted to a full-blown rejection of all that she had done for them to finally have a "good" life in Canada.

This desire for a good life was a recurring theme in the stories of respondents who were children of immigrant families, often surfacing in descriptions of their interactions with their parents. The desire for and emotional investment in a good life, as Sara Ahmed (2010) has argued, mediate immigrants' relationship with the nation and represent a promise of equality and happiness that is never fulfilled. Yet, to borrow from Stuart Hall (1996), no desire, including that of immigrants' longing for a good life, is innocent and free of power relations. Immigrants' longing for a good life, Sunera Thobani (2007) contends, implicates them in the ongoing colonization of Indigenous lands in Canada. The desire to acquire a good life orients immigrants towards a continual emulation of white settlers at the expense of dispossessing Indigenous peoples. Bonita Lawrence and Enakshi Dua (2005) have highlighted the ways in which immigrants can comply with, and even further, ongoing colonization in Canada.

Without discounting these realities, I would like to suggest that a rigid and negative dichotomy between immigrants and Indigenous peoples fails to account for the ways in which colonization of land and displacement of people are internally linked and co-produced. It is indeed important to account for the ways that immigrant longings for a good life on stolen lands inevitably contribute to dispossession of First Nations peoples in Canada. Yet the very processes that produce dispossession of lands also produce displacement of populations. Understanding Indigenous dispossession and migrant displacement as co-produced phenomena means understanding that one is not the *cause* of the other, but rather that both are *effects* of ongoing forms of colonialism, neocolonialism, imperialism, and geopolitical hierarchies.

All in all, my respondents' narratives repeatedly demonstrated that racialization was integral to their subjectivities and their everyday lives. Being racialized and/or of an immigrant background exceeded the limits of an encompassing and purely gendered and sexual identity. My respondents made it clear that their lives were not just about their non-conforming genders and sexualities. Yet, as Henie said, coming out had had the unfortunate effect of reducing everything to sex, and for her life was not "just about sex."

Out and Not Out: Compulsory Visibility and Agentic Invisibility

While it is tempting to suggest that the majority of my participants were not out about their sexuality and/or gender identity with their families, it is more accurate to say that my enquiries into this topic produced more uncertainties about the meanings and possibility of being completely out or absolutely closeted. Although respondents could often clearly state whether they had had "the talk" with their parents, this tangible moment did not seem to be a reliable indicator of their "outness." In some cases, respondents had been outed without being aware of it. Lily, for instance, had been outed to her grandfather, yet she had felt no difference in the way he continued to interact with her. Whether and to what extent she was outed was, thus, not completely clear to her. Hence, contrary to the common conceptions of coming out, being out was not necessarily an intentional, consciously planned, or even known state.

Moreover, having had the talk did not necessarily result in coming out. Elham, for instance, had, in fact, told her mother once about her same-sex desires years before without this affecting their relationship in any way. She had not told her father and had no intention of doing so. She deeply loved and respected her father and did not see any point in disturbing their close and peaceful relationship. For her, the information about her sexual life and partners was irrelevant to their relationship. The fact that she lived in Canada away from her family meant that she did not even feel that she was hiding anything that was culturally appropriate to disclose. Discussing sexual relationships with parents, she argued, was not part of her culture, regardless of whether the relationships were of a queer or straight nature.

Of course, in some cases, having the talk had dire consequences. Tino's relationship with their mother had gone through two years of turmoil before they were eventually able to reconnect. At the time I interviewed Tino, they had a close and loving relationship with their mother, even though their mother continued to perceive them as a cis-gender person with same-sex desires. Zubi, on the other hand, had been disowned by her family after coming out. Even though her mother had walked in on her twice having sex with a female partner, her non-heterosexuality was taken seriously only after she had come out verbally.

In a few cases, my participants had come out to, and were accepted by, their families. Afsaneh enjoyed the full support and protection of her loving mother. Amir and Pan were fully and comfortably out to their entire families. Many of the participants were out to their siblings but not parents. In other cases, particularly when participants lived with their families, the decision to come out was complicated by considerations about the anticipated tension such proclamations would create within the family.

Those of my respondents who had not declared their non-conforming genders and sexualities to their families had, nonetheless, left traces that revealed their defiance of the prescribed heterosexual path. Both Elham and Nishka had explicitly and successfully convinced their families of their lack of interest and belief in marriage. Contrary to the stereotypes that present racialized families as being incapable of listening to and respecting their daughters' unconventional choices, in particular, their families had been relatively understanding and supportive of them.

Writing about New York–based gay Dominican men, Carlos Decena (2011) has proposed the term *tacit*, in place of *out* or *closeted*, to describe his informants' states of being out. He describes being tacit as a state of being *and* not being out. Being tacit is distinct both from being silent and from speaking openly. Sometimes, Decena suggests, gender and sexual non-conformity is tacitly known and intuitively felt by family members, without being openly discussed. This seemed to apply to some of my participants' families, which in turn complicated the assumption that being out and closeted were mutually exclusive states of being.

AC's family, for example, appeared to have a very strong, unspoken knowledge of her non-heterosexuality. While she had never discussed her sexuality with her parents, other relatives had suggested to her that her family already knew. Her mother, generally a reserved and private person, had been particularly friendly and welcoming to AC's partner of two years, treating her like a member of their family. AC had also noticed her mother switching to gender-neutral terms, such as "partner" instead of "boyfriend," signalling to AC that she was aware and supportive of her relationship.

My participants' decisions to come out or not also involved the need to protect not only themselves but also their families. Since their racialized and/or immigrant families relied on networks of kin and community, safety and well-being were not merely personal but also familial concerns. The hesitations of a number of participants about coming out were informed by their desire to protect their families, particularly fathers, in the close-knit networks of extended family and community. Sometimes participants chose not to fully come out to avoid inflicting unnecessary pain on their loved ones. Decisions about disclosing or not disclosing their sexual and gender identities were made with considerable thought. While secrecy sometimes caused some nuisances in their lives, their silences were maintained agentically and allowed considerable control over the circumstances of their lives.

Many of the participants, furthermore, spoke about the call, or at times the pressure, to come out. Sometimes this pressure was experienced tacitly, while at other times, it was made explicit. Elham and AC recalled explicit conversations in which ex-partners, acquaintances, and strangers demanded that they declare their non-heterosexuality to their families. They had been told that coming out was a necessary step in becoming a proper queer subject, and even a real test of their families' worth. Elham and AC, of course, perceived these statements to be deeply individualistic, Eurocentric, and short-sighted.

Decisions about living open and visible queer lives clashed at times with decisions about self-presentation and racial and cultural embodiment. As Gayatri Gopinath (1997) has argued, queer South Asian women's seemingly "femme" presentations are often underwritten by continual negotiations between cultural and sexual identities. For

Nishka, for instance, the dominant modes of self-presentation that signify female non-heterosexuality clashed with her appreciation and love
for her culture. For example, she retained her long hair as a symbol
of her cultural background, even though this reduced her chances of
being read as a non-heterosexual woman. Letting go of culturally significant symbols was more painful to Nishka than compromising her
queer visibility.

Generally, my respondents' critical engagement with the politics of
coming out meant that they often evaluated coming out as a pragmatic
move, in terms of its practical usefulness, both to themselves and their
families. Safety was a significant factor in decisions to come out. Trans
informants, in particular, and for good reasons, were extremely cautious about whether and how they came out. Their narratives highlighted the particularly violent experiences of gender non-conforming
persons in Toronto. It is impossible to do justice to the experiences of
my trans respondents within the limits of this paper, yet I would like
to acknowledge the specificity and significance of their experiences in
this discussion.

In sum, my respondents presented coming out, *selective* coming out,
and *not* coming out as political, yet personal, choices that were made
in conversation with the realities of their racial positioning. Their decisions about coming out were informed by the politics that marked the
everyday existence of non-white subjects in the context of Toronto and
Canada.

Conclusion: Coming Out, Race, and Space

As this paper suggests, queer and trans Black and people of colour have
an ambivalent relationship to coming out. In spite of their critiques of
coming out, my respondents often considered coming out "unnecessary yet necessary." Although they rejected coming out as a political
responsibility for all, they also emphasized the importance of visibility. Those who were prominent community figures found that being
out enabled them to create more spaces for racialized trans and queer
people. These and other participants, however, also spoke about being
out as a "privilege" that, while not available to all, could be strategically
used to the benefit of queer of colour communities.

Being racialized *and* gender and sexually non-conforming in a political context that incorporates certain forms of non-heterosexuality into
the imperialist body of the nation (Puar 2007) is indeed a complicated

position. Hence, the processes through which we create our identities, and our decisions about coming out, are also complicated. Given the centrality of race and non-citizenship in the politics of homonationalism, we, as queer and trans Black and people of colour, have a troubled and troubling relationship with spaces of visibility. Our presences, and taking and making of space, at once unsettle the imagination of who can *be* queer and trans, and yet they are implicated in a landscape in which coming out is made into a necessity before *being* queer or trans can be conceived.

Acknowledgments

I am thankful to my participants for trusting me with their stories and thoughts. Meeting them and learning about their lives was the most joyful aspect of this research.

References

Ahmed, Sara. 2010. *The Promise of Happiness*. Durham, NC: Duke University Press. https://doi.org/10.1215/9780822392781.

Anisef, Paul, and C. Michael Lanphier, eds. 2003. *The World in a City*. Toronto: University of Toronto Press. https://doi.org/10.3138/9781442670259.

Bannerji, Himani. 2000. *The Dark Side of the Nation: Essays on Multiculturalism, Nationalism and Gender*. Toronto: Canadian Scholars' Press.

Decena, Carlos. 2011. *Tacit Subjects: Belonging and Same-Sex Desire amongst Dominican Immigrant Men*. Durham, NC: Duke University Press. https://doi.org/10.1215/9780822393900.

Edelman, Elijah Adiv. 2009. "The Power of Stealth: (In)visible Sites of Female-to-Male Transsexual Resistance." In *Out in Public: Reinventing Lesbian/Gay Anthropology in a Globalizing World*, edited by Ellen Lewin and William L. Leap, 164–79. Malden, UK: Wiley-Blackwell. https://doi.org/10.1002/9781444310689.ch9.

Eng, David L. 1997. "Out Here and Over There: Queerness and Diaspora in Asian American Studies." *Social Text* 15 (3/4): 31–52.

– 2010. *The Feeling of Kinship: Queer Liberalism and the Racialization of Intimacy*. Durham, NC: Duke University Press. https://doi.org/10.1215/9780822392828.

Fanon, Frantz. 1967. *Black Skin, White Mask*, translated by Charles Lam Markmann. New York: Grove Press.

Foucault, Michel. 1990. *An Introduction*. Vol. 1, *The History of Sexuality*, translated by Robert Hurley. New York: Pantheon Books.

Gopinath, Gayatri. 1996. "Funny Boys and Girls: Notes on a Queer South Asian Planet." In *Asian American Sexualities: Dimensions of the Gay and Lesbian Experience*, edited by Russell Leong, 119–27. London: Routledge.
– 1997. "Nostalgia, Desire, Diaspora: South Asian Sexualities in Motion." *Positions* 5 (2): 467–89. https://doi.org/10.1215/10679847-5-2-467.
– 1998. "On Fire." *GLQ: A Journal of Lesbian and Gay Studies* 4 (4): 631–6.
– 2005a. "Bollywood Spectacles: Queer Diasporic Critique in the Aftermath of 9/11." *Social Text* 23 (3–4): 157–69.
– 2005b. *Impossible Desire: Queer Diasporas and South Asian Public Cultures*. Durham, NC: Duke University Press.
Gosine, Andil, and Gloria Wekker. 2009. "Politics and Passion: A Conversation with Gloria Wekker." *Caribbean Review of Gender Studies* 3: 1–11.
Hall, Stuart. 1996. "New Ethnicities." In *Stuart Hall: Critical Dialogues in Cultural Studies*, edited by Dave Morley and Kuan-Hsing Chen, 441–9. New York: Routledge.
Haque, Eve. 2012. *Multiculturalism within a Bilingual Framework: Language, Race, and Belonging in Canada*. Toronto: University of Toronto Press.
Kinsman, Gary. 1996. *The Regulation of Desire: Homo and Hetero Sexualities*. Montreal: Black Rose Books.
Lawrence, Bonita, and Enakshi Dua. 2005. "Decolonizing Antiracism." *Social Justice* 32 (4): 120–43.
Manalansan, Martin F., IV. 2003. *Global Divas: Filipino Gay Men in the Diaspora*. Durham, NC: Duke University Press. https://doi.org/10.1215/9780822385172.
Nash, Catherine Jean. 2006. "Toronto's Gay Village (1969–1982): Plotting the Politics of Gay Identity." *Canadian Geographer* 50 (1): 1–16. https://doi.org/10.1111/j.0008-3658.2006.00123.x.
Plummer, Ken. 1995. *Telling Sexual Stories: Power, Change and Social Worlds*. London: Routledge. https://doi.org/10.4324/9780203425268.
Puar, Jasbir. 1994. "Writing My Way 'Home': Travelling South Asian Bodies and Diasporic Journeys." *Socialist Review* 24 (4): 75–108.
– 1998. "Transnational Sexualities: South Asian (Trans)Nation(alism)s and Queer Diasporas." In *Q & A: Queer in Asian America*, edited by David Eng and Alice Hom, 405–22. Philadelphia, PA: Temple University Press.
– 2007. *Terrorist Assemblages: Homonationalism in Queer Times*. Durham, NC: Duke University Press.
Rosser, B.R. Simon, William West, and Richard Weinmeyer. 2008. "Are Gay Communities Dying or Just in Transition? Results from an International Consultation Examining Possible Structural Change in Gay Communities." *AIDS Care* 20 (5): 588–95. https://doi.org/10.1080/09540120701867156.

Sears, Alan. 2005. "Queer Anti-Capitalism: What's Left of Lesbian and Gay Liberation?" *Science and Society* 69 (1): 92–112. https://doi.org/10.1521/siso.69.1.92.56800.

Stryker, Susan. 2006. "(De)Subjugated Knowledges: An Introduction to Transgender Studies." In *The Transgender Studies Reader*, edited by Susan Stryker and Stephen Whittle, 1–17. New York: Routledge.

Thobani, Sunera. 2007. *Exalted Subjects: Studies in the Making of Race and Nation in Canada*. Toronto: University of Toronto Press.

Walcott, Rinaldo. 2007. "Somewhere Out There: The New Black Queer Theory." In *Blackness and Sexualities*, edited by Michelle M. Wright and Antje Schuhmann, 29–40. Berlin: Lit Verlag.

– 2012. "Outside in Black Studies: Reading from a Queer Place in the Diaspora." In *Queerly Canadian: An Introductory Reader in Sexuality Studies*, edited by Maureen FitzGerald and Scott Rayter, 23–34. Toronto: Canadian Scholars' Press.

Zimman, Lal. 2009. "'The Other Kind of Coming Out': Transgender People and the Coming Out." *Gender and Language* 3 (1): 53–80. https://doi.org/10.1558/genl.v3i1.53.

11 The Sacred Uprising: Indigenous Creative Activisms

AN INTERVIEW WITH REBEKA TABOBONDUNG
BY SYRUS MARCUS WARE[1]

Rebeka Tabobondung is a multimedia artist who creates video and new media works. She is the co-founder of Maaiingan Productions, an Indigenous-led graphic design and arts company, and *MUSKRAT Magazine*, an online magazine of Indigenous activism, art, and movement-building. Rebeka divides her time between her reserve on Perry Island and Tkaronto. While head of the University of Toronto's Centre for Women and Trans People, Rebeka facilitated a large-scale town hall and several small-scale meetings to usher in a new era of gender freedom, which rooted trans and gender fluidity in an Indigenous world view. One of the results of her work was the renaming of the centre to be inclusive of trans and gender-variant people. Rebeka's well-known video, *The Original Summit: Journey to the Sacred Uprising*, documented the experiences of a bus full of queer, trans, and allied Black, Indigenous, and people of colour (BIPOC) from Toronto to the Free Trade Area of the Americas summit in Quebec City in 2001. Considering this large-scale movement-building as part of a much larger global uprising, Rebeka's film offers insights into BIPOC queer, trans, and allied communities in the late 1990s and early 2000s. She challenges the white-centred and -led activism that was prevalent in many early-2000s movement spaces in the city, instead remapping a genealogy of the BIPOC resistance that shaped the city.

In the following pages, Rebeka speaks about these projects and highlights how they resist the erasure of Indigenous people, histories, and lands, and help Indigenous and people of colour who are queer,

---

1 We thank Anupama Aery for transcribing this interview.

Two-spirited, or trans arrive at different understandings of themselves, their histories, and their presents. Rebeka is joined by Syrus Marcus Ware, a visual artist, community mobilizer, educator, and researcher from Toronto, with whom she shares part of her journey. In this conversation, the two discuss fifteen years of activism and point us to the power of artistic practice in not only challenging dominant histories but also building and sustaining communities. Along the way, they share their insights into archiving histories lost or buried through colonization, the spaces that brought them to reclaim their identities, and the connections among anti-colonial and anti-racist struggles, Indigenous self-determination, and queer and trans movements. In these histories, as Ferguson noted, struggles for space are tied to struggles of time (quoted in Dinshaw et al. 2007). Thus, the struggle to claim space for queer and trans Black, Indigenous, and people of colour at the University of Toronto is tied to that institution's history as a branch of settler-colonial conquest, and the struggle must therefore reject nationalist tellings of history by supporting Indigenous autonomy. This also applies to the struggle to claim space within activist movements. Thus, the fight against neo-liberalism in Quebec is shot through with Québécois calls for sovereignty, which reinscribe the erasure of Indigenous peoples.

REBEKA: My name is Rebeka Tabobondung, and I am of mixed ancestry. I am Anishnaabe Ojibway from Wasauksing First Nation. I'm Beaver Clan. My mother was born in Holland, and I grew up in over fifteen towns and cities across Canada, but I've been back in the traditional territories of my Anishnaabe ancestry for the last twenty years. I am a publisher and founder of *MUSKRAT Magazine*. I've been involved in media arts and activism for a very long time. I'm very passionate about storytelling, and it's kind of ironic that your project is archiving the work or activities we were involved in fifteen years ago because we didn't really archive it back then. In my own activism, the question of archiving has evolved to telling stories, to capturing and then disseminating them.

What I saw as a young Native person fifteen years ago within mainstream activist circles was a real lack of analysis or acknowledgment of the impacts of colonization and colonialism. It made the activism of that time and my involvement feel very, very shallow because it did not go into the depth of history, of Canadian history, or the history of any of the places in which the activism took place. So it was basically liberal people on stolen Native land that were espousing leadership around progressive values, while there was, like, a huge elephant in the room about colonial experience and devastation and theft. Basically the lies of what Canada is all about.

The power imbalances that were existing weren't discussed. At the time I was working at the University of Toronto, at what was then still called the Women's Centre. There were a lot of people of colour activists there who were really involved in embracing a larger analysis around colonialism but also around race and culture and identity. As an Indigenous person, I really connected to that cause. As a result of colonization I, and many Indigenous folks from my generation, were subject to an assimilationist policy against Indigenous people. Growing up, our culture was practically erased, as were our languages, by residential schools. I didn't even hear my language until I was in my twenties, not only because I was disconnected from my community physically but because my father's generation was shamed into not speaking their languages – my father's first language was Ojibway. This was probably reinforced by their own parents, who wanted them to be successful in the "white man's world," so they were encouraged to assimilate in order to survive. I could really relate to what the activists at the Women's Centre at the time called "identity politics." But I don't want to call it identity politics because it's really just acknowledgment of who we are, and that matters to me.

SYRUS: This moment in the late 1990s saw a lot of change around how we organized, and so much labour by those on the margins pushing for more intersectional analysis in our activist movements, making space for all of us to fight for self-determination. Can you say more about your experiences within the largely queer and trans activism at the centre at that time?

REBEKA: That's why I really connected to people like you, people who were valuing their cultural identity and looking at how it was impacted by the mainstream and by colonization. Those that considered how it's so important to make those connections to race and, of course, beyond that to gender and sexuality. Just understanding that this Western lens is so, so rigid and confining – that it's really just a lens, and there's so much more beyond that. That's how I became very passionate with my first documentary, *The Sacred*

Uprising, about our journey to Quebec City in 2001. We were going to protest this globalization – this neo-liberal globalization – but I felt I was also going with a lens of how that connects to Indigenous lands and Indigenous rights and environmental justice. It was really, really important for me, when I was in Quebec City, to understand what the Indigenous history there was. Because so much of the mainstream narrative at the time was just the question of Quebec sovereignty and how Quebecers had the right to self-determination, and while I think everybody has a right to self-determination, you can't silence one, erase their history, steal their land, and just assert your culture and yourself and dominate. That was the subject matter of my documentary. I was making those connections to our activism and colonialism. And I very much did it to share that with my fellow activists. I felt like they weren't, at the time, thinking very deeply, as deeply as they needed to, to really transform things.

SYRUS: Which is what we wanted to do: we wanted to transform and build a just society. We went together on a bus that was all people of colour, Indigenous people, and some white trans people. We were so frustrated by the open calls for "all activists" to head to Quebec to fight without any consideration of the different kinds of risk we would each experience on the front lines. So we hired a seventy-five-person bus and went as a big, solid group of Indigenous, [people of colour], and trans folks committed to making sure we all made it back out of Quebec together. And you had interactions with other Indigenous activists in Quebec, some of which are featured in *Journey to the Sacred Uprising*.

REBEKA: At the time, the late Rodney Bobiwash was a mentor of mine. He was an Anishnaabe activist who also had a very broad lens around making connections and valuing other forms of knowledge and building on that through activism. He was making links between people in the north and the south, especially among Indigenous people. At the time in Toronto, it felt like the Indigenous activist community, at the University of Toronto, was not exactly a big community. There weren't a lot of Indigenous students, and those that were there were in kind of survival mode. Many were older students coming back to school after being away for a while, and they had lots of family responsibilities, and so there was not a lot of leadership in that kind of activism stream. I remember at the time, too, the connections with OPIRG[2] and the Women's Centre. They really wanted to support Indigenous spaces, the creation of Indigenous spaces, and leadership for students at the University of Toronto.

I was the president of the Native Students' Association, and so one of the ways that we thought that it could be supported was through creating a new, autonomous Native Students' Association that was funded by the students themselves. I remember trying to build support for that with Indigenous students at the university at the time. They were very supportive, but the administration's stance was to "squash that as quickly as possible!" – to not rock the boat. They said that if we tried to push for too much, all funding for Indigenous programs at U of T could be threatened. So we were faced with quite a hostile environment. And, therefore, the support dwindled, too – people were scared to support us. It took a while. I felt like during the years spent at the Women's Centre, we were really dedicated. We recognized that it was a very special and unique place, where people of colour, trans people, and Indigenous people were actually the leaders. In a lot of other universities, that's not the case, right? We really wanted to build a foundation there. We recognized that student leadership doesn't usually last for years as people build their careers, get their education, and then move on. But we really felt that when the time did come to move on, we wanted to leave a strong foundation.

And so that's why it was really important to us to change the name of the centre to the Centre for Women and Trans People. That was huge! We needed to show our community that we [were] "walking the talk." The space was open to exploring gender beyond the binary. At the time, fields like women's studies weren't embracing gender variance. Not to say that we were the only ones; there was a centre in Montreal that did this, too. We had travelled to Montreal for "The Fire This Time," a grassroots conference in the early 2000s, and to meet with the Dragon Root Centre to find out

---

2 OPIRG stands for Ontario Public Interest Research Group. In Canada and the United States, the "PIRGs" have been key sites of radical and progressive student activism since the 1970s. On many campuses, they model queer of colour and other intersectional, anti-oppressive politics and employment practices in ways that surpass hiring, admissions, and curricular practices by the universities.

more about how they processed their name change and programming shifts. We were looking to them for leadership. Their name
was based on a flower that had both sexes. We were inspired by
them. But we also faced opposition back home. We had our funding threatened by the Graduate Students' Union, which showed
that many people were not able to accept the idea of gender beyond their traditional thinking.

SYRUS: How does this relate to the overlap in the other organizing?
It's so interesting that, in that specific building in which the centre
was located, you had (and still have) many activist orgs: you had
First Nations House, you had OPIRG, you had the centre. We were
all trying to decolonize our activism, and we were really thinking
about the ways that this forced gender binary was totally connected to an experience of colonialism. In a way, this illustrates the lack
of decolonization within those spaces, within the student movement. It showed the work that most student activists still needed to
do to try to understand the reality of [being] Two-spirited, gender-
variant, and really, just all humans be able to be in this space and
work together.

REBEKA: I identified as bisexual, but even in my own life, I was still
kind of in the closet. I felt like the attitudes in my community,
in Wasauksing First Nation, made it hard to be out. I was going
through a process of reconnecting with my community there. I felt
like, at that time, it was not an open space to be out. There was
a lot of judgment around Two-spirited people, so I felt that tension for myself personally because I wanted to be accepted there.
[Laughs.] But at the same time, being in the city, I felt, was also
tough. I was hearing some teachings about what Two-spirited
meant, what it means. And it was such a very positive perspective!
That really spoke to me, and it was just such an open, unconfining
analysis or perspective of what gender is. To me, it just resonated
so much. So I wanted to connect more with teachings around being Two-spirited. I wanted to share that kind of exploration, share
what is happening with other people like myself. When we would
do workshops, we would ask, What is gender? What is sex? We'd
always conclude that it was like a circle, with lots of different possibilities which you cannot define. [Laughs.] And that's the beauty
of it; that's a positive thing!

This was part of how we started Maaiingan Productions! My
partner, Dave, is a graphic designer, and we created a collective of

Indigenous artists, designers, and photographers that wanted to support each other's work. We also had a larger vision of sharing those skills with other Indigenous communities, supporting Indigenous messaging in Toronto and beyond. That was part of having grown up in Canada – we grow up with a lack of Indigenous media representation. We lack even just educational awareness. There is a silencing of Indigenous history in the public school system ... anything beyond the fur trade. [Laughs.] Just to see ourselves represented so poorly in the media, and always portrayed through a Western lens, one that paints Indigenous people with all of these myths – for example, that we live off subsidies. Meanwhile, Canada actually lives off Indigenous people subsidizing Canada – it's a contradiction! The reason why Canada is rich is because of Indigenous land and resources. All these stereotypes about Indigenous people being lazy, being drunks – these are the things that still dominate the media, that create a public impression.

I think that the 1990s was the era where we first had the technological access and the media arts skills, where we first had power. We had access to cameras, portable cameras, and editing suites, and so we could just go out and just do it. That was a super-exciting time! We could also become entrepreneurs because we could own that equipment for ourselves. It was interesting to watch the impacts of this work. I remember being at the centre, and you used to make the most beautiful posters. We would use collage and make photocopies. It's almost like a lost art now – it was such a creative process!

SYRUS: Exactly! We'd go make photocopies, and it would be a movement-building activity because while we're making and cutting and pasting, we'd be talking and brainstorming. It's that kind of interaction that becomes a collaboration, rather than just sitting alone at your laptop, clicking your mouse. Digital art-making is a fine way to work; it's just a different process.

REBEKA: Now we can look back on that – and it's nostalgic – we see the value of that. And we certainly valued the creative beauty of it. Because they were such beautiful posters that we hung up with pride! But the thing was, I think, we also saw the power of the Internet to get our messaging across. I looked at other social movements and was inspired by the Zapatistas and the Native Youth Movement in BC, how they were bringing their cameras out. And now we see it happening in the States: everyone's got a camera. At that point we didn't, but once we had access to them, we brought the cameras out when we protested. That was our security. A way to document and to share that with the world and hold the law enforcement accountable.

I remember at that time, every once in a while, you'd get these underground videotapes. We'd talk to other Native activists, and they would pass around videocassettes documenting these activist movements. For example, we received these underground videos about the Gustafsen Lake Stand-Off.[3] And we received other videos from the Native Youth Movement. The videos were proof of what was happening: "Yes, this really happened; look, watch this video!" I remember screening stuff like that at U of T. We had our own little video or film presentations in which we shared these videos. They were not out in the public discourse because uploading things to the Internet and sharing them via social media, the way we share videos now, hadn't even been invented. I think that technology has been so exciting! That is what I see now, how my activism has evolved. I just finished a short doc called *Spirit of Birth* (2015), which is about traditional birth knowledge and reclaiming space in Toronto through the Birth Centre. I'm still using technology to tell these stories.

As a result, I now have access to these pools of Indigenous people. Our communities are so connected; we can share information within our own networks. We're so networked, yet there's still so much work to be done to share messaging about an Indigenous point of view and an Indigenous lens on pretty much everything. And in Canada, where the political climate right now is very oppressive towards activism, towards dissent, the arts is a sector and field in which you can get away with saying a lot in the name of art. 'Cause art values expression! [Laughs.]

SYRUS: You've been making art that connects to your activism for decades. Can you tell us about the creation of your online publication, *MUSKRAT Magazine*?

REBEKA: *MUSKRAT Magazine* is an online Indigenous arts and culture magazine. We're funded through the arts councils, and it's

---

3 The Gustafsen Lake Stand-Off stemmed from the long-standing conflict over unceded Secwecmec/Shuswap land in the interior of British Columbia. In 2015, it resulted in a month-long stand-off at Gustafsen Lake between the Ts'peten Defenders and the Royal Canadian Mounted Police and Canadian military.

such a beautiful window to share Indigenous points of view and Indigenous world view. I felt extremely motivated to learn about connections [among] family, spiritual world, activism, and art. I'm glad to be able to document this for my child and my community and digitize and archive it. By doing so, I hope to breathe life into it, through different art projects, broadcasting, and publishing. What we share through art then leads to critical commentary. We're inspired by our recreation story: the story of the muskrat. At the time of a great flood, there was a sky woman who had rested on the back of a turtle. Muskrat was the weakest of all of the water animals that were there at the time. All of them had tried to dive down to the bottom to bring some earth back for sky woman to be able to make land, but couldn't. It was muskrat – the humble muskrat – who had the courage and the strength. In the end, he was the only one that was successful, and he brought that earth to the top.

I feel like that story has so many teachings; it's so important, and it helps to celebrate our values as Indigenous people: our celebration of who we are as people within the larger universe, that we're connected and dependent on the natural world and the animals, but also that we all have the power to change the world through our actions, even though we are led to believe that we don't have any power, when we actually do have power. We need to believe that we do and perceive that we do because, as I was saying, this is Indigenous land! We are resilient, and we have the tools via technology to share those perspectives and not be silenced. Hopefully we can share that with the broader world. I think that people could benefit from making connections to these teachings, but certainly *we* can benefit as Indigenous people by understanding and building a positive cultural identity.

MUSKRAT brings art, storytelling, articles together and then connects them to the idea of using all of the tools available to disseminate the information because having this online creates an access. We find that a lot of our content is shared immensely within our niche Indigenous networks, but then it does break through to other media as well. We see *MUSKRAT* as an archive. It is itself also a repository of things that happened in our community and all of the amazing work and elder people that should be heard. That's also reflected in our current partnership with Rez Radio 91, which is a storytellers' festival, interviewing local storytellers and keepers of stories and knowledge. They will be celebrated and honoured, and their stories will be documented through a combination of interviews, video, audio. That's content for us, but we also see it as documenting and preserving our cultural stories. If you go to our magazine, there's a really great little piece that explains the history of the muskrat and how it helps us shape our understandings. It's a great interpretation of the teaching.

References

Dinshaw, Carolyn, Lee Edelman, Roderick A. Ferguson, Carla Freccero, Elizabeth Freeman, Judith Halberstam, Annamarie Jagose, Christopher S. Nealon, and Tan Hoang Nguyen. 2007. "Theorizing Queer Temporalities: A Roundtable Discussion." *GLQ: A Journal of Lesbian and Gay Studies* 13 (2): 177–95.
Kahgee, Adrian, and Rebeka Tabobondung, dir. 2002. *The Original Summit: Journey to the Sacred Uprising*. Maaiingan Productions. Videocassette, 43 min.
Tabobondung, Rebeka, dir. 2015. *Spirit of Birth*. 11:49 min.

Epilogue: Caressing in Small Spaces

JIN HARITAWORN

We ought not to be able to keep from imagining the real assembly – the gathering of things in the flesh, of fantasy in the hold – as the fecund caress of earth/commune/school/lab/jam/(collective) head, where the performed devotion of calling and responding in an arrangement refuses every enclosure of its resources.

– Fred Moten

The eleven chapters in this book explore what it might look like to make space and take space beyond the enclosures brought here with European settlement. As Moten (2017) makes clear, this settler-colonial logic of enclosure pervades everything: from the university and the non-profit – reserved for the reproduction of bourgeois subjects destined to rescue and control Black, brown, and working-class populations – to the carceral, neo-liberal city – territorialized on land that is cyclically cleansed, flipped, fenced off, objectified, and "regenerated" for the productive and consumptive use of the properly alive.

The contributors to *Queering Urban Justice* approach the urban along with the political and epistemic logics that naturalize and evolve from it. The spaces that they make across all these different and related sectors resist territoriality, securitization, and ownership. These spaces are frequently ephemeral. Their inhabitants swap fecund caresses – both tender and critical – at the corner, on the steps, in the park, and at the kitchen table. They pursue socialities that are dangerous to the army of politicians, planners, police people, and business owners who are busily staking out the borders of gay villages and neo-liberal cities, here and across the postmodern world. The politics that result from these palimpsestic encounters are not meant to stay in the air-conditioned offices of an NGO. They go beyond a carceral, acquisitive politics of rights and protection. They seek not recognition by, but abolition of, the regime of murderous inclusions that variously uses and discards us. Their knowledges are frequently forged outside the academic classroom. They expropriate the resources that the racial and colonial university has extracted from Black, Indigenous, and racialized peoples and put them back in our communities' service.

The pages in this book thus make contributions along multiple scales. Love letters to the city they are rooted in, they both leave and remember their mark on social movements in Toronto – a city that has often disowned and forgotten the decades-long leadership of queer and trans Black, Indigenous, and people of colour (QTBIPOC). At the same time, they recognize that cities, and the presence in them of Black, Indigenous, and people of colour with vastly incommensurate relationships to the land, and immensely under-appreciated paradigms of using and sharing space, are the products of globalization.[1] Cities arrived on Turtle Island and in other colonized places along with Europeans, and they continue to grow as a result of what Harsha Walia (2013) refers to as "border imperialism": the ongoing dispossession, displacement, and often involuntary migration of poor, racialized, and Indigenous peoples, both here and in the Global South, as a direct consequence of Global North capital. In this genealogy of the neo-liberal city, the gay village – peopled by properly modern homosexuals who double as consumers and ascendant border guards against the dark masses – is but the latest outgrowth of the enclosure.

As explained in the editors' introduction to this book, the urban justice perspective that emerges here differs from existing accounts of sexual minorities and the city. An increasing number of authors now critique the celebratory takes on "queer space" for euphemizing queer gentrification and the replication of acquisitive and securitized

---

1 As Rikke Mananzala, former director of the queer of colour youth organization FIERCE and a member of Right to the City – New York City, puts it, "The daily issues in our communities – like the experiences of low-wage service workers or people getting displaced from their homes through gentrification – are expressions of national and international trends, specifically how neoliberalism has transformed our cities. That's why our local organizations have formed alliances that are national in scale with international analysis" (quoted in Goldberg 2008, n.p.).

approaches to land and territory by urban LGBT communities (FIERCE 2008; Hanhardt 2013; Manalansan 2005). In my book *Queer Lovers and Hateful Others*, on queer of colour organizing in Berlin, I propose the term "queer regeneration" to explain the classed and raced dynamics that frequently accompany the city-sanctioned development of queer neighbourhoods in neo-liberal cities (Haritaworn 2015). In the era of the creative city, queers with race and class privileges are hailed as first-wave gentrifiers and encouraged to move into neighbourhoods that are on the brink of gentrification. Meanwhile, racialized communities, the majority of whom in Berlin are made up of former guest workers and their descendants, are pushed out of areas in which they were long confined through racist and classist policies of residential segregation. White queers who are moving into these neighbourhoods have actively participated in marking their racialized neighbours as patriarchal, homophobic, violent, and criminal. Through moral panics over homophobic and transphobic hate crimes, they have delivered cultural scripts of vulnerable queers who need protection from hateful Others in the dangerous inner city.

Queer regeneration here describes the simultaneous revitalization of the inner city and of the white queer lifestyles, identities, and embodiments that get to rebrand this transitional space. The term *regeneration* is a play on gender and genre: it describes the (incomplete) transition of race- and class-privileged queers from "degenerates," whose genders and sexualities are considered criminal, mad and perverse, to aspiring citizens who are encouraged to reproduce socially, biologically, and spatially. It describes, simultaneously, the transfer of degeneracy from regenerating spaces to the degenerate bodies that linger there, whose expulsion is the condition for the revitalization of those spaces.

Like *Queer Lovers*, *Queering Urban Justice* is both invested in the local environment where we live, work, and play and highlights lessons that go beyond the local (see Gosine and Teelucksingh 2008). The anthology is indeed the first queer of colour–themed collection on urban justice internationally that we co-editors are aware of. At the same time, we look on a proud legacy of queer of colour–led urban interventions. Ever since the queer and trans of colour youth group FIERCE (Fabulous Independent Educated Radicals for Community Empowerment) defended the Christopher Street piers in New York as part of the Right to the City coalition, the link between urban justice and QTBIPOC cannot be unthought (see Right to the City – New York City 2009). Like few other sites, the piers, most famous as the setting for *Paris Is Burning*, the contentious documentary of the house/ball scene that introduced vogueing to a white, cis public, symbolize the queerness of urban justice. There, Stonewall warriors Sylvia Rivera and Marsha P. Johnson once sheltered houseless and sex-working youth as part of their legendary group Street Transvestite Action Revolutionaries (see chapter 1 by Haritaworn, Gossett, Rodríguez, and Ware). Long after Rivera's and Johnson's passings, low-income youth unable to perform consumer citizenship in the increasingly corporatized and securitized West Village fought to stay on the piers, which they claimed as a queer of colour, affirming cultural space where you do not need to consume to belong.

As discussed in the first chapter, our roundtable with Che Gossett, Río Rodríguez, and Syrus Marcus Ware, queer of colour spaces like the piers are not confined to New York, even if urban justice movements in other cities have been slower to incorporate a queer and trans analysis. In Toronto, "The Steps" in front of the Second Cup at the heart of the Church-Wellesley village, long a gathering spot for low-income youth, fell prey to a coalition of business owners and city planners seeking to "beautify" the "gaybourhood" (Ramirez, forthcoming; Rodriguez 2016). The street corner continues to be an important space where trans sex workers in Toronto prefigure alternative ways of organizing, however embattled by homeowners, condo developers, planners and politicians, and homonormative non-profits, which capitalize on trans of colour struggles by turning them into lucrative raw material that can be extracted for status and funding (Forrester, forthcoming).

As the authors in this book demonstrate, the right to the city always already intersects with racial, economic, gender, and disability justice. It addresses both material and cultural questions: How is city space distributed? Who is left with its costs and benefits (see Gosine and Teelucksingh 2008)? Who owns the city both materially and culturally? Who gets to brand it? Who is reflected in its design, its archives, and its monuments? Who is remembered and commemorated (see chapter 3 by Dryden)? Whose histories of arrival, whose contributions to artistic and political movements are honoured, taught, published, and institutionalized (see chapters 2 by Catungal; 4 by Diaz, Largo, and Pino; 6 by Ejiogu and Ware)? Whose presences are violently policed and displaced (see chapters 8 by Atluri, 7 by Khan and Newbold, 3 by Dryden)? What acts, identities, and socialities does the urban architecture of settler colonialism carve out for us?

What alternatives to these maps and moulds already exist – what methods of surviving and thriving have we innovated, often without knowing it? What contributions have QTBIPOC made to understanding and contesting colonialism and Occupation, both here and in Palestine (see chapter 9 by Abu Hatoum and Moussa, the interview with Tabobondung in chapter 11)? What possibilities of gender and sexuality exist beyond the narrow politics of visibility and coming out that is dictated to us as the only way to be queer (see chapter 10 by Masoumi)? What tools, skills, and experiences do QTBIPOC have to offer broader urban movements – sharing space, dealing with conflict, and building communities that prefigure the world we want to live in (see chapter 5 by Chin)? How do we refuse the biopolitical and geopolitical paradigm of space and its proper uses brought here by settler colonialism, and support and learn from Indigenous struggles to reclaim the land from its imposed status of enclosure into an agentic being (Simpson 2014)? How do those of us whose ancestries are not from here refuse settler cultures, while acknowledging our own complicities, and without further appropriating the struggles of the peoples on whose lands we arrived as uninvited visitors (Lawrence and Dua 2005; Thobani 2014)?

The chapters in this book thus go beyond the model of rights and inclusion that was always reserved for the entitled few. They denaturalize the assumptions that more of us need to own homes or businesses, which must be defended from dangerous Black and brown populations. They reject inclusion in a property and protection paradigm of space whose bases are properly located in settler colonialism, anti-Blackness, and border imperialism. In the place of citizenship rights, the authors gathered here assert a right to the city that QTBIPOC communities have ample practice of exercising. The spaces we have caressed in may be few and small. May we continue to use them well, fumbling our way beyond enclosure.

References

FIERCE. 2008. "LGBTQ Youth Fight for a S.P.O.T. on Pier 40." Press release (15 September). http://fiercenyc.org/media/docs/3202_PublicHearing PressRelease.

Forrester, Monica. Forthcoming. "Organizing on the Corner: Trans Women of Colour and Sex Worker Activism in Toronto in the 1980s and 1990s." In *Marvellous Grounds,* edited by Jin Haritaworn, Ghaida Moussa, and Syrus Marcus Ware.

Goldberg, Harmony. 2008. "Building Power in the City: Reflections on the Emergence of the Right to the City Alliance and the National Domestic

Worker's Alliance." *In the Middle of a Whirlwind* (website). Accessed 24 May 2017. https://inthemiddleofthewhirlwind.wordpress.com/building-power-in-the-city/.

Gosine, Andil, and Cheryl Teelucksingh. 2008. *Environmental Justice and Racism in Canada: An Introduction.* Toronto: Emond Montgomery.

Hanhardt, Christina B. 2008. "Butterflies, Whistles, and Fists: Gay Safe Streets Patrols and the New Gay Ghetto, 1976–1981." *Radical History Review* 2008 (100): 61–85.

Haritaworn, Jin. 2015. *Queer Lovers and Hateful Others: Regenerating Violent Times and Places.* London: Pluto. https://doi.org/10.2307/j.ctt183p5vv.

Lawrence, Bonita, and Enakshi Dua. 2005. "Decolonizing Antiracism." *Social Justice* 32 (4): 120–43.

Manalansan, Martin F., IV. 2005. "Race, Violence, and Neoliberal Spatial Politics in the Global City." *Social Text* 23 (84–5): 141–56.

Moten, Fred. 2017. "Collective Head." *Women & Performance* (online journal) 26 (2–3). Accessed 23 May 2017. https://www.womenandperformance.org/bonus-articles-1/26-2-3-moten.

Ramirez, Aemilius. Forthcoming. "Speaking Our Truths, Building Our Futures: Arts-Based Organizing in QTBIPOC Communities in Toronto." In *Marvellous Grounds*, edited by Jin Haritaworn, Ghaida Moussa, and Syrus Marcus Ware.

Right to the City – New York City. 2009. "Policy Platform." Accessed 20 May 2017. http://www.fiercenyc.org/sites/default/files/resources/0944_RTTCNYCPlatform.pdf.

Rodriguez, Gabriela. 2016. "Mapping QTBIPOC Toronto." A major portfolio submitted in partial fulfilment of a master's degree in environmental studies, York University, Toronto.

Simpson, Leanne Betasamosake. 2014. "Not Murdered, Not Missing: Rebelling against Colonial Gender Violence." Blog post, 8 March. Accessed 30 December 2016. https://www.leannesimpson.ca/writings/not-murdered-not-missing-rebelling-against-colonial-gender-violence.

Thobani, Sunera. 2014. Prologue to *Queer Necropolitics*, edited by Jin Haritaworn, Adi Kuntsman, and Silvia Posocco, xv–xviii. London: Routledge.

Walia, Harsha. 2012. *Undoing Border Imperialism.* Oakland, CA: AK Press.

Contributors

Nayrouz Abu Hatoum is a visiting scholar at the City Institute at York University and an adjunct professor in the Department of Sociology at Ryerson University, both in Toronto. She completed her PhD in social anthropology at York University. Her doctoral research, titled "Framing Absence: Visuals of the Wall and the Vanishing Landscapes in Palestine," explores both Palestinian and Israeli relationships with the bordered and violent landscapes in Palestine. Her work has been published in *Visual Anthropology Review* (2017) and *Min Fami: Arab Feminist Reflections on Identity, Space and Resistance* (Inanna Publications, 2014).

Tara Atluri has a PhD in sociology. She is part of artistic initiatives and social movements in the Indian subcontinent and around the globe. Her writing has been published in scholarly and popular media such as magazines, newspapers, and blogs. In 2016, she published *Āzādi: Sexual Politics and Postcolonial Worlds* (Demeter Press, 2016). This book discusses the protests that occurred following the 2012 Delhi gang rape case and the 2013 decision by the Supreme Court of India to uphold section 377 of the Indian Penal Code, which criminalizes "unnatural" sexual acts, thus effectively making queerness criminal in India. Atluri's second book, *Uncommitted Crimes: The Defiance of the Artistic Imagi/nation* (Inanna Publications, 2017), was published in 2017. This text discusses dissident art as a form of political protest. The title is taken from Theodor Adorno's assertion that "every work of art is an uncommitted crime."

John Paul Catungal is Instructor I (tenure-track) at the Institute for Gender, Race, Sexuality and Social Justice, University of British Columbia,

Vancouver. He received his PhD in geography from the University of Toronto, where he researched the racial geographies of ethno-specific, community-based, sexual health promotion and social service provision in Toronto. He is a recipient of the Governor General's Gold Medal for Academic Excellence, the Canadian Association of Geographers' Star-key-Robinson Award, and the American Association of Geographers' J. Warren Nystrom Award. He has co-edited *Filipinos in Canada: Disturb-ing Invisibility* (University of Toronto Press, 2012), a 2013 special issue of *ACME International Journal for Critical Geographies* on "Sexual Land-scapes, Lives and Livelihoods in Canada" (with Catherine Nash), and a 2017 special focus section of *TOPIA: Canadian Journal of Cultural Studies* on "Queer/Asian/Canadian" (with Dai Kojima and Robert Diaz). His current research examines, in part, the utility of queer of colour theoriz-ing for the scholarship of teaching and learning, with a focus on "for us, by us" mentorship efforts among Filipinx youth, and the politics of campus and classroom climate at universities.

Matthew Chin is assistant professor in the Graduate School of Social Service at Fordham University and a visiting scholar in the Depart-ment of Sociology at Columbia University, both in New York City. He completed his PhD in social work and anthropology at the University of Michigan. His research interests include community organizing, art, and political economy as well as race, gender, and sexuality in the Americas. He is currently working on a historical ethnography that analyses Jamaica's first sexual-minority activist organization, the Gay Freedom Movement (1977–84). He has received a Social Sciences and Humanities Research Council of Canada Doctoral Fellowship, and his work has been published in venues such as *Affilia, Time & Society, Cana-dian Social Work, Journal of Community Practice*, and *Gay and Lesbian Issues and Psychology Review*.

Robert Diaz is assistant professor of transnational feminisms, global-ization, and sexuality studies at the Women and Gender Studies Insti-tute at the University of Toronto. His teaching and scholarship focus on the intersections of sexuality, Filipino, Asian, and postcolonial studies. His *Diasporic Intimacies: Queer Filipinos and Canadian Imaginaries* (North-western University Press, 2017) brings together artists, scholars, and community workers to examine the contributions of queer Filipinos/as to Canadian culture and society. His research has appeared, or is forth-coming, in *Signs, GLQ, Women & Performance, Journal of Asian American*

Studies, Filipino Studies: Palimpsest of Nation and Diaspora, and *Global Asian Popular Culture*.

OmiSoore H. Dryden, PhD, is an interdisciplinary scholar who theorizes blood and examines the culture and politics of blood donation. His research explores how the history of racism and colonialism frame contemporary cultural understandings of healthy and tainted blood. Blood discourse is integral to the discussion of social justice and education, and Dr. Dryden's work provides the critical examination that deepens the interrogations into the relationships among science, health and disease, homophobia, and racism in the Canadian context. He has published in peer-reviewed journals and edited a collection (with Dr. Suzanne Lenon) titled *Disrupting Queer Inclusion: Canadian Homonationalisms and the Politics of Belonging* (UBC Press, 2015). Dryden's monograph, tentatively titled *Canadian Blood Services, 1998–2015: Donation, Black Life and the Politics of Homophobia*, is currently in progress. This project centres a black queer transnational/diasporic analytic through which a diverse set of archives, including the donor questionnaire, is analysed.

Nwadiogo Ejiogu (Honours BA, MA) has authored several texts, including the widely cited and taught "How Disability Studies Stays White and What Kind of White It Stays," which is anthologized here for the first time. She has worked as a researcher and teaching assistant at the University of Toronto and is earning her MD at Meharry Medical College in Nashville, Tennessee.

Che Gossett is a PhD candidate in women's and gender studies at Rutgers, New Jersey, and an archivist at Barnard Center for Research on Women, New York City. They are the recipient of the 2014 Gloria E. Anzaldúa Award from the American Studies Association Women's Committee, a Radcliffe research grant from Harvard University, the 2014 Sylvia Rivera Award in Transgender Studies from the Center for Gay and Lesbian Studies at the City University of New York, and the 2014 Martin Duberman Research Scholar Award from the New York Public Library. Che was a member of the 2013 Archivists and Librarians Delegation to Palestine.

Jin Haritaworn is associate professor of gender, race, and environment at York University, Toronto, and has been involved in queer of colour–centred research and community-building in London, Berlin, and Toronto. They have authored multiple publications, including two books, several articles (in journals such as *GLQ*, *Society and Space*, and *Sexualities*), and four (co-)edited collections (including *Queer Necropolitics*). Their latest book, *Queer Lovers and Hateful Others: Regenerating Violent Times and Places* (Chicago University Press, 2015), deals with queer space-making and criminalization in gentrifying Berlin. Jin has made contributions to several established fields on both sides of the Atlantic, including gender, sexuality, and transgender studies; critical race and ethnic studies; and urban studies, and has participated in numerous debates, including on homonationalism, gay imperialism, intersectionality, and queer space.

Janaya Khan is the co-founder of Black Lives Matter Toronto and has become a leading voice in the global crusade demanding social transformation, justice, and equality. Known as *future* within the Black Lives Matter (BLM) movement, Khan is a Black, queer, gender-nonconforming activist, staunch Afrofuturist, boxer, and social justice educator. Khan's dedication and bold approach to social justice work has created opportunities to contribute to academic and front-line community dialogue, engaging audiences on the global impacts of the BLM movement. An accomplished lecturer and author, their writings have been featured in *The Feminist Wire, The Root, Huffington Post Black Voices,* and *Al Jazeera.*

Marissa Largo is a PhD candidate in the Department of Social Justice Education at the Ontario Institute for Studies in Education, University of Toronto. In 2013, she was awarded the Joseph-Armand Bombardier Canada Graduate Scholarship from the Social Sciences and Humanities Research Council of Canada for her doctoral project on contemporary Filipino/a Canadian visual art. As a Toronto-based artist, she has presented her work in festivals, galleries, and museums such as the Royal Ontario Museum (2015), the Robert Langen Gallery at Wilfrid Laurier University (2013), Scotiabank Nuit Blanche (2011 and 2012), Mayworks Festival of Working People and the Arts (2012), A Space Gallery (2008), and MAI (Montréal, arts interculturels) (2007). Marissa also works with many progressive arts and cultural organizations that connect social activist art practices with community engagement.

Azar Masoumi is a doctoral candidate in the sociology program at York University, Toronto. Her research explores the interplay among gender, sexuality, imperialism, and asylum, particularly in relation to women and sexual-orientation and gender-identity refugees from Iran.

Ghaida Moussa is a doctoral candidate in the Graduate Program in Social and Political Thought at York University, Toronto, where she interrogates how gendered, racial, and neo-liberal regimes of knowledge inform our understanding of chronic, unidentified illness. She was awarded the 2010 Lambda Foundation for Excellence Award for her master's work on queer Palestinian resistance to oppressive national, colonial, and neo-colonial narratives at the University of Ottawa. Her poems "Ghourbeh" and "Tazakar" have appeared in *Sinister Wisdom*. She is, with Ghadeer Malek, the co-editor of *Min Fami: Arab Feminist Reflections on Identity, Space and Resistance* (Inanna Publications, 2014). Along with Shaista Patel and Nishant Upadhyay, she is also co-editor of the recent *Feral Feminisms* special issue, "Complicities, Connections, and Struggles: Critical Transnational Feminist Analysis of Settler Colonialism."

LeRoi Newbold is a community organizer, parent, educator, and art curator for Black Lives Matter Toronto. LeRoi is a founding member of St. Emilie Skillshare and, for the past eight years, has taught and written curriculum for Canada's first public Africentric school. LeRoi is the director of Black Lives Matter – Toronto Freedom School, which teaches young children about Black pride and resistance through arts-based programming.

Fritz Luther Pino (MSW, RSW) is a PhD candidate in social justice education, Ontario Institute for Studies in Education, University of Toronto. He is a registered social worker and works as a program coordinator and consultant at the Silayan Filipino Community Centre and at the Filipino-Canadian Seniors' Club. He received the Social Sciences and Humanities Research Council of Canada Doctoral Fellowship Award for his dissertation on Filipino gay seniors in Toronto. Fritz currently teaches mental health and diversity and social justice courses at the School of Community Services at Seneca College of Applied Arts and Technology, Toronto.

Gabriela (Río) Rodríguez is a Toronto-based latin@ queer educator working in queer, trans, and people of colour communities. Río is pursuing a masters in Environmental Studies from York University, Toronto, and is about to graduate with a major portfolio that examines the history of Toronto's

Church and Wellesley district. The project focuses on key moments in the history of the Gay Village that highlight the simultaneous displacement and erasure of queer and trans bodies of colour from public space. Río's work interrogates urban and neighbourhood planning that has claimed lasting public space for white gay safety, while simultaneously criminalizing trans people, people of colour, and sex-working people.

Rebeka Tabobondung is the publisher of *MUSKRAT Magazine* and a former festival director of imagineNATIVE Film & Media Arts Festival. She is a community documentary filmmaker, poet, and Indigenous knowledge researcher with an MA in sociology and equity studies in education. Her documentary work has screened at festivals across Canada and around the world, and her written works have been published in numerous journals and anthologies throughout North America. Rebeka's latest research and film work document traditional birth knowledge from Wasauksing First Nation, of which she is a member. She is the co-founder of Maaiingan Productions; research coordinator of the Indigenous Knowledge Network for Infant, Child, and Family Health at St. Michael's Hospital, Toronto; and a former director of the Centre for Women and Trans People at the University of Toronto.

Syrus Marcus Ware is a Vanier Scholar, visual artist, community mobilizer, educator, and researcher pursuing his PhD in the Faculty of Environmental Studies at York University, Toronto. Syrus holds degrees in art history, visual studies (University of Toronto), and sociology and equity studies (Ontario Institute for Studies in Education, University of Toronto). In 2014, he was awarded the Slyff Fellowship/Graduate Fellowship for Academic Distinction by York University. Syrus's research focuses on experiences of marginality and the ways that the presence of racialized, trans, and disabled people can challenge "static" social environments. Syrus has authored several book chapters, journal articles, and peer-reviewed publications about disability, the diversification of museums, trans parenting, and sexual health for trans Men who have Sex with Men, including the widely cited "How Disability Studies Stays White and What Kind of White It Stays" and "Going Boldly Where Few Men Have Gone Before: One Trans Man's Experience of a Fertility Clinic and Insemination" (Sumach, 2009). Syrus was awarded the TD Diversity in the Arts Award in 2017. Additionally, he was voted Best Queer Activist by *Now Magazine* (2005) and was awarded the Steinert and Ferreiro Award (2012) for LGBT community leadership and activism.